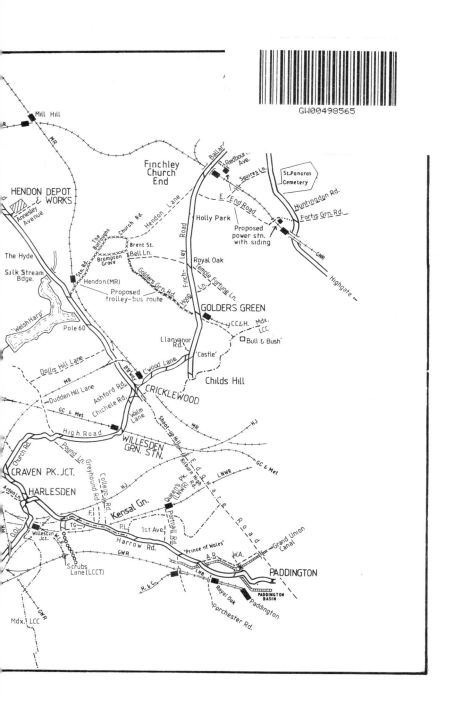

THE METROPOLITAN ELECTRIC TRAMWAYS

ELECTRIC TRAMWAYS

Volume One, Origins to 1920

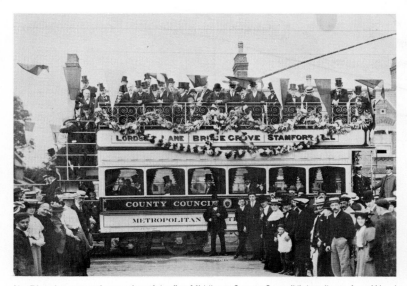

No. 71 and guests at the opening of the first Middlesex County Council light railway, from Wood Green to Bruce Grove, on 20 August 1904. The procession started from Bruce Castle.
(Greater London Record Office

Front cover—
Metropolitan Electric Tramways were the first of the London company operators to introduce top-covered cars. No. 214 of Type F was selected for this official posed photograph in the summer of 1908. (Leicestershire Museums, Brush Collection

The Metropolitan Electric Tramways

Volume One, Origins to 1920

by
C. S. SMEETON

Published in London by

THE LIGHT RAIL TRANSIT ASSOCIATION
13A The Precinct, Broxbourne, Herts EN10 7HY
in association with
THE TRAMWAY AND LIGHT RAILWAY SOCIETY

1984

Printed by W. J. Ray & Co. Ltd., Warewell Street,
Walsall, West Midlands WS1 2HQ.

CONTENTS

MAPS

FOREWORD

by D. W. K. Jones

The Metropolitan Electric Tramways—'The M.E.T.' as we knew it—differed from most tramway systems in that it was conceived and planned as a whole, to serve areas of northwest and north London, many of which at the turn of the century were thinly populated. Its main lines, coherent and logical, were realised in little over five years. It was a rare example of fruitful co-operation to a common end between local authorities—the Middlesex and Hertfordshire County Councils in this instance—and the operating company, the MET, and later the Underground group of which it became a subsidiary. Though not without vicissitudes, as the following chapters will demonstrate, the partnership endured and was generally profitable to all parties, unlike many townships in Britain where blocking tactics and political in-fighting seemed to determine progress, or rather the lack of it.

Thus was created almost overnight a bold enterprise which opened up new areas to relieve London's expanding population—Hampstead Garden Suburb, Finchley, Whetstone, Palmers Green, Winchmore Hill, Sudbury, and later the London County Council's Watling, White Hart Lane and Burnt Oak housing estates. The very names conjure up an era.

For twenty years or so the MET prospered as an exemplary, well-maintained but conventional tramway, as is related in detail in the ensuing chapters. Then, in the mid-twenties, something happened—bus competition, largely unregulated. Even the MET's nominal partner in the Group, the London General Omnibus Co, was forced to throw competing services on to the tram roads to save its own skin. Many contemporary tram networks round the country faltered under this assault and were lost—caught with out-of-date material and insufficient reserves. Quite substantial undertakings were going under by the late twenties or early thirties. Not so the MET—*this* tramway was going to fight back.

Perhaps this is what gave the MET its special place in the affections of the London tramway enthusiast. It was smart, it was disciplined, it was efficient within its limits. But now it challenged the bus competitor with a whole series of brilliant innovations, and it nearly won.

We youthful students—the word 'fan' had mercifully not been invented—watched fascinated as experiment after experiment was launched: coupled cars, high-speed motors, air brakes, new catenary and new bow collectors to match it, trolley skids, trolley reversers, welded rail, passenger flow, ticket-issuing machines, new standards of passenger comfort with transverse sprung-seating, heaters, improved lighting and decor and more covered top decks to entice the busward-looking customer. Not all these ideas were successful, or universally adopted. But perhaps the watershed can be defined as March 1926, when the statutory maximum speed was raised from 16 mile/h to 20 mile/h over the greater part of the system. Design work was then pushed ahead on higher-powered cars with modern equipment and lightweight bodywork to take advantage of the new possibilities thus opened up.

We were witnessing the birth of a modern tramway. First there came two unique and quite different new cars: Bluebell, full of new ideas, speedy, graceful, and a full four tons lighter than her predecessors, was designed to maintain a scheduled speed of 12 mile/h with four stops a mile. Then came the less-successful Poppy, built like a bus by bus engineers; and in 1929 the first of the prototype 'Felthams', the cars which set the seal on the experiments of the preceding years. Quickly followed in 1931 the production run of 54 Felthams for the MET (and 46 for the London United Tramways), and commercial success for the new policies was assured. Passengers flocked back to the trams wherever the Felthams ran. Nothing in the contemporary bus world could touch them for comfort, while superb acceleration and braking gave them the edge for speed of service in suburban conditions. Nor were the older cars inferior in performance; with their newly-installed high-speed motors, modernised equipment and with the remorseless use of the magnetic brake they sailed into the fray like rejuvenated old ladies on a last-fling holiday.

Why was the MET able to rise to the challenge like this? The answer must lie largely in the personality of one man, Christopher John Spencer, General Manager during the critical years of transformation. Spencer had vision, ingenuity and persistence, and he had a first-rate technical team to back him, led by his deputy, A. V. Mason, MIEE. Spencer needed all these attributes to succeed in rebuilding 'his' tramway, and a sound political sense too, for he had to secure the support not only of the Middlesex County Council, which had its own internal battles between pro- and anti-tram factions in the twenties, but of his own Board, a subsidiary of the normally bus-orientated Underground group, which had to be convinced that a case could be made for further capital investment in tramway development, at a time when they were obliged to accept cross-subsidy from the LGOC through pooled receipts on shared sections of route.

Ranged against Spencer were first and foremost the Metropolitan Police, whose attitude at that time to all innovation can only be described as negative at best, uncomprehending and prejudiced as a norm. As private ownership of cars spread, the motoring organisations were becoming a powerful lobby against the trams which seemingly blocked their members' path, while the Press added their irresponsible voice for change, then as now. Yet Spencer and his team battled on. As A. V. Mason put it: "The tramcar must remain, but it must progress in speed and comfort . . . Capacity alone, speed alone or comfort alone will not do. We must have all".

What Spencer and Mason recognised, and others chose not to, was that the torque of the electric motor is at its greatest at low speeds, while the reverse is true of the petrol engine; torque increases with the speed of the engine. In practical terms this implies that the tramcar can get away far more quickly than a bus, and in heavy traffic with frequent stops this is what counts in mounting a speedy service at close time-intervals. Effective braking also counts. Top speed matters little.

Enough has been said to explain the hold the MET had on a young enthusiast such as myself, who daily used the cars and loved every inch of track, every swirl of finely-shaded gilded numbering, lettering and lining which adorned the trams, and perhaps above all the sights and sounds of action—the tremendous deep hum of a heavily-laden car getting under way, the note gradually rising to a near-scream as the statutory limits of speed were exceeded (they usually were), and then the sudden sharp descending note as the brakes clamped to the rails and another shattering stop ensued. Ten passengers, five seconds, two bells and away. Not a moment lost!

But speed and safety is a commercial attribute too, and signs were that the general public was not slow to recognise the advantages offered. Receipts rose, but so did expenses. How far could it have gone? We shall never know. The MET story ended abruptly with the Company's absorption into the London Passenger Transport Board on 1 July 1933. On that day, tramway development in London virtually came to an end, for the policy of the new Board ran strongly in favour of the bus and trolleybus. The trams lingered on for some years, but no more truly-new cars were built and the Felthams remained as the sole legacy of the great effort at modernisation. And they were to serve London well, far beyond the MET era, until 1950 in fact in South London and for nine more years after that in Leeds, a lasting memorial to the only Company-owned tramway in Britain to modernise.

On the Continent, far-sighted engineers and local politicians have continued to work together to fashion superb people-movers for their cities—quiet, pollution-free electric cars running in subways or on reservations. It might have been so here.

INTRODUCTION

The area served by the Metropolitan Electric Tramways consisted of the North-west, North and North-eastern suburbs of London which fell within the County of Middlesex, together with a line which followed the route of a horse tramway which ran from Harlesden Green along the Harrow Road to a terminus near Westbourne Park and which was originally planned to reach the South-east end of the Edgware Road at Paddington, but which was finally reached by the electric trams of the MET (always known to its familiars as "the M.E.T.," never "the Met."). The MET trams also penetrated into the Southern part of Hertfordshire at two points, and from 1912, following an agreement with the London County Council joint services were worked into Central London and it became possible to travel by London County Council and MET cars over three counties without changing trams.

The author was born in a house in High Street, North Finchley in 1916; this was on the Great North Road route, which at this point carried heavy traffic from both the trunk route from Central London through Highgate to Barnet and the routes from Paddington and Cricklewood by way of Golders Green which had joined the Great North Road a little to the south at Tally Ho Corner junction. His imagination was aroused at an early age by the beautifully-proportioned red and white tramcars which passed back and forth daily in an unceasing stream and an upper window was used as a vantage point from which to observe the tramway scene, and later, in the second half of the 1920s, to watch for the many experimental trams which from that time were coming into use on the Golders Green route and were the forerunners of the renowned Feltham cars of 1931.

Because of the wide-ranging nature of this history, it is being presented in two volumes, the publication of which will be separated by an interval of two to three years. The division between Volume One and Volume Two is, for most purposes, taken as the end of 1920, but for the convenience of the reader some specialized aspects of the story have been dealt with wholly in one or the other volume; thus, the present volume deals comprehensively with the track and overhead, depots, power supply and biographies, but excludes detailed consideration of services, fares, tickets, rolling stock and ancillary vehicles and staff matters, which will be dealt with in Volume Two.

The MET system was based mainly on a unique partnership between the Metropolitan Electric Tramways Ltd. and the Middlesex County Council; the nucleus of the system was a horse tramway, nine miles in extent, which operated from termini at Finsbury Park and Stamford Hill northwards to Wood Green, Tottenham and Edmonton. This system, owned and operated by the North Metropolitan Tramways Company, was bought by the MET in 1902 and reconstructed for electric traction and over a period extending to 1911 was extended to a maximum of 54 miles, almost the whole of which was double line. Apart from the already well-built up areas of Tottenham and Edmonton and to a lesser extent, Wood Green, the greater part of Middlesex was at the beginning of the 20th century thinly populated, and such settlements as Finchley, Hendon, Edgware and Enfield in Middlesex, and Barnet and Waltham Cross in Hertfordshire were distinctly separated by extensive tracts of open country; the advent of the tramways in these areas was quickly followed by urban development on a huge scale, a process which was continued and intensified in the 1920s and later by the Underground railways which were extended in some cases beyond the existing outer tram termini in North Middlesex and South Hertfordshire.

In addition to their part in the urban development of the area, the MET and its associated North Metropolitan Electric Power Supply Company played a leading part in the industrialisation of Enfield, Ponders End, West Hendon and North Acton with the Park Royal district, much of this development taking place during and subsequent to the Great War.

The Metropolitan Electric Tramways Ltd. was part of the huge British Electric Traction Group of companies, headed by Emile Garcke, and was in fact the largest tramway undertaking in that group, which consisted mainly of tramway and power companies with a smaller number of omnibus undertakings which became larger in number as some of the tramways were converted to motor buses in later years. The BET provided finance for these various companies and in most cases was the majority shareholder.

Although there have down the years been numerous articles published on various aspects of the MET, no detailed history has previously been attempted; its memory has been kept alive mainly by personal recollections, and no-one has up to now had the time to study and bring together the vast volume of historical material, some of which has only recently become available to researchers. The present author has devoted several years to bringing this material together to produce this detailed history much of which has not previously seen the light of day. Little attention has previously been given to the vital rôle of the Middlesex County Council in the formation and operation of the system, and the sequence of events which led first to the through running agreements with the London County Council starting in 1912 and later to the MET joining the Underground group of companies in 1913. Other aspects dealt with are the trolley-bus experiments of 1909, the searchlight trams of the Great War, the development of the North Metropolitan Electric Power Supply Company, and the complex relationships between the MET and the County Councils of Middlesex and Hertfordshire which were governed by a complicated series of agreements between the parties.

Because early students of the system did not have the benefit of access to detailed official records various misconceptions have come to be accepted over the years; in particular some opening dates given earlier have been found to be incorrect; all opening dates have been verified and where necessary corrected. In addition the Board of Trade inspection dates are given together with salient points from the Inspectors' reports.

Among a number of interesting facets of the MET history, the story of the short single line link between the MET and the London United Tramways at King Street, Acton which was laid in 1915 has been told in detail; the story of the failure to reach Harrow and beyond is likewise told for the first time, and the many attempts to reach Watford, none of which materialized mainly owing to sustained opposition by frontagers, are chronicled and illustrate the manner in which comparatively small groups of individuals could influence developments designed to benefit the population as a whole.

Throughout the lifetime of the system it was burdened by heavy out-goings in the form of the rent of the Middlesex lines, which was based upon the capital expenditure of the County Council on the "Light Railways"; one-third of the total expenditure on the MET system went on improving nearly fifty miles of trunk roads in North London. These roads were transformed from narrow, ill-kept thoroughfares into fully-paved highways mostly in wood-block with foot-ways of Victoria stone slabs, and of widths between fifty and sixty feet. These roads have benefited all users ever since and would certainly not have been constructed to such standards at that time but for the advent of the trams. Numerous other improvements were made, such as the reconstruction or widening of a large number of bridges, the expenditure being borne by the Company in the case of the tramways in Wood Green, Tottenham and Edmonton and along the Harrow Road, and by the County Councils in the case of the Light Railways.

The MET operated in the areas of no less than eighteen district councils in the counties of Middlesex and Hertfordshire and eight Metropolitan Borough Councils in the county of London; under successive reorganisations of local government some of these have disappeared and others have merged to form a smaller number of much larger authorities. In this history all are described as they were at the inception of the MET system and during its lifetime.

As originally conceived this book was presented in strictly chronological narrative form; however, the complexity of the subject proved to be such that this would place too great a reliance on the reader's memory. The author is indebted to Mr. J. H. Price for suggesting that the work should be re-arranged in mainly geographical form and for showing how this could be done. Accordingly Mr. Price's guidance has been followed in the presentation of this book and the succeeding Volume Two.

A debt of gratitude is also owed to Mr. A. W. McCall who has provided the sections covering tickets, fares and routes, a highly complex story in itself. These will be included in Volume Two.

C. S. Smeeton

Ambergate, Derbyshire.

Autumn, 1983.

ABBREVIATIONS IN THE TEXT

BET	The British Electric Traction group
BTH	The British Thomson-Houston Co. Ltd.
Brush	The Brush Electrical Engineering Co. Ltd.
GE	The General Electric Company (USA).
GER	Great Eastern Railway Company
GNR	Great Northern Railway Company
FDET	Finchley District Electric Traction Co. Ltd.
HR&P	Harrow Road and Paddington Tramways Company
HCC	Hertfordshire County Council
L&ST	London and Suburban Traction Co. Ltd.
LCC	London County Council
LGOC	London General Omnibus Co. Ltd.
LNWR	London and North Western Railway
LPTB	London Passenger Transport Board
LTAC	London Traffic Advisory Committee
LUT	London United Tramways Ltd.
MCC	Middlesex County Council (see below)
MET*	Metropolitan Electric Tramways Ltd.
MTOC	Metropolitan Tramways and Omnibus Co. Ltd.
M&G	Mountain and Gibson Ltd.
NLT	North London Tramways Company
NMT	North Metropolitan Tramways Company.
NorthmeT§	North Metropolitan Electric Power Supply Company.
RDC	Rural District Council
SMET	South Metropolitan Electric Tramways & Lighting Co. Ltd.
UDC	Urban District Council
UERL	Underground Electric Railways of London Ltd.

Except where otherwise indicated, references to 'MCC', 'Middlesex', 'the county' or 'the council' refer to the Light Railways and Tramways Committee of the Middlesex County Council, which was set up in April 1901. In October 1919 it became the Light Railways and Tramways Sub-Committee of the council's Highways Committee.

* These initials were always pronounced separately, viz. 'M.E.T.'.

§ The shortened name 'NorthmeT' is used for brevity throughout this history, though the power company did not adopt it until the 1920s.

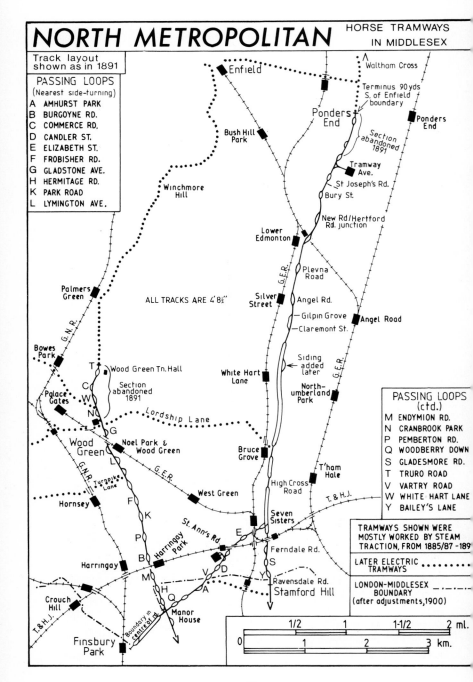

NORTH METROPOLITAN

HORSE TRAMWAYS IN MIDDLESEX

Track layout shown as in 1891

PASSING LOOPS
(Nearest side-turning)
- A AMHURST PARK
- B BURGOYNE RD.
- C COMMERCE RD.
- D CANDLER ST.
- E ELIZABETH ST.
- F FROBISHER RD.
- G GLADSTONE AVE.
- H HERMITAGE RD.
- K PARK ROAD
- L LYMINGTON AVE.

PASSING LOOPS (ctd.)
- M ENDYMION RD.
- N CRANBROOK PARK
- P PEMBERTON RD.
- Q WOODBERRY DOWN
- S GLADESMORE RD.
- T TRURO ROAD
- V VARTRY ROAD
- W WHITE HART LANE
- Y BAILEY'S LANE

ALL TRACKS ARE 4'8½"

Enfield

Waltham Cross

Terminus 90 yds S. of Enfield boundary

Ponders End

Ponders End

Bush Hill Park

Section abandoned 1891

Tramway Ave.

St Joseph's Rd.

Bury St.

Winchmore Hill

New Rd/Hertford Rd. junction

Lower Edmonton

G.E.R.

Plevna Road

Palmers Green

G.N.R.

Silver Street

Angel Rd.

Gilpin Grove

Claremont St.

Angel Road

G.E.R.

Bowes Park

Wood Green Tn. Hall

Section abandoned 1891

Siding added later

White Hart Lane

North-umberland Park

Palace Gates

Lordship Lane

Wood Green

Noel Park & Wood Green

G.N.R.

Bruce Grove

T'ham Hale

G.E.R.

Turnpike Lane

West Green

High Cross Road

T. & H.J.

Hornsey

Harringay Park

St. Ann's Rd.

Seven Sisters

Ferndale Rd.

Harringay

Crouch Hill

T. & H.J.

Boundary in centre of rd.

Manor House

Ravensdale Rd.

Stamford Hill

Finsbury Park

TRAMWAYS SHOWN WERE MOSTLY WORKED BY STEAM TRACTION, FROM 1885/87 -189

LATER ELECTRIC TRAMWAYS ....

LONDON-MIDDLESEX BOUNDARY (after adjustments, 1900)

| 1/2 | 1 | 1-1/2 | 2 ml. |
| 0 | 1 | 2 | 3 km. |

10

CHAPTER ONE

THE HORSE AND STEAM ERA

The electric tramways which are the subject of this history were in part descended from a group of horse and steam tramways which in the later years of the nineteenth century served the Wood Green, Tottenham and Edmonton areas and a horse tramway which, in the South-western part of the electric tramways' area, provided a service between Harlesden Green along the Harrow Road in the direction of Paddington to a point near Westbourne Park station with a branch which, for a short time, ran from Harrow Road to Carlton Road (the present Carlton Vale) serving the Maida Hill and Kilburn Park districts.

As a detailed history of London horse tramways is being produced by another author, only an outline resumé of these tramways will be given in this history in order that the reader may be acquainted with the influence these early lines had on their electric successors.

The North London Suburban Tramway Company Ltd. was incorporated in 1878 as a joint stock limited company, and in 1879 secured powers under the Tramways Act, 1870 for a line from Stamford Hill via Tottenham and Edmonton to the Middlesex-Hertfordshire county boundary at Freezywater, a distance of 7.703 miles. There were plans to extend the line beyond the boundary through Cheshunt but these did not materialize. Contracts to the value of £38,500 were entered into for the construction of the line; of this sum £3,000 was allocated for the purchase of land for use as a depot and offices. The depot site was on the east side of the main Hertford Road at Lower Edmonton and was approached by a road which was named Tramway Avenue. The contract included the provision of twelve one-horse cars seating twenty passengers each, 75 horses and uniforms for the platform staff.

The first horse cars of the North London Suburban Tramway Company were of the Eades Patent Reversible type. These single-horse cars seated twenty passengers.

Construction commenced at Lower Edmonton in May 1880 of the single line and passing loop route, and the first section, from Tramway Avenue southwards as far as the Tottenham—Edmonton boundary near Union Row, a distance of two miles was opened on 10 April 1881; on 16 May a further 1.625 miles was opened from the Tottenham—Edmonton boundary to High Cross, Tottenham and on 4 June the line was extended from High Cross to an end-on junction with the North Metropolitan Tramways line at Stamford Hill, a distance of 1.073 miles. From Tramway Avenue northwards to a point 90 yards south of the Edmonton-Enfield boundary at Ponders End the final section of 1.037 miles was inspected on 5 January 1882 and opened by 7 January. This marked the end of construction by the Company; the remainder of the line authorized to the Middlesex—Hertfordshire county boundary at Freezywater was not constructed.

The car fleet was increased to twenty, with 116 horses by the end of 1881, and although traffic was reasonable a loss was incurred for the year's operations. A Provisional Order was obtained in August 1881 for new lines from Seven Sisters Corner, Tottenham along Seven Sisters Road to Finsbury Park and from Finsbury Park via Seven Sisters Road and Green Lanes to Wood Green, a total distance of 4.475 miles. The financial position of the company was giving some cause for concern at an early date, and while the directors considered that these new lines had good prospects for increased traffic receipts, they were reluctant to commit the company to the necessary expenditure; they called an Extraordinary General Meeting which took place on 30 January 1882 at which it was resolved to dissolve the existing company and seek Parliamentary powers to form a statutory company in its place, which would have powers to work the existing tramways and construct additional ones. The Bill was presented to Parliament in the Spring Session of 1882 and received the Royal Assent on 10 August. It empowered the dissolution of the North London Suburban Tramway Company Ltd. and the incorporation of the statutory North London Tramways Company. The powers for the lines from Seven Sisters Corner to Finsbury Park and from Manor House to Wood Green were confirmed to the new company, and it was proposed to enter into a contract with the City of London Contract Corporation Ltd. for the construction of the new lines.

The shareholders of the Company were still concerned about the financial position, and pressed the directors to stay their hand on the new lines; it was suggested that the company might merge with the North Metropolitan Tramways Company, whose lines from Inner London terminated at Finsbury Park and Stamford Hill. It was thought that the adoption of steam as motive power would solve the company's problems and at a shareholders' meeting it was agreed that the sanction of Parliament should be sought for the use of steam power. The Bill in the 1883 Session was duly enacted as the North London Tramways Act 1883, sanctioning the use of steam on the Company's lines for a period of seven years, and the abandonment of the powers to build beyond Ponders End to Cheshunt.

Fourteen steam tram engines were obtained from Merryweather & Sons, together with twenty double-deck bogie trailers from the Falcon Engine & Car Works Limited; the engines were Nos. 1-14 (Merryweather works numbers 142-155 of 1885), were four-coupled with two horizontal cylinders of $7\frac{1}{2}$ in. dia. bore and 12 in. stroke and a wheelbase of 5 ft. 0 in. The trailers had six windows a side and seating on the upper decks was of the knifeboard type. The first trial run of a steam tram was made on 28 January 1885.

Meanwhile, construction of the line from Seven Sisters Corner to Finsbury Park had commenced, a heavier section rail being used to carry the increased weight of the steam trams. The formal introduction of steam hauled services between Stamford Hill and Ponders End took place on 1 April 1885 and until 31 May 1885 the steam trams ran alternately with horse cars; the last horse car ran on the latter date. A small two-road depot was built south of St. Anns Road with an access line in Kingsford Terrace, Seven Sisters Road.

12

In 1885 the horse trams between Edmonton and Stamford Hill were replaced by the steam trams of the North London Tramways Company. This photograph shows Merryweather engine No. 1 and Falcon trailers 11 and 12 in the approach to the depot in Tramway Avenue, Edmonton, when new. (Merryweather & Sons

An early view near Stamford Hill with a Merryweather engine and Falcon trailer working on the service from Ponders End to Stamford Hill. (London Borough of Newham Libraries

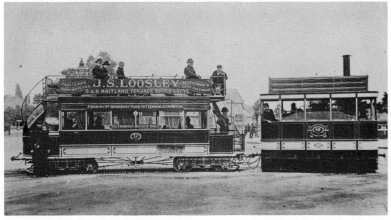

In December 1885 the steam trams started running from Edmonton to Finsbury Park, using the new line in Seven Sisters Road. The route-board "Woodbury Town" probably refers to Woodberry Down, a road which diverges from Seven Sisters Road at the Manor House. Engine 10 with trailer 17. (Merryweather & Sons

The new section of line between Seven Sisters Corner and Finsbury Park was opened as far as the Manor House on 24 October 1885, and from the Manor House to Finsbury Park on Saturday 12 December with a through service of steam trams between Finsbury Park and Ponders End. During 1885 an additional engine was purchased, from Merryweather and Sons, which was numbered 15 in the company's fleet and was Merryweather works number 164. This engine was a heavier and more powerful machine than the earlier Merryweathers, with 8 in. cylinders and 14 in. stroke. It was followed in 1886-7 by ten from Dick, Kerr & Co. Ltd. of Kilmarnock, Nos. 16-25, and a further seven trailers built by the Falcon Engine & Car Works. These differed from the first cars in having seven windows a side and garden seats on the upper decks.

Construction of the line from the Manor House to Wood Green commenced on 6 October 1886, but owing to difficulties with the local authorities, mainly over widenings, the work was not completed until August 1887; the section was sanctioned by the Board of Trade on 10 August, but did not commence working to Wood Green, where the line ended at the Town Hall, just short of Truro Rd., until 24 December 1887. A further 40 yards from Truro Road to Sidney Road was authorised, but not built. The line to Stamford Hill from Seven Sisters Corner became a branch following the opening of the Finsbury Park section in December 1885 and was worked irregularly; no service was worked on the section during 1887. It is possible that a service of horse cars was provided from the Manor House to Wood Green (Lordship Lane) during the weeks preceding the start of the steam service, but this is unconfirmed.

While the new sections of line from Seven Sisters Corner to Manor House and from Finsbury Park to Wood Green had been laid with heavier section rail than the line between Stamford Hill and Edmonton, the track on both the new and older sections began to deteriorate, the weight of the steam engines proving too much for them. Derailments became frequent, complaints about noise and smoke from the engines were reaching the local authorities and the Board of Trade, and above all the company were in extreme financial difficulties.

Services of an indifferent nature continued through 1888 and 1889, and the time was approaching when the company's permit from the Board of Trade to use steam traction was due for renewal.

By 9 June 1890 the company went into voluntary liquidation; a Receiver, W. J. Carruthers Wain, former Chairman of the Board of Directors, was appointed and meanwhile the permit to use steam traction was due for renewal on 2 August 1890; the Local Boards of Health (forerunners of the Urban District Councils) objected to the steam permit being renewed. Maj. Gen. C. S. Hutchinson of the Board of Trade told the company that steam traction could be continued until 31 October 1890 on condition that certain repairs were carried out, and if other repairs and recommendations were carried out a further extension of two years would be granted. In the event, following a further inspection of the engines

In readiness for the extension to Wood Green in 1887, the North London Tramways Company bought ten Dick Kerr engines (Nos. 16-25) of the type shown above, and seven larger Falcon trailers with transverse top deck seats and seven windows per side, as shown below. The upper picture of engine 18 with an 1885 Falcon trailer was taken at Wood Green terminus near Truro Road.   (Author's collection, Lens of Sutton

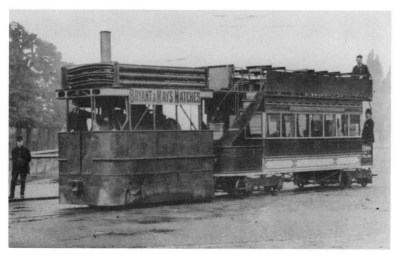

by Maj. Gen. Hutchinson, which were again found to be in an unsatisfactory condition, an agreement was arrived at on 25 November 1890 whereby the company would deposit £600 with the Board of Trade as a guarantee that maintenance would be carried out, and a further six months' licence would be granted. The Company offered to pay at the rate of £100 per month during which time the Board would issue monthly permits as long as this sum was paid.

The Debenture holders were now up in arms, and on 14 March 1891 the Company was offered for sale; it then transpired on 2 April that agreement had been reached on 26 February for the sale and reconstitution of the Company as 'The London Electrical Tramways Company Ltd.' It appeared that Carruthers Wain and one of the Debenture holders had attempted to arrange this deal with Charles John Westwood and Frederick Charles Winby, who were described as tramway contractors and engineers. The directors of the proposed new company were to be Westwood, Winby, Clifford Docwra and four gentlemen named Sanders, Knights, Relf and Hurrell. Nominal capital of the company was to be £150,000 in £1 shares.

On learning this, the Board of Trade expressed doubts that the new arrangements would be successful in restoring the fortunes of the North London Tramways Company; Hornsey Local Board of Health opposed the scheme unreservedly, whilst some of the other Boards agreed to the proposals with reservations, others wanting an inquiry. None of the local authorities were interested in taking the undertaking over.

A solution was found when Middlesex County Council took a hand and made an approach to the North Metropolitan Tramways Company to see if they would take over the system and work it with horse cars. The North Metropolitan Company agreed to purchase the undertaking at the liquidation value of £22,600, pointing out that they would have to spend a further £30,000 to bring it up to the necessary standards of safety and efficiency. The North Metropolitan took over operation with horse cars on 1 August 1891, the last steam tram having run on 31 July. The purchase was completed on 12 April 1892, the North Metropolitan Tramways Company's Act of 1892 sanctioning the purchase

On 1 August 1891 the steam trams were replaced by horse trams operated by the North Metropolitan Tramways Company, one of which is shown here at Tramway Avenue on the Edmonton-Finsbury Park service. (Tramway Museum Society

and empowering the company to double some of the single track in Tottenham. The rolling stock was not included in the purchase by the North Metropolitan Tramways Company and was sold off by the liquidator mainly at scrap value; two of the Merryweather engines were bought by the Dewsbury, Batley & Birstal Tramways Co. Ltd., in whose fleet they became Nos. 10 and 11. This purchase took place as late as 1900, so presumably the engines, perhaps with others, had been taken back by Merryweathers and kept in store.

The lines continued to be worked by the North Metropolitan Tramways Company until they were sold to the Metropolitan Electric Tramways Ltd. in 1902.

After taking over operation of the Finsbury Park-Wood Green service, the North Metropolitan introduced a through service of horse cars between Wood Green and Moorgate. A new depot was built for the horse cars at Jolly Butchers Hill, Wood Green, and the section of line north of this point was given up. (Tramway Museum Society)

The other progenitor of the electric lines, in the South-west of the Metropolitan Electric Tramways area, was the Harrow Road & Paddington Tramways. The Harrow Road & Paddington Tramways Company was incorporated as a statutory company by the Harrow Road & Paddington Tramways Act of 1886; the Company was empowered to construct a line from the Royal Oak at Harlesden Green, along the Harrow Road to a point west of the Lock Hospital Bridge over the Grand Junction Canal at Amberley Road in Paddington consisting of 2.33 miles of double and single track on the standard gauge. From a point about 0.162 miles from the Amberley Road terminus a branch left the main line at Chippenham Road to proceed along Chippenham Road, Malvern Road, and Cambridge Road to terminate in Cambridge Road at the intersection with Carlton Road (now Carlton Vale), Kilburn Park. This line, double track at its commencement in Harrow Road and in Chippenham Road became a single line from the Chippenham Hotel along Malvern Road and Cambridge Road to its termination, and was 0.638 miles in length. At the time these lines were promoted the area served lay wholly in Middlesex, but most of the company's lines were in areas which passed to the newly-formed London County Council on 21 March 1889.

17

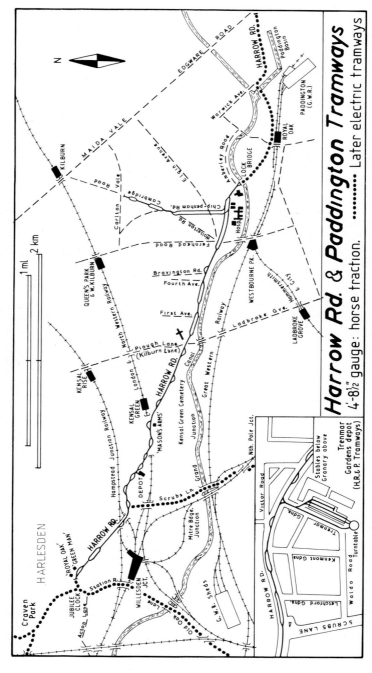

Harrow Rd. & Paddington Tramways
4-8½" gauge: horse traction. ⋯⋯⋯ Later electric tramways

N

1 ml
2 km

HARLESDEN

Craven Park

JUBILEE CLOCK
'ROYAL OAK'
'GREEN MAN'
Acton Lane
Station Rd.
WILLESDEN JCT.
Old Oak Lane
G.W.R. Sheds
Mitre Bdge. Junction
Scrubs Ln.
Nth. Pole Jct.
DEPOT
'MASONS' ARMS'
KENSAL GREEN
KENSAL RISE
Kensal Green Cemetery
Grand Junction Canal
Great Western Railway
London & North Western Railway
Hampstead Junction Railway
HARROW RD.
Plough Lane (Kilburn Lane)
First Ave.
Fourth Ave.
Bravington Rd.
QUEEN'S PARK & W.KILBURN
KILBURN
MAIDA VALE
Carlton Vale
Cambridge Rd.
ELGIN AVENUE
EDGWARE ROAD
Warwick Ave.
Amberley Road
Chippenham Rd.
Wolverton Rd.
Fernhead Road
WESTBOURNE PK.
LADBROKE GROVE
Ladbroke Gve.
Hammersmith & City
LOCK BRIDGE
Hospl
ROYAL OAK
PADDINGTON (G.W.R.)
Paddington Basin
HARROW RD.

Trenmar Gardens depot (H.R.&P. Tramways)
Stables below Granary above
Trenmar Gdns.
Kenmont Gdns.
Letchford Gdns.
Victor Road
HARROW RD.
SCRUBS LANE
Waldo Road
Turntable

There are few surviving records of the Company, which was incorporated with share capital of £60,000 in £10 shares, and the first directors were John Kerr, Frederic Manuelle, John Metcalfe, Benjamin Nowell and Joseph Robson; at a later date new directors were appointed and some of them were also directors and shareholders of the North Metropolitan Tramways Company. The original proposals in the Cricklewood, Kilburn and Harrow Road Tramways Bill of 1886 covered a much larger system; the line along Harrow Road was planned to continue across Lock Bridge for a further 0.70 mile as far as the Stafford Hotel near Royal Oak Station, and that in Cambridge Road to continue across Carlton Road through Cambridge Road and Cambridge Gardens to reach Maida Vale LNWR station in Kilburn High Road, a distance of 0.206 mile. From Maida Vale station the line was projected north-westwards along Kilburn High Road and Shoot-up Hill (the main Edgware Road) to the Crown Hotel at Cricklewood for a distance of 1.612 miles. Objections by Willesden Local Board of Health, Hampstead Vestry and other bodies resulted in the whole of the line between Cricklewood and Maida Vale station and the part of the line from Maida Vale station to the Prince of Wales in Cambridge Road being struck out, and as the canal company thought that the Lock Hospital Bridge at Amberley Road could not carry tramway traffic the section between Amberley Road and the proposed terminus at the Stafford Hotel near Royal Oak station was likewise struck out. The Lock Hospital Bridge was an iron structure dating from 1866.

Of the authorized mileage all but 0.19 mile between the Prince of Wales in Cambridge Road and the south side of Carlton Road, and about fifteen yards at the west end of the route at the Royal Oak, Harlesden, was constructed by July 1888. Maj. Gen. C. S. Hutchinson carried out the inspection for the Board of Trade on 2 July and subject to the correction of some minor faults he recommended the Board of Trade to issue their certificate of fitness for use; this was issued on 9 July but meanwhile the lines had opened for public service on Saturday 7 July. Initially the car fleet consisted of twelve two-horse seven-windows per side double-deck cars and 110 horses; these totals varied from year to year. In 1895 there were 110 horses and 19 cars, and in 1897 the number of horses had risen to 139 and the number of cars decreased by three, whilst at 1901 the number of horses stood at 157 with 21 cars. The Knifeboard-seat cars of 1888 were supplied by G. F. Milnes & Co. of Birkenhead and were in a red livery; later additions came from the Falcon Works at Loughborough, with top deck garden seats, and were painted brown.

The Company's depot was in Trenmar Gardens, on the College Park Estate near the west end of the Harrow Road line; this building was about 250 ft. long and some 75 ft. wide with two tracks entering the building at the front and emerging at the back into a small yard situated at the end of Waldo Road. A single line from Harrow Road ran alongside the depot for its full length to meet the two tracks in the yard at the rear of the building, adjacent to the stables. The company's office was at 24 Kenmont Terrace, a house near the College Park Hotel.

The Harrow Road & Paddington Tramways Company applied to Parliament for further powers in 1891; an extension of the line at Lock Hospital Bridge eastwards as far as Edgware Road, and a continuous line from the Crown Hotel at Cricklewood through Kilburn and Maida Vale to reach the proposed extension of the Harrow Road line were accompanied by a proposal to construct a short line from Harrow Road along Walterton Road to meet the existing line in Chippenham Road at the Chippenham Hotel, and to continue the Cambridge Road line from Carlton Road northwards into and along Kilburn Park Road as far as High Road, Kilburn. Another line, to commence in Harrow Road at a junction with the existing line at the Royal Oak, Harlesden was planned to pass into and across High Street, Harlesden and into Manor Park Road, continuing along Manor Park Road and regaining the Harrow Road in Craven Park to continue along the main Harrow Road to terminate at the entrance to Stonebridge Park.

Very few photographs of the Harrow Road horse tramway have survived; this view is at the Harlesden terminus. It is reproduced from a coloured commercial postcard showing the car in a livery of brown and cream. (Courtesy E. D. Chambers

From the east end of Manor Park Road the line was to continue along High Street, Harlesden joining the line through Manor Park Road in Craven Park. High Street, Harlesden, Craven Park and Hillside, Stonebridge Park are all named sections of the main Harrow Road. The total mileage in the Bill was 6.120, in a mixture of double and single line, and of this only 1.80 miles was sanctioned in the Harrow Road and Paddington Tramways Act which received the Royal Assent on 28 July 1891. Objections by Willesden Local Board of Health, the London County Council and other bodies resulted in the major extension westwards of the Harrow Road line to Stonebridge Park and the proposed new line from Cricklewood to Paddington along the Edgware Road being struck out. The extension of the Harrow Road line eastwards across Lock Hospital Bridge to Paddington, the short connection between Harrow Road and the line in Chippenham Road through Walterton Road and the extension of the line up to Kilburn High Road from Cambridge Road into Carlton Road and Kilburn Park Road with a terminus in the latter at the junction with Kilburn High Road, a total of 1.810 miles, were sanctioned, and the abandonment of the authorised but unbuilt section in Cambridge Road from Carlton Road to the Prince of Wales was authorised by the Act. None of this construction was undertaken, although the powers were twice extended, by Acts of 1893 and 1894.

By early in 1891 it is clear that traffic on the Chippenham Road branch had not come up to expectations, and from January there were contradictory reports in the local Press and at meetings of the Paddington Borough Council and Willesden Local Board of Health's various committees. The first of these, at an unstated date in 1891 was a statement by the Willesden Engineer and Surveyor to the effect that the line "was not in any way worked for the last twelve months". On 13 January 1893 the *Kilburn Times* said that the line had not been worked for three years, but by 20 January this was contradicted by a statement by the Company that "a tram had run every two or three months". On 21 February 1893 the Willesden Works and General Purposes Committee was told that traffic on Cambridge Road had never ceased for the space of three months—"a constant service was now being run". But in the Engineer and Surveyor's Report for 1892/3 he stated that the line was "practically discontinued in the year 1892/3".

However, it is established that service along the route had definitely ceased by August 1894 and it has to be assumed that up to that time occasional cars traversed the route, probably to retain the statutory powers. On 11 June 1895 it was reported to Willesden Urban District Council (successors to the Local Board of Health from 1894) that the line in Cambridge Road, i.e., from the Chippenham Hotel northwards into Malvern Road and Cambridge Road was now abandoned, and by the end of the year that part of the line had been taken up. The line in Chippenham Road, in the Metropolitan Borough of Paddington and in the County of London remained in place although not worked; on 9 January 1896 the Works Committee of Paddington Council recommended the Council to consent to the Company setting back the kerb in Harrow Road near Ashmore Road so the Company could widen the roadway to 32 ft. and double the track there, the work to be done by the Council at the Company's expense. This was subject to the Company agreeing to the removal of the Chippenham Road track, the cost of which was estimated at £166.

Later, on 5 October 1897 the track was still in place and the Works Committee recommended that the Company should be advised that unless the track was removed the Council would apply to the Board of Trade for an order for its removal. On 19 September 1899 the Works Committee withdrew the motion to take up the track, and by 4 October 1900 the Council were advised that the Company were within their statutory rights in retaining the Chippenham Road track. From this it appears that the Company had been running statutory cars over the Chippenham Road section and had preserved their Parliamentary rights; this continued after the purchase of the Harrow Road and Paddington Tramways by the Metropolitan Electric Tramways in 1904. One of the Harrow Road company's horse cars, No. 1, was retained after electrification and stabled at Stonebridge Park Depot whence it sallied forth once every three months carrying a fare-paying passenger over the section as far as the Chippenham Hotel. The Works Committee of Paddington Borough Council reported on 5 November 1907 that the MET were now prepared to lift the rails at the Harrow Road and Shirland Road ends of Chippenham Road provided the Borough Council did not object to the Company derailing a horse car in Harrow Road and taking it across the carriageway paving every three months to comply with the requirements of the Tramways Act. It is evident that those interested in this line at this time, the MET and the LCC still wished to retain the powers. The Company's request was agreed to and the Council confirmed the Committee's recommendation on 19 November.

By 30 January 1912 the London County Council had acquired the Chippenham Road line and those sections of the Harrow Road line in the County of London; on that day A. L. C. Fell, the London County Council Tramways Manager asked the Borough Council what surface they would require if and when the County Council removed the track and setts. The Borough Council wanted the road paved with bituminous macadam, and on 22 May 1912 the LCC advised the Borough Council that they were prepared to remove setts and rails and pave with macadam at a cost not to exceed £700. Paddington Borough Council accepted the offer on 9 December 1912.

Following agreement to sell the lines to the MET, the Harrow Road and Paddington Tramways Company had obtained Parliamentary powers in their Act of 11 August 1903 to reconstruct and electrify their lines and to lease their undertaking to the Metropolitan Electric Tramways. A second Act of 22 July 1904 sanctioned the sale of the Harrow Road and Paddington undertaking to the MET, and the history of these measures and subsequent history of the electrified lines is detailed in another chapter.

Unrealised Proposals in the Metropolitan Electric Tramways Area

In addition to the numerous Light Railway and Tramway schemes of the Middlesex and Hertfordshire County Councils and the Company and their direct progenitors, there was a number of attempts to obtain powers in parts of the Metropolitan Electric Tramways area, many of which did not reach fruition; some companies were formed which did not put forward any specific proposals for powers. These are here outlined briefly for the sake of completeness.

The first proposal of any kind for tramway powers anywhere in the area was that of the Common Road Conveyance Company, which was incorporated on 14 December 1870 with nominal share capital of £5,000 in £1 shares; in 1871 the Company obtained a Provisional Order under the terms of the Tramways Act of 1870 for a horse tramway 12.10 miles in length to run from the Essex Arms, Watford through Bushey, Great Stanmore, Little Stanmore, Edgware, The Hyde, Hendon, Cricklewood and the Slade to a terminus at the Edgware Road station of the Hampstead Junction Railway. Other powers were sought for lines between Southall and Shepherds Bush, Kew and Richmond, Ealing and Brentford and Uxbridge and Southall. The Watford—London line was entitled "The Common Road Conveyance Tramway". The Provisional Order was confirmed in the Metropolitan Tramways Orders Confirmation Act of 7 July 1873. The Company's authorised capital was increased in October 1873 to £500,000 in £5 shares, of which 120 were taken up by the original subscribers. Evidently the Company was unable to attract sufficient investors in their schemes and on 26 February 1875 it was wound up by the High Court on a creditor's petition.

On 14th November 1878 the North West Metropolitan Tramways Co. Ltd. was incorporated with an authorised share capital of £100,000 in £10 shares. The stated objects of the Company were to construct, purchase, lease or work tramways in Middlesex, to obtain additional powers and leases and to operate omnibuses and act as general carriers. The first subscribers to this company, taking one share each were an impressive group of individuals; they were Sir Wilfred Brett, KCMG, Chairman of Sheffield Tramways Company; William Barfoot, Chairman of Leicester Tramways Company; C. E. Davison, a director of Wolverhampton Tramways Company; Francis J. Heseltine, a director of Swansea Tramways Company; Clement Shelton, Mayor of Leicester; Alexander Wood, Chairman of Edinburgh Street Tramways Company and William Mousley, contractor, of Westminster. Despite this array of highly-placed subscribers, the company did not proceed with any proposals and on 8 September 1879 an extraordinary general meeting of the shareholders resolved that the Company should be voluntarily wound up. Essex White Layton was appointed liquidator and the Company was finally wound up on 28 November 1879. However, on 14 November 1884 the same promoters gave notice of application for a Provisional Order for a line along the Harrow Road from the Crown Inn at Harlesden Green to Cottage Road in the borough of Paddington, for which they intended to form a statutory company of similar title, but this scheme did not proceed.

The Edgware Road and Maida Vale Tramways Company was formed in 1883 and applied on 19 November 1883 for a Provisional Order for a line commencing in Edgware Road, Paddington, at Church Street and continuing for 2.950 miles north-westwards along Edgware Road to terminate outside the Edgware Road (now Brondesbury) station of the North London Railway. The line was to be worked by horse traction on the standard gauge. As was so often the case, opposition by frontagers and the local authorities ensured that no progress was made, and the Company was dissolved.

The London, Highgate and Finchley Tramways Company was registered on 22 December 1885 with authorised share capital of £50,000 in £10 shares; the first subscribing shareholders and directors were Henry Fishwick; Edward Daniel Stone; Frederick Hudson; John Lees and Edward H. Carter. The engineers were Edward Pritchard and Robert Vawser, and the Company applied to Parliament in the 1886 Session for powers to construct a line commencing at the Archway

Tavern, Highgate and passing along Archway Road, Highgate, the Great North Road, East and North Finchley and Whetstone to terminate at the Middlesex—Hertfordshire county boundary north of Whetstone, a distance of 5.80 miles, on the standard gauge, the line to be single track with passing loops. Sanction was sought to use steam or animal traction. The Bill failed and there was no further activity on the part of the Company, which was struck off the register on 10 May 1892.

The London Street Tramways Company was incorporated in 1870 with nominal capital of £100,000 and operated a network of horse tramways in mainly the North-west Metropolitan area of London, i.e., that area covered by the Metropolitan Board of Works and which later became the County of London. Although prior to the formation of the London County Council in 1889 the area North of the Thames was part of the County of Middlesex there was at that time no administrative county, and the Metropolitan Board of Works was the administrative body for that part of old Middlesex which formed part of the Metropolitan area, together with the old areas of Metropolitan Essex, Surrey and Kent.

The London Street Tramways Company obtained powers in their Act of 1888 to continue their line terminating at Archway Tavern, Highgate northwards along Archway Road for 1.725 miles as far as the Hornsey—Finchley boundary, about 250 yards south of East Finchley station. Of this mileage, 0.575 miles was double line and 1.150 miles single. This took the line beneath the old Highgate Archway, a narrow stone arch where the road was only 16 ft. wide (and where it was at one time proposed a tunnel should be constructed); the Act provided that the line should not be constructed until the Archway was rebuilt and the Company were to pay to Hornsey Local Board of Health £3,000 towards the cost of this reconstruction. The Local Board of Health and Islington Vestry had agreed the specification of the work (only some 6 ft. of the width of the arch was in Islington, the rest in Hornsey). The powers for the Archway Road line were to lapse two years after the completion of reconstruction of the arch. The line was not built, and the Company's Act of 1895 relieved them of their obligations in respect of both the arch and the line. The arch was replaced by the present structure in 1897.

Yet another attempt to obtain powers North of the Archway Tavern came about when the Highgate and Finchley Tramways Company Ltd. was registered on 18 December 1897, with authorised share capital of £20,000 in £10 shares. The first subscribers were Arthur Collins Bromley; W. J. Kershaw; Charles Massey; Robert Green and James Bruton. Charles A. Wilkinson was the Secretary. The Company proposed to seek powers for a line from the Archway Tavern along Archway Road and the Great North Road through Highgate and East Finchley to terminate at Strawberry Vale, East Finchley, about 150 yards south of the present North Circular Road. The total distance was 3.50 miles of double line, of which 0.380 mile would be interlaced. A branch from the Wellington at North Hill left the Great North Road to traverse North Hill and terminate at the terminus of the Highgate Hill cable tramway in High Street, Highgate; this branch was intended to be single line with passing loops, 0.836 mile in length. The line at the Archway Tavern was proposed to connect with the North Metropolitan Tramways line which terminated there in Holloway Road, and both lines were intended to be constructed on the standard gauge; a wide variety of traction forms was mentioned in the intended Bill, i.e., overhead electric, conduit electric, cable, gas, oil and compressed air. In the event the Bill was not proceeded with and the company was dissolved and struck from the register on 26 October 1900.

In 1899 and 1900 Willesden Urban District Council considered the question of tramways in their district. There were lengthy discussions in the district on the subject of tramways, almost invariably in acrimonious terms, local residents' and ratepayers' bodies being strongly opposed to proposals that the Urban District Council should promote tramways or light railways in the district. At a Special Meeting of the UDC on 30 October 1900 Councillor Cowley, seconded by Councillor Pinkham, proposed that the UDC should promote a Bill in the 1901 Spring Session of Parliament for powers to construct lines in the District extending to a little under six miles; one of these was planned to commence in Malvern Road at the end of the still extant but unused Chippenham Road branch of the Harrow Road and Paddington Tramways, thence proceeding via Malvern Road, Salusbury Road, Winchester Avenue, Willesden Lane and Cavendish Road as far as High Road, Kilburn near Brondesbury station. From Willesden Lane a line continued north-westwards along Willesden Lane into and along High Road, Willesden, Church Road, Craven Park, Craven Park Road, High Street, Harlesden and Station Road, Harlesden to terminate at Willesden Junction station. A short branch left Church Road, Willesden at Taylors Lane to proceed along Taylors Lane, Harlesden and terminate in the yet-to-be-built Gibbons Road, adjacent to the Taylors Lane site on which a generating station was proposed to be built. The two main routes were described as Route A: along Cavendish Road, Willesden Lane, Church Road, Craven Park, High Street, Harlesden to Tubbs Road (adjacent to Willesden Junction station) and Route B: Winchester Avenue, Salusbury Road, Canterbury Road, Malvern Road to Chippenham Gardens. The costs of the two routes were estimated at £40,937 and £12,850 respectively.

The Council's Bill sought powers for other projects, including the construction of the generating station on land they owned at Taylors Lane, Harlesden, and the tramway proposals were the subject of heated debate within the district and between the UDC and the County Council. There was a suggestion that if the UDC won their powers they would grant running powers to the MCC, but in the event local opposition developed to such an extent that a town poll was held by the UDC which resulted in a vote of 2,532 in favour of the scheme and 3,633 against. The Council removed the tramway proposals from their 1901 Bill but proceeded with the powers for the generating station, which they obtained and constructed the station which was in 1903 sold to the North Metropolitan power supply company.

The Charing Cross Euston and Hampstead Railway Company had still not constructed their line to Hampstead and Golders Green when, in 1901 they deposited a Bill in Parliament seeking powers to form a company to be called the Finchley and Hendon Tramways Company with £160,000 authorised capital to construct and work lines in connection with the projected Tube railway at Golders Green. The Bill sought powers for a line 3.262 miles from Golders Green Tube Station (when constructed) to the junction of Ballards Lane and the Great North Road at Tally Ho Corner, North Finchley. This line would traverse Finchley Road, Temple Fortune, Regents Park Road and Ballards Lane, and be double track throughout. A second line, 1,775 miles in length continued southwards from the commencement of this line along Finchley Road and into North End Road (now Golders Green Road) and Brent Street to terminate in Hendon at the intersection of Brent Street and Church Road. A short line, 70 yards in length left Finchley Road on the east side 50 yards north of Golders Green Station's intended entrance and terminated in open land alongside the intended Tube line and Works where depot facilities were to be shared with the Tube Railway.

A further short line, 70 yards in length, left Finchley Road on the east side 50 yards south of the commencement of the line at Golders Green to terminate in the field on the east side of Finchley Road which is now part of the forecourt of Golders Green Tube Station, and a third length of 70 yards left Finchley Road on the east side 130 yards south of Mutton Brook (about 150 yards south of the present North Circular Road) and terminated in a field which would later become part of the Hampstead Garden Suburb. All sections were double track throughout.

Objections by Finchley Urban District Council caused the line north of Mutton Brook through Finchley to Tally Ho Corner to be struck out and the Bill achieved a second reading thereafter as the Hendon Tramways Bill. However, there were further objections and the Minutes of the Charing Cross Euston and Hampstead Railway Company simply record that "the Bill did not pass".

CHAPTER TWO

PLANS AND PROPOSALS

The north-eastern side of Middlesex developed as a residential and industrial area by the latter half of the nineteenth century, the railway facilities offered by the Great Eastern Railway and Great Northern Railway having encouraged large numbers of people from inner north and north-east London to migrate to the healthier and less crowded districts to the west of the Lee Valley. By the 1880s Tottenham, Edmonton, Wood Green and the eastern part of Hornsey were already served by horse and steam tramways.

No such facilities then existed in the much larger, but more sparsely populated central and western parts of Middlesex, other than the Harlesden end of the Harrow Road & Paddington company's horse tramway. The large area consisting of the Urban Districts of Finchley, Friern Barnet, Hendon, Harrow, Willesden, Wembley, Kingsbury, Enfield, Southgate, much of Hornsey, the Barnet and Hendon Union Rural Districts, and the Urban Districts of East Barnet Valley and Barnet in South Hertfordshire relied solely for public transport on the rather poor services provided by the GNR, LNWR and Midland Railway, and on infrequent horse omnibuses.

The Light Railways Act of 1896, although not intended by Parliament as a means of authorising street tramways, was soon used as a cheaper and less onerous form of tramway legislation than the Tramways Act 1870. One of the first such applications was made on 23 October 1897 by the Finchley District Electric Traction Company Ltd., for lines from Canfield Gardens (Hampstead) near Finchley Road Metropolitan Railway station through Childs Hill and Golders Green to North Finchley and from Golders Green to Hendon Midland Railway station. The London County Council said that if this scheme was approved they would ask Parliament to change the Light Railways Act to exclude lines along urban streets, but the Light Railway Commissioners in March 1898 rejected the scheme.

The promoters of the Finchley District Electric Traction Co. Ltd. were J. T. Firbank, a contractor who had built much of the Great Central Railway, and W. M. Murphy, a well-known figure in the tramway sphere, particularly in Dublin. The secretary was Joseph Barber Glenn, a leading figure in the Provincial Tramways group, and other subscribers were A. A. Tyler, E. F. Vesey-Knox, M.P., Edward Wragge, A. L. Hookings and Stacy Bates. Sir Douglas Fox was civil engineer to the company, and the lines would have been of standard gauge with electric traction.

Nothing daunted, the Finchley District Electric Traction Co. Ltd. made a fresh application in November 1898, this time for a different pattern of routes. They now envisaged building a U-shaped line from the North Metropolitan company's horse tram terminus at the Archway Tavern, Highgate, along Archway Road to The Wellington and then across country to Bell Lane, Hendon, following the line of a proposed road. The line would traverse Hendon to reach the Edgware Road and follow it southward through Dollis Hill and Cricklewood to Brondesbury (North London Railway) station, with a terminus in Iverson Road. A half-mile branch would run northwards from Hendon to The Hyde, and another short branch would serve the Church Road area of central Hendon. Most of the lines would have been single line track with passing loops. The total sought was

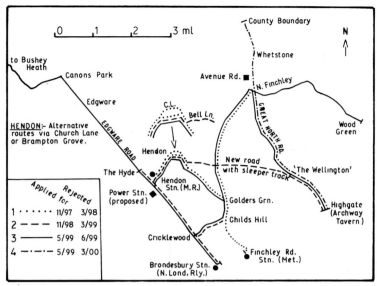

Rival applications for Light Railway Powers in Middlesex included those of the Finchley District Electric Traction Co. (1, 2, 3) and Finchley and Hornsey Councils (4) in 1897-99. All these were rejected or withdrawn.

9.81 miles, and powers were sought to buy a five-acre site for a generating station near the Brent reservoir (Welsh Harp) in Hendon.

At the inquiry, held on 28 March 1899, it emerged that the new road from Archway Road to Hendon would be 80 feet wide with a sleeper track tramway. Much of the land was owned by the Ecclesiastical Commissioners and Eton College, who had agreed in principle to the proposals, which would have aided the development of the area. However, all the local authorities except Hendon and Islington were opposed to the scheme, and the application was rejected. The proposed route is now covered by parts of the Barnet By-Pass and North Circular Roads.

By this time, other tramway schemes were being proposed for the area, but the Finchley District Electric Traction Co. Ltd. was back with a fresh application a few weeks later, this time for 26 miles of line (shown on the map) covering the Edgware Road, Great North Road, Cricklewood—North Finchley, Golders Green—Hendon and North Finchley—Wood Green routes. This was dismissed on procedural grounds. The Light Railways Act 1896 required applications to be made and published during the months of May and November in two consecutive issues of the local newspapers in the areas concerned (and the *London Gazette*). The FDET notice appeared in the *Hendon & Finchley Times* on 26 and 31 May 1899, but the Commissioners held that as this special edition of 31 May had been specially produced to carry the notice of application within the time limit, it did not comply with the Light Railways Act. The application was summarily rejected, and no public inquiry took place.

This third attempt by the FDET company was its swan-song. No return was made to the Registrar of Companies in 1900 or 1901, and when the Registrar asked Joseph Barber Glenn about this in October 1901 he was told that the company had not traded in the past year and that no shares had been issued. The company was struck off the register on 18 November 1902.

The second attempt to obtain light railway powers for the area was made in April 1898 by the Metropolitan Tramways and Omnibus Company Limited, and although its first application was unsuccessful, this was the scheme that eventually succeeded. The MTOC was incorporated on 21 November 1894, and although its stated objects in the tramway field were very far-ranging, including manufacture, it would seem that it was set up to work those parts of the North Metropolitan company's horse tramways that lay outside the County of London after the main North Metropolitan system was purchased compulsorily by the LCC. As a first step, the MTOC built horse tram depots at Wood Green and Forest Gate and leased them in 1897 to the North Metropolitan Tramways, but meanwhile the LCC had agreed to grant the NMT a lease of the lines, and so the need for separate operation of the outlying portions did not arise. The MTOC company therefore remained inactive for several years. Its directors throughout the period were Charles H. Fox, S. A. Cosser, H. S. Headington, O. Wethered, H. K. Heyland, J. Jenssen and D. P. Kingsford.

The British Electric Traction Co. Ltd., which had been founded by Emile Garcke and his associates in 1896, was seeking to obtain a financial interest in as many tramways as possible, and to obtain concessions for districts where scope existed for electric tramways. Although this is not evident from the MTOC papers, it is likely that during 1897 the BET had approached the MTOC directors with an offer to back them in applying for powers to build a network of lines in Middlesex, for which the BET would take over the powers once they had been obtained.

In consequence, the MTOC applied to the Light Railway Commissioners in April 1898 for a London, Barnet, Edgware and Enfield Light Railways Order, and published a brochure to acquaint the public with the overhead trolley system. It was profusely illustrated with views of electric tramways in such places as Bristol, Coventry, Leeds, Rouen and Versailles, and contained statements in support of the proposals from the general managers of the Corporation Tramways of Glasgow and Sheffield. The total mileage applied for was 31¼, of standard gauge and mostly double track, to be worked on the overhead system.

The routes of this and later applications are shown on the maps, and will therefore be described only briefly in the text. The April 1898 MTOC application comprised Cricklewood (The Crown) to Edgware (Church Lane), Cricklewood to Childs Hill, Golders Green and North Finchley, Highgate Archway to Barnet, from Wood Green via New Southgate, Oakleigh Road South and Oakleigh Road North to join the Barnet line in High Road, Whetstone and from Wood Green to Enfield, continuing via Ponders End to join the North Metropolitan company's line at Tramway Avenue. The Wood Green and Tottenham routes were also to be linked by a line along Lordship Lane, and sites were planned for depots and power stations at Oak Lane, East Finchley, near High Barnet GNR station, and at the corner of Edgware Road and Pipers Green Lane in Edgware.

The proposed lines were opposed by the local authorities, frontagers and other interests, and all were withdrawn except Wood Green to Tottenham and Wood Green to Enfield. These were the subject of an inquiry at Wood Green on 13 July 1898, but were rejected. The opposition was based largely on the feeling that the public roads should not become the preserve of a private company aiming to make a profit.

The promoters, it is assumed, then took steps to win the support of at least some of the objectors, and submitted three new applications in November 1898. One was for Cricklewood—Edgware, Childs Hill—North Finchley, Cricklewood—Childs Hill and Golders Green—Hendon, the second was for Wood Green—Tottenham, Highgate—Whetstone and Wood Green—Whetstone, and the third was for Edmonton to Waltham Cross and Ponders End to Enfield. The promoters had agreed to widen various roads, and to the lines in Middlesex being purchasable by the local authorities under the provisions of the Tramways Act, 1870.

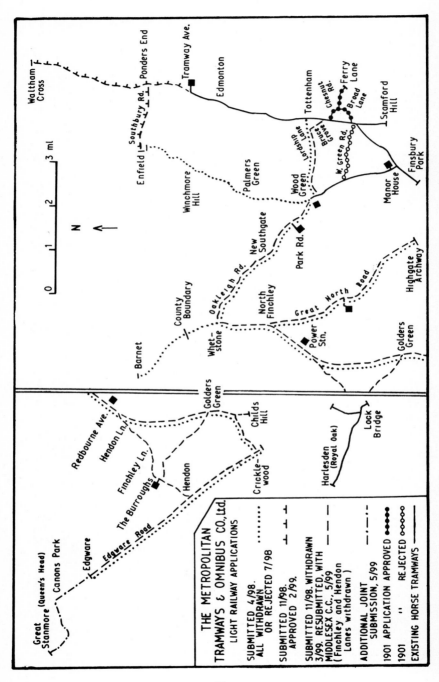

THE METROPOLITAN
TRAMWAYS & OMNIBUS CO., Ltd.
LIGHT RAILWAY APPLICATIONS

SUBMITTED 4/98.
ALL WITHDRAWN
OR REJECTED 7/98 · · · · · · · ⊥⊥⊥⊥⊥⊥

SUBMITTED 11/98.
APPROVED 2/99. — · — · —

SUBMITTED 11/98. WITHDRAWN
3/99. RESUBMITTED WITH
MIDDLESEX C.C., 5/99 — — — —
(Finchley and Hendon
Lanes withdrawn)

ADDITIONAL JOINT
SUBMISSION, 5/99 — · · — · · —

1901 APPLICATION APPROVED ●∘∘∘●

1901   "   REJECTED ∘∘∘∘∘

EXISTING HORSE TRAMWAYS ——————

3 ml

N

0   1   2

28

As a result, when the first inquiry took place at Enfield on 22 February 1899, the lines from Edmonton to Waltham Cross and Enfield were approved. This was the first application under the 1896 Act in the area covered by this book to receive the blessing of the Light Railway Commissioners, but confirmation by the Board of Trade was deferred pending the submission of other applications in Middlesex.

The other MTOC applications were heard on 15 March 1899, at the same inquiry as those of the Finchley District company. When local authority opposition caused the FDET plan to be rejected, counsel for the MTOC offered to withdraw his company's application for Edgware and Hendon and defer that for Wood Green and Finchley. This was accepted by the Commissioners, who saw little purpose in proceeding until the parties concerned had reached agreement.

In fact there had been a change in the attitude of the Middlesex County Council, who had previously opposed the company schemes. The MCC, like the London County Council, had felt that the Light Railways Act was not a proper means of obtaining powers for electric tramways, but the London United Tramways had obtained a Light Railway Order for their line from Southall to Uxbridge, the first street tramway to be so authorised. The Board of Trade confirmed the LUT Order on 2 February 1899, and at the next meeting of Middlesex County Council, on 23 February, a motion was carried that the County Council should promote its own light railways. The council felt that they were the right and proper authority for tramway or light railway promotion within the county, though the London United were already in possession of the south-west part.

From the outset, the MCC envisaged that they would construct and own the lines and lease them to a company to operate. The company they favoured was the Metropolitan Tramways and Omnibus Co. Ltd., backed by the BET, and after discussions an application was made to the Light Railway Commissioners in May 1899 in the joint names of the County Council and the MTOC. The lines requested were the same as in the MTOC's application of November 1898, excluding Edmonton—Enfield and Waltham Cross (already authorised to the company) and Hendon to Finchley (withdrawn) and with the addition of a line from Edgware to the Queens Head at Great Stanmore. Depots and power station sites would be at Burroughs Lane in Hendon and at Redbourne Avenue and East End Road in Finchley.

However, the county now found itself face to face with a new opponent, Finchley Urban District Council. Finchley were in the process of obtaining Electric Lighting Orders and planning their own generating station, and wished to build and operate their own light railways to provide a useful load for their generators. Finchley had persuaded Hornsey Council to join in promoting a joint municipal line from the Archway Tavern, Highgate along the Great North Road to the Finchley—Barnet boundary north of Totteridge Lane. Their applications were published on 16 May 1899. The power station would have been at Redbourne Avenue, and the depot in High Street, North Finchley, at Avenue Road.

The LCC had promised Finchley and Hornsey its support, but then withdrew it on learning of the comprehensive scheme now planned by Middlesex. Hornsey then withdrew, earning hard words from Finchley, who prepared to dig in for a battle with Middlesex. Finchley called a meeting of local authorities on 13 June 1899 at which the MCC was condemned for entering into an arrangement with a private company, but in the months that followed the MCC gained the goodwill of the councils of Hendon and Hornsey, and the general agreement of Tottenham, Southgate and Wood Green. Finchley was therefore isolated, and when its application was eventually heard, on 14 March 1900, it was rejected on the grounds that a line contained wholly within a single urban district was outside the scope of the Light Railways Act. Finchley appealed to the Board of Trade in June 1901, but this was rejected. Finchley accepted this with ill grace, and kept up a stern opposition to everything Middlesex put forward for some years to come, accepting the county's light railways only if accompanied by extensive road-widening, resurfacing, street lighting and other improvements, at county expense.

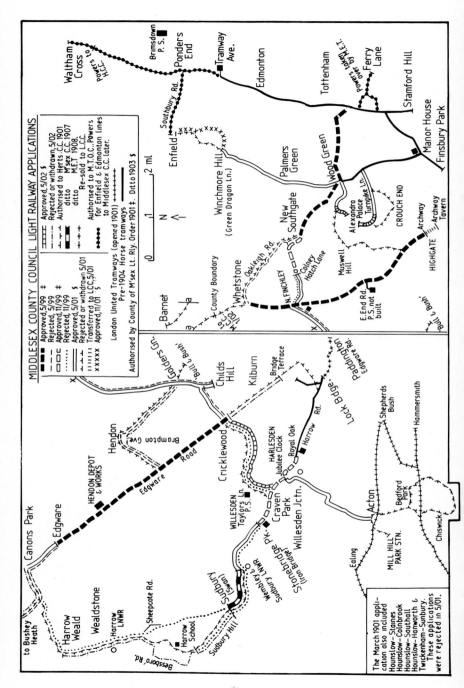

MIDDLESEX COUNTY COUNCIL LIGHT RAILWAY APPLICATIONS

Approved, 5/99 ‡
Rejected, 5/99
Approved, 11/99 ‡
Rejected, 11/99
Approved, 5/01 §
Rejected or withdrawn 5/01
Transferred to LCC, 5/01
Approved, 11/01 §

Approved, 5/02 §
Rejected or withdrawn 5/02
Authorised to Herts. C.C. 1901
ditto   M'sex. C.C. 1907
ditto   M.E.T. 1908.
Re-sold to L.C.C.
Authorised to M.T.O.C. Powers
for Enfield & Edmonton lines
to Middlesex C.C. later.

London United Tramways (opened 1901)
Pre-1904 Horse tramways
Authorised by County of M'sex Lt. Rly. Order 1901 ‡ Ditto 1903 §

0   2 ml

30

During 1899, Middlesex County Council discussed its joint application with the Board of Trade and the Light Railway Commissioners, and it was agreed that any lines approved would be sanctioned to the County Council, in their name only. Consideration of the May, 1899 applications was deferred to await plans for the rest of a comprehensive county scheme, and in November 1899 the MCC applied for additional lines. The two applications were considered together on 14, 21 and 25 March 1900.

The result of these inquiries, as shown on the map, was that the MCC were given powers for Tottenham—Wood Green, Wood Green—Friern Barnet, Whetstone—Highgate, Cricklewood—Edgware and Harlesden—Stonebridge Park, which were confirmed in the County of Middlesex Light Railways Order 1901. Lines rejected were from Stonebridge Park to Sudbury Hill and Stanmore (see Appendix 5), Edgware to Stanmore, Craven Park to Cricklewood, Cricklewood to Childs Hill, Golders Green to Hendon, Childs Hill to North Finchley, North Finchley to Friern Barnet (Colney Hatch Lane), and Whetstone to New Southgate. However, the lines granted together with the existing North Metropolitan lines in Wood Green, Tottenham and Edmonton formed a basic framework, on which work could proceed.

The year 1900 passed comparatively quietly, with many negotiations with district councils on the subject of road widenings, pavings and other preliminaries, with the aim of re-submitting those applications which failed in 1900. The county engineer's staff were busy preparing the necessary drawings and tender documents, and in April 1901 the county set up a Light Railways and Tramways Committee, as described in the next chapter.

A fresh application was made to the Light Railway Commissioners in May 1901, covering Wood Green to Enfield, New Southgate to Whetstone, Friern Barnet to North Finchley, North Finchley to Childs Hill and Cricklewood, Cricklewood to Craven Park, and Golders Green to Hendon. These had been considered before, but there were also some new lines. One was a circular route to serve Turnpike Lane and Crouch End, another was from Wood Green to Archway Road via Palace Gates Road, Dukes Avenue and Muswell Hill Road, and a third was from Golders Green crossroads to the Hendon—Hampstead boundary, near the famous Bull and Bush hostelry. In the southwest, the MCC applied for a line from Harlesden to Mill Hill Park (now Acton Town) station and for an interesting circular route in Chiswick and Bedford Park. There was a further attempt to obtain powers for the Harrow and Stanmore districts (see Appendix 5) and, for the first time, an attempt by the MCC to build a line in LCC territory, from Cricklewood through Kilburn and Maida Vale to the Harrow Road. This and later proposals for Kilburn are described in Appendix 7.

The May 1901 MCC application also included some lines in south-west Middlesex, centred on Staines and Hounslow. At the inquiry at Hounslow on 22 July 1901 these were opposed by the London United Tramways. The MCC suggested that the LUT might lease the lines, but the LUT made it clear that they would press for their own powers. Charles Tyson Yerkes, the American financier, who had recently gained control of the Metropolitan District Railway, offered to lease the lines, but most of the local authorities preferred the alternative LUT scheme, and the MCC application was rejected. The MCC put forward no further proposals for West Middlesex.

The Finchley applications were considered on 30 October 1901, after the MCC had persuaded Finchley UDC to withdraw its opposition, and Friern Barnet—North Finchley—Childs Hill—Cricklewood was approved, though Golders Green—Hendon was rejected and New Southgate—Whetstone was withdrawn. Two days later, the Commissioners learned that an agreement had been reached between the LUT and MCC regarding lines in Acton, as a result of which the MCC would not build south of Horn Lane. Cricklewood—Craven Park was rejected, and so were all the Harrow and Stanmore lines, save only for Edgware to Canons Park. However, powers were granted for the line from Stonebridge Park to Sudbury & Wembley station.

The inquiry for the other Wood Green lines was held on 10 November, and resulted in powers for Wood Green to Winchmore Hill, Turnpike Lane to the western entrance to Alexandra Park, and Wood Green to Palace Gates, the other applications being rejected. The wish to avoid steep gradients in Bush Hill, and opposition from residents of Bush Hill Park led to a plan to build a new road and light railway through the Red Ridge Estate from Winchmore Hill to Enfield, and this was granted in the county's 1903 Order, as described in Chapter 4.

In the autumn of 1901 Middlesex County Council applied for a Bill in Parliament making the Council a tramway authority under the Tramways Act 1870 and giving it powers to purchase or lease tramways in the county; it received the Royal Assent on 23 June 1902.

No mention has yet been made of the line from Whetstone (Totteridge Lane) to Barnet. This had been applied for in November 1899 jointly by the MTOC and Hertfordshire County Council, and was an attempt by Hertfordshire to penetrate Middlesex territory. At that time Middlesex and Finchley UDC had submitted rival plans for the Finchley area, and Hertfordshire evidently wished to remain neutral and retain the option to connect its line with whichever party obtained powers from Whetstone southwards. In the event the MCC scheme proceeded and Middlesex took over the powers south of the county boundary.

By the end of 1901, the MCC had thus obtained powers for almost all the lines that were eventually built, save for the gap between Cricklewood and Harlesden. This was applied for again in May 1902, this time with success, and powers were granted at the same time for the two short lines in the grounds of Alexandra Palace. Of the other May, 1902 applications, Golders Green—Hendon and the lines in Harrow were again rejected and were now dropped, but Cricklewood—Kilburn though rejected was revived later by the LCC. Further details of these three proposals will be found in Appendices 3, 6 and 7.

This account has brought the record of light railway proposals in Middlesex up to the point when the first MET and MCC lines were opened in the summer of 1904. A few more proposals were made, or revived, in subsequent years (including Wembley to Sudbury, which was built) and these are described in the chapters dealing with the areas concerned.

Construction of the MET system took eight years. The final section (from Enfield to Ponders End) was opened with car 147 on 20 February 1911, driven by County Councillor Weston.
(London Borough of Enfield Libraries

32

CHAPTER THREE

THE BET-MCC PARTNERSHIP

We have seen in Chapter Two that more than one group of tramway promoters was interested in north and central Middlesex. The number of contestants would have been even greater if three of them had not already joined forces in 1898; the Metropolitan Tramways & Omnibus Co. Ltd. (MTOC), the British Electric Traction Co. Ltd. (BET) and British Thomson-Houston Co. Ltd. (BTH).

Under an agreement of 30 September 1898, BET and BTH agreed not to seek powers for the area, and to use their best endeavours to help the MTOC obtain them. The parties evidently recognised that the MTOC, representing the interests of the North Metropolitan Tramways Company, was in a strong position through the latter's ownership of the horse tramways to Wood Green and Edmonton, and BET, BTH, North Metropolitan directors George Richardson and John Goddard and solicitor H. C. Godfray each lent the MTOC £1,000 towards the cost of obtaining Light Railway powers. If they were obtained, the MTOC would issue each lender with shares to a value four times the sum advanced. It was evidently already envisaged that the BET would equip and operate the lines, for the agreement placed an obligation on the BET (and not the MTOC) to give BTH the option of supplying the electrical equipment, subscribing for one-fifth of the shares or debentures, and nominating one director. In fact, the scheme did not proceed as envisaged, and the original MTOC directors continued in office until September 1901, but the agreement was still in force in May 1903, when it was modified to allow the BET to order equipment from Brush, who would sub-contract where possible to BTH.

In February 1899 the Middlesex County Council, learning that the Board of Trade was prepared to grant light railway orders to companies wishing to build lines along public roads, decided to promote its own light railways. The London County Council supported the proposal, preferring the Middlesex proposals to those of Hornsey and Finchley councils, and Middlesex had led the LCC to believe that it was going to be both owner and operator of the lines in its area. Some councillors may have envisaged this, but the point was at that time undecided.

The withdrawal by the MTOC of its March 1899 application for lines in Edgware, Hendon, Wood Green and Finchley may have been due to local opposition, as stated at the inquiry, or it may indicate that informal talks had already begun between the MCC and BET, with the latter offering to lease and operate lines to be built and owned by the county council. An agreement was reached along these lines, and on 18 June 1899 the Highways Committee of the London County Council was dismayed to learn that Middlesex was promoting a light railway scheme *jointly with a private company*. It was holy writ with the LCC that tramway and other public undertakings should be municipally owned and operated, and London would not entertain the intrusion of private capital into any scheme with which it was associated. One speaker said, 'We have been diddled by Middlesex, which has sold its birthright to a company'. One result was that the LCC withdrew its November 1899 application for the piece of line from the Archway Tavern to Highgate Archway, though it was revived later.

In fact it seems unlikely that Middlesex had ever seriously envisaged working the lines itself. Unlike many members of the LCC, the members of Middlesex

County Council were mostly successful businessmen and farmers, and Herbert Nield, M.P., vice-chairman of the MCC light railways committee, later said that the Middlesex method was to be preferred to that of the London County Council, since it gave municipal control 'without the evils attaching to municipal working'. The council had powers to ensure that the cars were kept in order, ran to time, and could step in, if necessary, and compel the lessee company to keep up to a standard.

Apart from two minor examples in later years (in Glamorgan and Lanark-shire) of light railways being built by county councils and leased to tramway companies, the arrangement reached between the Middlesex County Council and the Metropolitan Tramways and Omnibus Company Ltd. (renamed The Metropolitan Electric Tramways Ltd. on 12 October 1901) was unique, and must therefore be described in some detail. The formal agreement between the parties was signed on 16 November 1900, and its provisions can be summarised as follows:

—the Council would construct the lines, widen roads and bridges, and lay the track (the method of construction to be agreed beforehand with the company);

—the Council would provide the land needed for road widening and the sites for generating stations and depots;

—the Council would lease the undertaking to the company from the date of opening until 6 August 1925 (in April 1902 this was extended to 31 December 1930);

—the Company would erect the necessary depots, generating stations and other buildings and provide and own the generating equipment, overhead equipment and distribution mains;

—the Company would provide and own the rolling stock, the design of which would be agreed with the Council;

—the Company would maintain the track, cars and equipment to the Council's satisfaction;

—the Company would maintain the road between the tracks and for 18 inches on either side;

—steam or cable traction would not be used without the special permission of the Council.

The company had to satisfy the Council that it was financially able to carry out the agreement, and had to deposit £20,000.

The rent payable by the company to the council was calculated on a two-part formula, with an element of profit-sharing. Part would be a fixed annual percentage of the council's capital expenditure, assessed half-yearly, being 4% per annum initially, rising to 4½% for the middle one-third of the lease and 5% for the final third, though subsequent expenditure would be charged at a flat 4%. From this sum, the company would deduct a similar annual percentage of its own outlay on cars, depots, generating equipment, mains and overhead. In addition, the council would receive 45% of the net receipts, after the company had deducted its working charges including repair and renewal of track, cars and equipment, its engineering and management expenses, rates, taxes, insurance, licences, compensation, and not more than £3,000 in directors' fees.

This agreement was signed on 16 November 1900 by Ralph Littler (chairman) and Walter George Austin (deputy clerk) for the Middlesex County Council, and by Oliver Wethered and Herbert Headington (directors) and George Bance (secretary) for the Metropolitan Tramways and Omnibus Co. Ltd. Headington and Wethered had been among the original MTOC directors of 1894, though it can be assumed that they were now acting for the BET.

At first it was left to the MTOC to continue working on its plans for the area, but on 16 April 1901 the county council set up a Light Railways and Tram-ways Committee, which was thereafter closely involved in nearly every aspect of the scheme. Its first chairman was County Alderman Cory Francis Cory-Wright,

Herbert Nield, M.P., was vice-chairman, and the other 19 original members were Aldermen Adams and Huggett, and county councillors W. King Baker, Barker, Beck, Bradshaw, Henry Burt, de Salis, L. S. Devonshire, de Wette, Furness, Goodyear, Holmes, Little, Norman, Pinkham, Walcott and Warren. A quorum was four members, and the full committee usually met at fortnightly intervals (later monthly), except for a summer recess.

The size of the committee reflects the size and scope of the light railway undertaking, which was to involve the reconstruction and improvement of some 50 miles of main roads in the county, with an expenditure that by 1909 had reached £1,290,000 and was to strain the council's borrowing powers. One of the committee's first actions was to appoint a consulting engineer (Vivian Bolton Douglas Cooper, a partner of Stephen Sellon of the BET), and a sub-committee of councillors Burt, Bradshaw and Pinkham was appointed to deal with the plans. Cooper was to work with the county engineer, Henry Titus Wakelam, who had been given extra staff.

ENTER THE M.E.T.

Meanwhile, on 1 October 1901, the Metropolitan Tramways and Omnibus Company Ltd. became a full member of the British Electric Traction group of companies. The original MTOC directors retired and were replaced by Emile Garcke, William Leonard Madgen and James Devonshire of the BET, with H. S. Price of BET headquarters as secretary. One of their first decisions (on 12 October 1901) was that the company's name should be changed to The Metropolitan Electric Tramways Ltd., and this change was registered on 15 January 1902. Four additional directors were appointed on 9 July 1902, of whom Sir Ernest Spencer and Charles Tegetmeier were BET men, but George Richardson and John Goddard were respectively chairman and deputy chairman of the North Metropolitan Tramways Company, operators of the large horse tramway system in North London. A full-time secretary, A. L. Barber, was appointed on 1 June 1902.

At this date the North Metropolitan company operated mainly over tracks owned by the LCC and leased back to the company, but the NMT both owned and operated the lines in Middlesex (to Wood Green and Edmonton). Under the MTOC/MCC agreement of November 1900, these were supposed to be sold to the county council, but because the North Metropolitan was a statutory company and only part of its undertaking was involved, the council's parliamentary committee found this to be too difficult. The parties therefore decided that the North Metropolitan would sell these lines to the MET.

The method chosen was an exchange of shares, which had the effect of giving the MET a controlling interest (75%) in the North Metropolitan company. The MET company's capital was increased from £1M to £1.5M, and the BET paid the MET to acquire 78,504 North Metropolitan shares, receiving 78,504 MET shares in return. The way was now clear for the MET to buy the horse tramways, and on 7 November 1902 a price of £220,000 was agreed, comprising £103,050 for lines and depots, £31,200 for cars, horses, plant and harness, and £15,750 for goodwill, the latter figure being calculated on the average annual profit of £11,021 earned by the NMT's lines in Middlesex. The sale took effect on 26 November 1902.

Under the November 1900 agreement, the MET had to obtain the council's agreement to each item of capital expenditure, a percentage of which would be charged each year against the revenue. For much of 1902 the MET officers were busy preparing estimates, and on 7 October A. H. Pott, who had been appointed MET chief engineer, gave the county council provisional estimates for the entire 48 miles of light railways proposed at that date. The company's outlay was calculated as £103,000 for Brimsdown generating station, £130,000 for a generating station at Cricklewood, £142,000 for high-tension mains and ducts, £77,000 for 48 miles of overhead construction, £138,000 for six car sheds with substations, and £210,000 for 300 cars, a total of £800,000. Some of these figures were later amended; only five car sheds were found to be necessary, and the

The Metropolitan Electric Tramways Ltd. began operations in November 1902 with 62 horse trams taken over from the North Metropolitan Tramways Co. and used on the lines to Wood Green and Edmonton. From mid-1904 their numbers were gradually reduced as the lines were electrified, until by early 1905 only eight cars remained, working a shuttle service between Edmonton (Tramway Avenue) and the Tottenham Boundary, as shown in this photograph. The last MET horse tram ran in July 1905.   (Courtesy L. A. Thomson

proposed Cricklewood power station was replaced by the purchase of one at Willesden, described in Chapter 16.

On 23 October 1902 the council awarded the contracts to build the first three sections of its Middlesex Light Railways. They accepted the tenders of W. Griffiths & Co. Ltd. for Wood Green to Tottenham (£28,329) and Highgate Archway to Whetstone (£50,224) and that of J. G. White & Co. Ltd. for the line from Cricklewood to Edgware (£49,981). The contracts were for laying the tracks, including foundations and road surfaces. Separate contracts for associated road-widenings went to Willesden public works contractor Clift Ford for Wood Green—Tottenham (£20,514), to A. Kellett & Sons Ltd. for Highgate—Whetstone (£12,778) and to R. Ballard Ltd. for Cricklewood-Edgware (£6,716).

The MET board considered that these contract prices were excessive, and asked to be consulted in future before tenders were accepted, since the high capital expenditure would increase the company's rent. MET director James Devonshire was particularly concerned at those cases where the local district councils were demanding wood block paving across the whole width of the roads, and lighting and other amenities where none had existed before, particularly in Wood Green and Friern Barnet. He considered wood block paving to be a highways improvement and therefore the responsibility of the county Highways Committee. However, council policy at the time was that the trams should pay for the road improvements, and the practice continued.

By early in 1903 the council had sent to the Board of Trade the plans and estimates for the future lines approved by the Light Railway Commissioners during 1902, and on 22 June 1903 Major Pringle of the BoT sent his report to Middlesex county engineer H. C. Wakelam. It was generally favourable, but he suggested some minor alterations. Work was now proceeding on the Council's three 1901 lines, but less rapidly than had been hoped, due partly to the many complaints from the district councils about traffic obstruction, quality of materials, drainage, and lighting, a typical example being Finchley UDC's complaint that the wood blocks being laid on the Great North Road were 'insufficiently pickled.' There were also delays by the contractors.

The council also had the right to approve the design of the cars to be used on the Middlesex Light Railways (or, more precisely, the cars that were to be charged against their revenue). This excluded the first 70 MET cars, which were charged to the account of the ex-North Metropolitan lines and were the sole responsibility of the MET, but the next 80 and many subsequent batches were to be 'County Council' cars and would bear the council's name. As described in Chapter 11, the council favoured the double-deck uncanopied type of car with divided staircase used by the London United Tramways, and the result was an order for cars to a design which by 1904 was already obsolescent. Because of the council's ruling, all subsequent double-deck cars up to 1908 were built with the costly internal monitor ceiling, a form of construction which most tramways had long since abandoned.

In February 1904 the council decided that the next lines to be built would be Wood Green to North Finchley, Wood Green to Palmers Green, and the two lines to Alexandra Palace. Two weeks later Harlesden—Stonebridge Park and Craven Park—Cricklewood were added to the programme, with Palmers Green to Winchmore Hill added later that year. The contracts for these and all subsequent lines are set out in the chapters describing each group of routes. These lines would have involved an outlay of about £180,000, but the costliest portion (Wood Green—Winchmore Hill) was deferred for two years, the MCC finding conditions in the money market unfavourable.

One of these contracts, for Turnpike Lane and Priory Road, had been awarded to J. G. White & Co. Ltd., but this firm then withdrew, and the contract was transferred to Dick, Kerr & Co. Ltd. J. G. White's withdrawal was due to a dispute with the county council over a subsidence on the Edgware line, described in Chapter 8, which went to arbitration, the council having to pay £4,000 of the £5,276 costs. As a result of this incident, the MET asked the county council to exercise closer control over the contractors' activities, or to permit such control to be exercised by the company. The council responded by appointing

This view of a Type C/1 car body on accommodation bogies at the Brush company's Loughborough works reflects both the involvement of the County Council of Middlesex in MET car design and also the links between the MET and the British Electric Traction Company, of which both MET and Brush were subsidiaries.

(Brush Electrical Engineering Co. Ltd.; Author's collection

additional Clerks of Works, and from 1905 there was some improvement. There were still some lapses from grace, especially by the smaller contractors, and many later contracts were awarded to Dick, Kerr & Co. Ltd., the acknowledged experts in tramway construction, whose methods gave virtually no cause for complaint.

It had been hoped to open both the first company and first council lines in May 1904, but various delays occurred and the first electric cars did not enter service until 22 July 1904, on the company's own lines from Finsbury Park and the Manor House to Wood Green and Seven Sisters Corner. The first council line, from Wood Green to Tottenham via Lordship Lane and Bruce Grove, was opened on 20 August 1904 amid great ceremony, described in the next chapter.

This gala opening was the occasion for a number of speeches which deserve to be reported in detail, so well do they sum up the unique relationship between the Middlesex County Council and the lessees of its light railway system, Metropolitan Electric Tramways Ltd. The most significant speeches were those of Sir Francis Cory-Wright, chairman of the council's Light Railways and Tramways Committee (who had been knighted in June 1903); Emile Garcke, chairman of the BET; and Sir Ralph Littler, chairman of the county council.

Sir Francis Cory-Wright said that the county council had been concerned at the lack of cheap and convenient travelling facilities in and around the county of Middlesex, and had realised that if they did not provide light railways or tramways, somebody else would. Companies would have come in and built the lines and taken profits which, he thought, rightly belonged to the county, because the county roads would be used for the purpose. Thus the county council had taken the matter up and prepared their first scheme, which was for about 50 miles of routes and would cost about £1.5M. They had joined hands with the MET, who were the lessees of the county lines, and at the end of 1930 all the lines would revert to the county council, who could then renew the lease, lease the lines to another company, or run them themselves. He was confident that the light railways, operating in conjunction with the company's tramways, would be a very profitable scheme besides being of enormous benefit to the public. He hoped that the county council would have the first 50 miles completed within three years, and by that time the county would have another 50 miles in readiness to come forward.

Emile Garcke, chairman of the MET, said it was the duty of the company to give satisfaction to the county council and the travelling public. The company hoped to remove some of the difficulties of the housing problem by the removal of factories and other industrial establishments to outlying districts. This was made possible by the co-operation between the MET and the North Metropolitan Electric Power Supply Company. The county council had agreed at once with the suggestion that the company should take the current for working the system from the Power Supply Company rather than go to the expense of building another power station. The arrangements with the county council retained the council's control over the roads, relieved the council of speculative risks, and entitled the county to share in the profits of the undertaking to the extent of nearly one half, and the interests of the two parties were thus very nearly identical.

Sir Ralph Littler, chairman of the MCC, then spoke of his own part in securing the light railways to the county council. He tried in 1891 to have the North London steam tramways handed over to the local authority, but this had not materialised. If this had happened, Middlesex could have had the first overhead trolley system in the country. Prejudices were strong against the overhead system at that time, and he did the next best thing by persuading the North Metropolitan Tramways Company to take over the steam lines; he was happy that after twelve years everyone was converted to his way of thinking. The MCC had been accused of handing over the interests in the west of the county to the London United Tramways, but this was nonsense; the LUT had had a very long start over the county council. The county council had the credit of having proved that light railways could, under the 1896 Light Railways Act, be made along public roads, and the County had also, in 1902, obtained an Act giving them powers as a tramway authority. Prior to that, the county council were not even allowed to be heard when schemes of the London United Tramways were before Parliament, as they were not a tramway authority.

By the end of 1904 both company and council were becoming concerned at the heavy expenditure on the light railways, and no major contracts were let until 12 July 1906, when the council awarded a £65,910 contract to Dick, Kerr & Co. Ltd. for the line from Wood Green to Winchmore Hill, and one of £67,000 to Dick, Kerr for Edmonton (Tramway Avenue) to the county boundary near Waltham Cross. Later in 1906 contracts were placed for Willesden Green to Craven Park, New Southgate station to North Finchley and Harlesden to Willesden Junction, followed in February 1907 by Willesden Junction to Acton.

By 1906 a large number of cases had come to light where local improvements which had no bearing at all on the light railways were being charged to the light railways account. When in 1905 the council was considering an extension from Cricklewood through Kilburn (described in appendix 7), Willesden Council demanded road widenings that could cost between £360,000 and £500,000. James Devonshire of the MET flatly said that if sums of that size were to be spent, the company would have nothing to do with the scheme.

In 1907 the County Council's Accounts Sub-Committee tried to change the basis for charging for repairs and renewals. They proposed to place the whole burden of repairs and renewals of permanent way, equipment and rolling stock upon the company, which would greatly increase the council's share of the revenue. The company threatened to refer the whole question of the lease to the Board of Trade, and it was referred back to the Accounts Sub-Committee as being contrary to both the letter and the spirit of the 1900 agreement. No more was heard of the proposal, and from July 1907 the light railways account was relieved of some burden when the Highways Committee agreed to take responsibility for all work on the roads along which light railways ran, from the dates when the lines were opened.

A combination of disputes over paving, road-widening and bridge widening delayed the placing of contracts for the New Southgate—North Finchley and North Finchley—Cricklewood lines to a point where in 1907 an extension of time had to be sought. This was granted by the Board of Trade, despite Finchley UDC's objections, and extended the period to 31 December 1908. The disputes over paving in Hendon, Finchley and Friern Barnet were settled by arbitration in April 1908, and the Board of Trade upheld the county council's view that it was unnecessary to widen Friern Barnet Road bridge before trams could run there.

When on 9 July 1908 the council awarded a £116,978 contract to Dick, Kerr & Co. Ltd. for the line from North Finchley to Childs Hill and Cricklewood, a comparison of costs with the Edgware Road line showed that construction costs per mile had doubled in four years. However, the cost per mile of the different lines did vary considerably, this one involving some expensive alterations to the road levels in order to reduce the gradients. The contract for Winchmore Hill to Enfield was awarded on the same day to George Wimpey & Co. Ltd., and extensions of time were sought in November (and granted in 1909) for certain unbuilt lines and proposed road widenings.

It had now become quite clear that the capital expenditure by both parties would exceed the original estimates, and the MET had to issue £200,000 of Second Debentures. The county council's expenditure to 31 March 1908 had amounted to £748,500, and a further £400,000 would be needed to complete the scheme. The council applied to increase its borrowing powers, and in May 1909 the council's total expenditure on light railways was quoted as £1,290,000. There were fears that the scheme was not going to prove financially viable, and there was a strong faction at the Middlesex Guildhall who were against any further expenditure on light railways. No more was heard of Sir Francis Cory-Wright's confident 1904 prediction that the first 50 miles of council light railways would be followed by another 50, and he had died on 30 May 1909, after a lifetime of service to business and public work in Middlesex, Hornsey and the City.

The last two construction contracts placed by the county were awarded on 22 July 1909 to Dick, Kerr for Ponders End to Enfield GER station (£45,000) and to George Wimpey & Co. Ltd. for Wembley station to The Swan at Sudbury (£27,132). The Sudbury line was opened on 24 September 1910, and the final extension, from Ponders End to Enfield, was opened in a snowstorm on 20 February 1911.

The construction of the light railways authorised to the Middlesex County Council was now complete, and no new applications were pending, though later proposals would be made by both council and company. From this date, there was a lessening of activity at Guildhall, though the county was much involved in the dispute over the 'boundary tramway' at Finsbury Park (Chapter Ten) which preceded the start of through running between the MET and LCC.

The MET company in 1910 was in a reasonably sound financial position, having in 1909 paid 5% on the ordinary shares, £25,000 on the 5% preferred shares and put £6,000 to reserve. However, they considered that a lease expiring in 1930 would not give them time to recoup their expenditure, and in 1911 offered the county council 50% of receipts from 1 January 1913 (instead of 45%) if the council would extend the lease to 1946. Negotiations took place in March 1911, but no agreement was reached.

From about the middle of 1915 the county council relaxed the strict surveillance they had exercised over the operations of the company, and by mid-1917 almost allowed the company a free hand apart from the regulation of fares. Meetings of the Light Railways and Tramways Committee between mid-1917 and 1919 were infrequent, as it was realised that the company was largely in the hands of wartime government control of inland transport, which could over-ride the views and wishes of local bodies.

The council's Light Railways and Tramways Committee ceased to exist on 13 October 1919, when it was reconstituted as a sub-committee of the Highways Committee. County Alderman Henry Burt, who had been chairman of the committee since 1909, did not seek re-election and County Alderman Charles Pinkham was elected chairman of the new committee. There was a resumption of Parliamentary activity over the Kilburn proposals, and the new committee decided to apply for powers to run motor buses. The LCC and Hertfordshire were seeking similar powers, and there were talks about a possible joint scheme between the three counties, perhaps also with Essex, but by the summer of 1920 all three county council Bills had failed.

In the Spring of 1920 discussions took place between the MET and MCC about the future relationship between the company and the county council. The company would shortly be faced with heavy capital expenditure, but could not raise the necessary capital unless their tenure was substantially extended (the London United Tramways had in 1918 secured an extension of purchase date to 1950, mainly on this account). Numerous informal discussions followed, but progress was infinitely slow, and it was not until December 1922 that the sub-committee recommended the county council to grant a new lease to run until 1951 at a fixed annual rent of £110,000 per year. Even this was shelved pending a full report by the council's solicitor, and its subsequent slow progress will be described in Volume 2. In the event, the original lease ran its full course until December 1930, and was succeeded by a new 42-year lease from 1 January 1931.

Constructing the tramways at Enfield Town in 1908. The top four pictures show various aspects of tracklaying without mechanical aids, including a gang manhandling a length of rail and the progress of the wood-block paving. In the bottom picture a patient horse is about to receive his feed; all haulage was still by horse and cart.
(London Borough of Enfield Libraries

41

CHAPTER FOUR
WOOD GREEN AND ENFIELD

During all the activity that brought into being the Middlesex Light Railways, described in the previous chapter, the Metropolitan Electric Tramways Ltd. went about the business of reconstructing and electrifying its own lines, the horse tramways from Finsbury Park and Stamford Hill to Wood Green and Edmonton. Perhaps because it did not have to consult the county council to the same extent, the company made somewhat better progress and parts of these lines were the first MET-worked electric tramways to open.

Early in 1902, it had been found impracticable for the Middlesex County Council to buy the North Metropolitan company's horse tramways in Middlesex, and a new agreement was signed between the NMT, MCC and MET on 21 May 1902 under which the North Metropolitan was to sell these lines to the MET, who would reconstruct and electrify the lines and then operate them. A separate agreement was drawn up for these lines, under which the county council would still receive 45% of the net revenue, but the company could first deduct all its working expenses, 6% per annum of its capital expenditure on the lines, and a further sum calculated from the proportion which these lines bore to the whole system as a contribution to the company's central charges.

The North Metropolitan Tramways introduced a Bill in the Spring Parliamentary Session of 1902 to authorise the electrification of the lines, and this received the Royal Assent on 31 July 1902. The MET then acquired a controlling interest in the North Metropolitan company, as already described, and on 26 November 1902 the MET became the owner and operator of 9 miles of horse tramway from Manor House and Stamford Hill to Wood Green and Edmonton, and the operator of the short section from Finsbury Park to the Manor House which due to LCC objections had been excluded from the sale. The Board of Trade had approved its inclusion in the MET scheme, despite the fact that the county boundary ran down the middle of the road, and after the LCC had accepted the position this line was sold to the MET on 30 December 1903.

Rather than transfer the powers, it was arranged that the electrification would nominally be carried out by the North Metropolitan company, under the direction of MET officers. Contracts were placed in November 1902, the main contractor being Dick, Kerr & Co. Ltd., who were to relay the track and carry out the necessary road-widenings for £92,788. Other contracts were placed with Hadfields Ltd. for special trackwork (£2,550), John Spencer Ltd. for traction poles (£93,520), F. Smith & Co. Ltd. for trolley wire (£2,835), British Insulated Wire & Helsby Cable Co. Ltd. for supplying and laying high tension cables (£32,163) and Callenders Cable & Construction Co. Ltd. for low tension cables (£30,738). The contracts (with the Brush Electrical Engineering Co. Ltd., since 1901 a BET subsidiary) for the substations are described in Chapter 16.

Further contracts for items required to complete the electrification were placed early in 1903; cast-iron pole bases, finials and collars and wrought-iron scrollwork from John Forster & Co. of St. Helens and W. Lucy & Co. of Oxford at £6,880, stranded galvanised steel span wire and guard wire from Rylands Bros. Ltd. of Warrington at £70, overhead fittings (ears by Estler Bros., frogs from Thos. Noakes & Sons) at £1.300, feeder and section pillar boxes and their equipment from BTH and R. W. Blackwell & Co. for £830.

Laying the MET electric tramways at the Manor House junction in early 1904, looking towards the boundary tramway in Seven Sisters Road. On the extreme right is a temporary horse car track; the centre curves were presumably intended for the Wood Green-Moorgate horse car service (until electric working began), and the left hand curves were for depot working.

(Tramway Museum Society

Work began on 3 June 1903, and it was hoped that the first lines would open in May 1904. However, in January 1904 the LCC objected to the line from Finsbury Park to the Manor House being electrified without their consent and asked that work should cease. By this time the reconstruction and electrification was almost complete, and the North Metropolitan refused to comply. Negotiations dragged on until May, when agreement was reached that the LCC would not exercise their powers of purchase of any part of this line until 10 April 1910, and this removed the last obstacle to the start of MET electric services. The horse tram services had meanwhile continued to operate, using the new electric tracks.

Seventy open-top bogie trams were purchased from the Brush Electrical Engineering Co. Ltd. to work the electrified horse tramways, and are described in the rolling stock chapter. They were of a maximum-traction canopied design somewhat reminiscent of the LCC A Class cars, and were numbered from 1 to 70. The contract was placed with Brush on 9 September 1903, and the first 35 were ready in April 1904. The dates on which they arrived at Wood Green depot are not known, but the order was completed in August, when the second 35 cars were delivered to the depot at Tramway Avenue, Edmonton.

On 19 July 1904, Major J. W. Pringle, R.E., of the Board of Trade, who was to be the inspecting officer for most of the MET and MCC lines, inspected the 1.877 miles along Seven Sisters Road from Finsbury Park (Blackstock Road) to High Road, Tottenham at Seven Sisters Corner, and the 2.08 miles from the Manor House along Green Lanes through Harringay to the 'Three Jolly Butchers' at Wood Green. The two routes were connected by a triangular double-track junction at the Manor House with 40 ft. radius curves, and a photograph shows that there was also a (temporary?) connection with the horse tram tracks towards Mildmay Park. Mr. A. P. Trotter inspected the electrical equipment. All was in order except for a requirement to alter the car lifeguards within two months, and the Board of Trade issued its Certificate of Fitness on 20 July. It imposed a maximum speed of 10 miles/h, with lower speeds over junctions.

The two lines opened for traffic on Friday 22 July 1904, with very little ceremony. The directors and chief officers of the BET and MET, with press representatives, went by special train from Liverpool Street to Brimsdown, inspected the new power station, and drove in carriages via Edmonton depot to Wood Green depot. Here they boarded three special trams and traversed the new routes, after which public services commenced forthwith. Some of the horses and horse cars were sold back to the North Metropolitan tramways for use on the lines they leased from the LCC, but others were kept to work between Stamford Hill and Edmonton.

NEW ELECTRIC TRAMS AT FINSBURY PARK.

The first MET electric lines, from Finsbury Park to Wood Green and Seven Sisters Corner, were opened on 22 July 1904 and were worked by cars 1-35, based at Wood Green depot. These two photographs were taken at Finsbury Park terminus shortly after service began; in the top picture the tower wagon stands ready to deal with any teething troubles with the newly installed overhead. At Finsbury Park the MET electric trams met the horse cars of the North Metropolitan Tramways. (Commercial postcard by G. Smith; courtesy D. W. K. Jones

At the opening of the first Middlesex County Council line (from Wood Green to Bruce Grove) on 20 August 1904, the first car to arrive at Bruce Castle for the ceremony was this Type B MET car. The official opening procession was headed by County Council car No. 71, shown in the frontispiece. (Commercial postcard by G. Smith, Author's collection

The new services were worked by MET cars 1-35, based at Wood Green depot and running alternately from Finsbury Park to Wood Green and to Seven Sisters Corner. The third side of the triangle at the Manor House was used by cars of the Seven Sisters route going to or from the depot. Fares were very low compared with those charged on the horse cars, one penny for the full journey on either route. The horse cars had charged twopence for the same journeys, with penny stages to or from Harringay Park Station or Amhurst Park. It was known at the time that electric traction would prove cheaper to operate than the horse cars, but higher fares were charged on later routes, reflecting the fact that the MET as lessees of the Middlesex County Council would have to pay to use the MCC tracks.

Meanwhile, contractor William Griffiths was completing the 1.843 mile council line from Wood Green to Tottenham via Lordship Lane and Bruce Grove, which virtually amounted to building a new road. Lordship Lane was very narrow right through to Bruce Castle, and the first part of Bruce Grove (to Hartham Road) was just a footpath, becoming Bruce Grove Road from Hartham Road until it joined High Road, Tottenham. It was a pleasant rural spot with many ancient elms and with the Sailmakers Almshouses and a row of recently-built villas on the south side of the footpath, Lordship Lane being mostly bordered by fields and smallholdings. Despite the extent of the work, a determined effort was being made to complete the line ready for a grand opening during the summer.

The Wood Green—Bruce Grove line was inspected by Lt. Col. E. Druitt, R.E., on 6 August 1904 and the Board of Trade certificate was issued three days later. The opening of the company's own lines on 22 July had been a comparatively quiet affair (the press does not even record the number of the first car) but the opening from Wood Green to Bruce Grove on Saturday 20 August 1904 was a gala occasion, centred on Bruce Castle, the picturesque old mansion in Bruce Castle Park which today serves as the Local History Museum and Art Gallery of the London Borough of Haringey, successors to Wood Green, Tottenham and Hornsey Councils.

45

The MET and Middlesex County Council had invited a large number of local dignitaries, and those attending included the Lord Lieutenant of Middlesex, the chairmen of all the district councils affected by the light railways scheme, their clerks and engineers, members of Tottenham and Wood Green councils, Clerks to Justices, Chairmen of Boards of Guardians, the mayors of Stoke Newington and Hackney, and others representing many local and city interests. Emile Garcke, James Devonshire, W. L. Madgen and J. S. Raworth represented the BET, and James Clifton Robinson came as general manager of the London United Tramways. The guests were received by the chairman and members of the Light Railways & Tramways Committee, who were accompanied by county council chairman Sir Ralph Littler and the High Sheriff of Middlesex, Alderman James Bigwood.

When the formalities inside the Castle were over, the guests adjourned to a huge marquee in the grounds for refreshments, accompanied by the band of the Scots Guards. The speeches reported in the previous chapter were then delivered, and Emile Garcke asked Sir Francis Cory-Wright to accept a silver and ivory mounted controller handle, with which he would be able to start the first car. It was presented as an emblem of the control which the County Council were to exercise over the company, control which he hoped they would use wisely but not too much. The High Sheriff then moved a vote of thanks to Sir Francis Cory-Wright for his great work on the light railway scheme, Sir Francis declared the line open and the party proceeded to the six cars drawn up at the park gates.

The six cars were heavily decorated, and the poles for some distance along the route were adorned with bunting, flags and replicas of the County coat of arms. The leading car was No. 71, and Sir Francis Cory-Wright took up his position on the platform. Cheered by the huge crowd, the procession moved off in the direction of Wood Green, continuing over the company's line to Finsbury Park and reversing there to cover the line to Seven Sisters Corner and then the section from there to Bruce Grove which had been sanctioned by the Board of Trade on the previous day and awaited opening on 24 August. Some reports speak of the procession completing the circuit, but the journey

Type A car No. 78 waits at "Spouter's Corner" at Wood Green to commence the journey to Finisbury Park. This view dates from 1905/6.   (London Borough of Haringey Libraries

46

No. 35 near Wood Green on the service from Finisbury Park to Bruce Grove via Wood Green. The "B" route indicator disc is for Bruce Grove.   (Courtesy D. W. K. Jones

ended at the corner of High Road Tottenham and Bruce Grove, where the two lines were not yet connected. The day ended with a fireworks display and illuminations in Bruce Castle Park, and at last the Middlesex County Council Light Railways had become a going concern.

The council later learned that the day's celebrations had cost the MET £801. This compared with a mere £120 spent by the MET on opening its own lines on 22 July, including the special train.

The new line opened later on the same day, 20 August 1904, and was worked at first as a self-contained local service, every six minutes, between Wood Green (Lordship Lane) and the west side of the GER railway bridge in Bruce Grove, at a fare of one penny. There were complaints about the lack of half-penny workmen's fares and the fact that the first cars on the route were too late for people starting work at 8 a.m.

Agreement was reached in November 1905 between the MET and Tottenham UDC for lowering the road under the railway at Bruce Grove GER station and joining the tracks with those in High Road, Tottenham. This 150-yard line was inspected by Major Pringle on 6 April 1906 and found to be in good working order, except that the overhead wires were within reach of upper deck passengers under the bridge. The Board's certificate, issued on 7 April, required this to be rectified before double deck cars could be used. Until this was done, only single deck cars could run there, so the MET (after a formal opening on 9 April 1906 when Sir Francis Cory-Wright drove a car from Bruce Castle to Alexandra Palace East) opened the line on 11 April 1906 with a service of single deck cars from Alexandra Palace East to Bruce Grove. A local press report gives the service as running through to Finsbury Park, suggesting that the single-deckers were augmented by double deck cars turning short of the bridge and this is supported by the photograph reproduced on this page.

The wires were later re-arranged under the bridge, and later in 1906 a six-minute service of double deck cars was put on from Finsbury Park via Wood Green

47

and Bruce Grove to Stamford Hill. It was a very roundabout route, but provided useful connections from Stamford Hill to Wood Green and from Finsbury Park and Harringay to points along Lordship Lane, and continued without alteration until 1915.

The opening of the two Alexandra Palace branches in December 1905 and April 1906 is described in Chapter Six, and this left only the continuation of the main line north from Wood Green to Southgate and Enfield to be completed. These two routes would share tracks as far as the top of Jolly Butchers Hill, and this section led in 1906 to some interesting discussions.

Wood Green depot was about 75 yards north of the junction with Lordship Lane, and this piece of line had been electrified by the MET in 1904 so that cars could reach the depot, though passenger cars turned at the foot of the hill. There was a curve allowing cars to enter and leave the depot from the north, the contractor had therefore completed the line to just short of the junction of Jolly Butchers Hill (Green Lanes) and Bounds Green Road.

Middlesex County Council also had powers to build this line, because Light Railway No. 1 of their 1903 Order was deemed to commence at the junction with Lordship Lane. The company therefore said that this piece of line was part of the Middlesex Light Railways, and that the county should pay its construction cost of £1,613. The county took the view that as the line was used by the company's cars to reach the depot, the company should bear half the cost of construction. MET secretary A. L. Barber then pointed out that the company's tramways in Wood Green were purchasable by Wood Green council in 1930, and if Wood Green exercised these powers the county council would not have access to the depot except by obtaining Wood Green's consent. The county accepted this argument, and paid the whole cost plus £413 for the special trackwork at the depot entrance.

The county's 1901 Order included powers for the line from Wood Green via Bounds Green Road to New Southgate, and construction was authorised in February 1904. However, probably for financial reasons, a contract was not placed for this line until 19 October 1905, when it was awarded to George Wimpey & Co. Ltd. of Hammersmith for £35,884. It was built during 1906, and in October of that year the county extended Wimpey's contract to cover the short section along Station Road, New Southgate to the junction with Friern Barnet Road. Beyond this point it could not be built until a decision had been reached on whether or not to widen the bridge over the GNR.

The first 1.075 miles from Green Lanes to the Ranelagh public house in Bounds Green Road was inspected by Major Pringle on 23 November 1906; the certificate was issued three days later, and it was opened for public service on 28 November by Sir Francis Cory-Wright in a short ceremony, after which public service commenced with single deck cars from Wood Green.

Friern Barnet council in 1907 demanded that all the poles in Station Road, New Southgate should be lit at night, even though it was not wholly in their district. The MCC had certain obligations under the 1903 Order, but not that of providing 'general illumination', and declined to comply.

The 0.9-mile line from The Ranelagh in Bounds Green Road to the junction of Station Road, New Southgate and Friern Barnet Road was inspected by Major Pringle on 7 May 1907 and approved; the certificate was issued on 9 May, and the line was formally opened next day with Sir Francis Cory-Wright driving the first car, double-deck number 94. However, when public service between Wood Green and New Southgate began on the following day, 11 May, it was provided by extending the single-deck service. No photographs of them on this section have come to light, but a resident interviewed some years ago by the author spoke of 'the continental *(sic)* single-deck trams that worked up to New Southgate station.'

The terminus remained at New Southgate station until 8 April 1909, when the service was extended through to North Finchley as described in Chapter 7. Some time prior to that, possibly on 8 April 1908, a through service of double deck

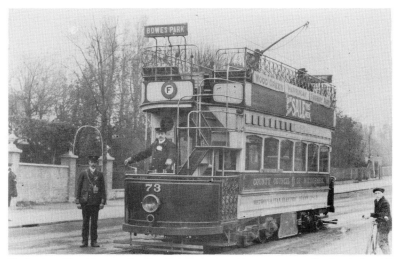

The line from Wood Green to New Southgate was opened in two stages, to The Ranelagh on 28 November 1906 and to New Southgate Station on 11 May 1907. No. 73 is shown on a short working to Bowes Park; the location is probably in Green Lanes north of the Manor House.
(Courtesy G. E. Baddeley

cars was put on from Finsbury Park to New Southgate station at a through fare of 2d. (1d. to or from Wood Green), and the single deck cars were withdrawn from the route. When in 1909 the service was extended to North Finchley, it ran every six minutes and an additional penny was charged between New Southgate and North Finchley.

The single deck services between Wood Green and the Alexandra Palace are described in Chapter 6, and the other route at Wood Green was the important one to Enfield. It was built in sections, the first contract being placed with Dick,

The connection between the Wood Green and Finchley routes was made on 8 April 1909. Car 107 of Finchley depot heads for Finsbury Park in Bounds Green Road. (Courtesy D. W. K. Jones

A first-day photograph of Type A car No. 89 at Palmers Green, 6 June 1907. The publisher of this commercial postcard captioned it wrongly as 7 June 1906, which has misled past historians.
(J. B. Series

The next section of the Wood Green-Enfield route, from Palmers Green to Winchmore Hill, was opened on 1 August 1908. Type B/1 car 65 stands at Winchmore Hill ready to return to Finsbury Park. The "W" route indicator is for the Wood Green route. (Courtesy J. H. Price)

Kerr & Co. Ltd. on 12 July 1906 at £65,910 for the 3.05 miles from Wood Green to Winchmore Hill (Green Dragon Lane). The first 1.126 miles from the junction of Bounds Green Road to Palmerston Crescent, near the New River bridge in Palmers Green was finished first and was inspected by Major Pringle on 4 June 1907. The certificate was issued next day, and a formal opening took place on 6 June with Sir Francis Cory-Wright officiating as usual. Public service commenced next day with a through service between Palmers Green and Finsbury Park.

The other 1.612 miles from Palmers Green along Green Lanes to Vicars Moor Lane, Winchmore Hill was not ready until July 1908. Major Pringle inspected it on

23 July and found it satisfactory, though widening was not quite complete; the certificate was issued on 26 July and the line opened for public service, apparently without ceremony, on 1 August 1908, with through cars to Finsbury Park.

Beyond this point, the original MTOC plan of 1898 had been to continue to Enfield Town by way of Bush Hill, London Road and Church Street. The Light Railway Commissioners had rejected this in July 1898 due to local opposition, and a similar application by the county council in May 1901 was withdrawn, when a new opportunity was found to approach the town by a more level route avoiding the steep Bush Hill and the descent into Enfield past Old Park.

The council had been negotiating with Urban Freeholds Ltd., who had acquired the large Bush Hill House Estate for development, and were willing to allow the line to be taken across part of their estate, then open land. The plan was to build a new road, 0.4 miles long, which would diverge from Green Lanes opposite Green Dragon Lane and run through the estate to meet Village Road, Bush Hill Park. The line would then continue into Enfield along Village Road, Park Avenue and London Road.

Agreement was reached between the parties by October 1901, and the line was included in the county's successful application of November 1901, authorised in the 1903 Order. The formal agreement with Urban Freeholds Ltd. was signed on 15 December 1902, by which time the land had been renamed the Red Ridge Estate. The landowners would provide the land free of charge, and the county would build a 60 ft. road, including bridges over the New River and Salmon's Brook. Urban Freeholds Ltd. would contribute £850 towards the council's estimated outlay of £10,000.

The contract to build the new road, to be named Ridge Avenue, was placed with Thomas Turner on 11 May 1905 at £6,975 including the two bridges, but

The opening-day scene at Enfield Town on 1 July 1909. No. 109 carried the official party, with County Alderman Henry Burt, chairman of the MCC Light Railways and Tramways Committee, at the controls. (London Borough of Haringey Libraries

VILLAGE ROAD, ENFIELD.

Southbury Road, Enfield.

Three tramway scenes in Enfield, reproduced from commercial postcards. The top picture shows No. 73 in Village Road, part of the new line through the Red Ridge Estate between Bush Hill Park and Enfield; the centre picture of No. 53 at Enfield Town terminus also shows the short length of single track laid in anticipation of a connection with Southbury Road which was never realised; the lower picture shows single-decker 138 in Southbury Road before the Enfield-Ponders End service was taken over by double-deckers.

(Courtesy J. B. Horne, Author's collection, and J. H. Price

housing development did not begin at that time and it was not until 9 July 1908 that a £40,220 contract was given to George Wimpey & Co. Ltd. to build the 1.62-mile Winchmore Hill—Enfield light railway. It took eleven months to build, and was inspected by Major Pringle on 21 June 1909, together with a 0.175-mile section in Green Lanes from Vicars Moor Lane to Green Dragon Lane which was still incomplete at the last inspection. The certificates for both lines were issued on 24 June 1909.

The formal opening of the Winchmore Hill—Enfield line on Thursday afternoon 1 July 1909 was a red-letter day in Enfield, with flags, bunting and other decorations much in evidence. The official party assembled at Wood Green depot to board car No. 109, which had been driven over from Finchley by the newly-opened route through Friern Barnet. The car was driven to Enfield by County Alderman Henry Burt, who had succeeded the late Sir Francis Cory-Wright as chairman of the county committee. Guests included members of Southgate, Edmonton and Enfield councils, the county engineer, other local dignitaries and representatives of the MET and the contractor. The route into Enfield was lined with large crowds, held back by police, and on reaching the Market Place terminus Henry Burt made a speech from the platform of No. 109, which was followed by three cheers from the crowd.

Public service began on Saturday 3 July 1909, with a through service from Enfield Town to Finsbury Park. The through fare was 4d. for the 6.992 miles, with a 2d. workman's fare from Enfield Town to Wood Green. The route from Wood Green had now reached its most northerly point, and it was to beome one of the busiest routes on the MET system. However, parts of the Red Ridge Estate were not completed until the inter-war years and a fare stage in Ridge Avenue was officially known simply as Pole 170, and later Pole 169.

Enfield's tramways were not yet complete, for another line was planned to enter the town from a junction with the Hertford Road line at Ponders End. It had been proposed by the MTOC in 1898, approved at an inquiry held in Enfield on 22 February 1899, deferred pending the transfer of powers to the county council, and finally authorised by the Board of Trade on 16 March 1906. The original application was for single track with passing loops, but the county decided in November 1903 to lay it as double track.

These powers did not specifically authorise a link with the line from Wood Green which ended in the Market Place, but the council considered that they already had powers under a clause in their 1903 and 1906 Orders which allowed them to lay crossovers, junctions and other connections for access to depots and other buildings and to facilitate the working of the lines. This line was wanted to enable cars to run to and from Edmonton depot, and although the clause did not specifically prohibit the carriage of passengers over such lines, this was implied.

The end of Southbury Road was very narrow, a bottleneck bounded on one side by the GER station and goods yard and on the other by the New River. The Great Eastern Railway had declined to sell land at a reasonable price for the road-widening that would have been required for a passenger service, but in May 1909 the county surveyor notified Enfield UDC of his intention to lay the connection as a single line, and asked their approval to the first 200 ft. in the Market Place being laid at once, to avoid having to take up the new wood block paving at a later date.

Enfield UDC felt that the council should widen the road to 50 ft. and lay a double line, but on 26 May 1909 they agreed by 8 votes to 7 to the county's request, and the contractor soon afterwards laid the turnout in the Market Place. Enfield council then had second thoughts, for on 28 May a petition with 250 signatures had been sent to the Board of Trade asking for a public inquiry. Major Pringle visited the site, rejected an alternative proposal to take the line through Genotin Road, and in December the Board approved the construction of a single line connection without any road-widening.

Enfield council still made difficulties, so in the hope of obtaining specific Parliamentary powers the MET included the connecting line in their 1911 Bill, with the approval of the county council. Enfield council, whose consent was required under Standing Orders, still refused and the line was struck out of the Bill. Surprisingly, in April 1914 Enfield UDC underwent a change of heart and asked that the line be laid, but the MET told the council they were no longer interested. Enfield council had tried the patience of the county council and the company for too long, and the connection was never made.

The 1.397-mile line from Ponders End along Southbury Road to Enfield GER Station was built by Dick, Kerr & Co. Ltd. under a July 1909 contract and was inspected by Major Pringle on 6 February 1911. All was found to be in order, except that the powers granted under the Light Railway Order had expired on 31 December 1910; however, the Board decided to overlook this, and issued its certificate on 10 February. The line opened on 20 February, with County Councillor Weston driving the first car, in a snowstorm. It was No. 147, one of the Alexandra Palace single-deckers, and these cars worked the route for a short time. They were soon replaced with double deckers, and for a very long time two double deck cars sufficed for the traffic on this route, known to MET staff as the Chicken Run.

Short working cars on the Enfield route reversed at Aldermans Hill, Palmers Green, and the MET and the council wished to construct a double track lay-by there, on the south side of the triangle. Southgate UDC had given their consent, and on 26 March 1911 Major Pringle inspected the site and recommended approval. The Winchmore Hill Ratepayers Association opposed the idea, and the county council reduced the proposal from double to single line, but opposition persisted. From July 1911 this section of roadway became a bus terminus and Southgate UDC said that it would need to be widened for trams; the residents opposed taking any part of the land or removing any trees, and nothing more was heard of the proposal.

The lay-by would have been useful in keeping short-working cars clear of the main line, for the service consisted of a car every three minutes from Finsbury Park to Palmers Green, with alternate cars continuing to give a six-minute headway to Enfield. At summer weekends, all cars would sometimes run through to Enfield to assist in moving the crowds.

The first five top-covered MET cars, Nos. 211-216, arrived during 1908 and the official photograph (of 214) shows it with route boards for Finsbury Park to Winchmore Hill. However, the Board of Trade first required the curves at Aldermans Hill, Palmers Green to be respaced for greater clearance, and the cars probably made their public debut on the Edmonton route. In February 1910 they were also authorised from Wood Green to Stamford Hill.

The Enfield route was selected as the first candidate for through running to Central London, jointly with the LCC. This first MET-LCC joint service, from Enfield to Euston (Tottenham Court Road) is described in Chapter 10, and was worked by some of the first MET cars to be fitted with plough carriers (297-316) and by 15 nearly-new LCC E/1 cars (1590-1604) which had been hired by the MET. Open top MET cars with plough carriers were also used after the first few months.

When the LCC route numbering system was introduced in January 1913, the Enfield workings were numbered 29 and the Palmers Green short workings became 31. Two numbers in the appropriate MET series (20 and 22) were left vacant and may have been reserved for use if through running were to lapse, but were never needed. When numbers were allocated to the other Wood Green routes (by 1914) they became 18 Stamford Hill—Finsbury Park via Bruce Grove and Lordship Lane, 28 Muswell Hill—Finsbury Park, 30 Turnpike Lane (The Wellington)—Alexandra Palace West, 32 Wood Green—Alexandra Palace East, and 34 Finsbury Park—North Finchley; the Southbury Road shuttle became service 26. Within a few months, services 28 and 34 had become through services to London using LCC numbers 51 and 21.

CHAPTER FIVE

TOTTENHAM AND EDMONTON

In his book *Semi-Detached London,* published by George Allen & Unwin in 1973, A. A. Jackson explains how the Great Eastern Railway, having accepted in 1864 an obligation to run workmen's trains to Walthamstow and Edmonton, tried to concentrate this cheap traffic in one part of its territory in order to discourage it from spreading to other districts capable of yielding more lucrative traffic. One result was that the market gardens of Tottenham and Edmonton were quickly covered with thousands of low-rent houses, Edmonton's population increasing by 160 per cent between 1881 and 1901.

This development along the road to Hertford had attracted tramway promoters and from 1885 the North London Tramways Company had operated steam trams from Stamford Hill and Finsbury Park to Edmonton and Ponders End. The company failed financially and the lines were sold in 1891 to the North Metropolitan Tramways Company, who worked them with horse cars. The section from the Edmonton depot at Tramway Avenue to Ponders End was abandoned.

Middlesex County Council had hoped to acquire these lines to form part of its light railway scheme, but this was found impracticable and instead the Metropolitan Electric Tramways Ltd. bought the lines from the North Metropolitan company on 26 November 1902, together with 62 cars, 600 horses and the depots at the Manor House and Edmonton. The horse tram services continued under MET auspices while electrification got under way.

A contract to reconstruct the lines from Finsbury Park and Stamford Hill to Wood Green and Edmonton was awarded in November 1902 to Dick, Kerr & Co. Ltd., as described in chapter four. The lines from Finsbury Park to Wood Green and Seven Sisters Corner were inspected by Major Pringle on 19 July 1904 and formally opened on 22 July, as already described. The widening at MET expense of Seven Sisters Road between Candler Street and St. Ann's Road had not then been completed, and this portion was at first worked as a single line, with a compulsory stop at each end. A service of horse cars continued between Stamford Hill and Edmonton, perhaps with some interruptions where work was in progress.

By August 1904 the line was complete from Stamford Hill as far as Brantwood Road, just short of the Tottenham—Edmonton boundary. The entire 2.410 miles was inspected and passed by Lt. Col. Druitt on 19 August 1904. It was double track throughout, with centre poles in the area of Tottenham council and span wires from the Tottenham—Hackney boundary to Stamford Hill terminus, but there was a temporary piece of single line at High Cross, Tottenham where the road widening was still incomplete.

The first passengers to use the section were the guests on the six cars that formed the opening procession along the first section of the Middlesex Light Railways on 20 August 1904, described in the Wood Green chapter. Starting from Bruce Castle Park, which Tottenham UDC had made available to the county council for the gala opening, these cars went via Wood Green to Finsbury Park and then via Seven Sisters Road to Bruce Grove station, where the guests alighted. Public service with electric cars began on Wednesday 24 August, the service from Finsbury Park being extended to Brantwood Road.

Type B car No. 29 at Seven Sisters Corner during the period from 22 July to 23 August 1904, when the electric cars from Finsbury Park worked only as far as this point. The other vehicle is a horse tram, but the postcard publisher has painted out the two horses and has added a headlamp. (Commercial postcard, Author's collection

The MET had probably hoped to start a through service from Wood Green via Bruce Grove to Stamford Hill, but agreement had not yet been reached with Tottenham council and the GER for lowering the road under the railway at Bruce Grove station, and there was a 150 yard gap between the line in High Road, Tottenham and that in Bruce Grove. Perhaps for this reason, no electric service was at this stage introduced to Stamford Hill. Horse cars continued to run from Brantwood Road to Edmonton and from Seven Sisters Road via Stamford Hill to Aldgate, those for the latter section probably operating from the North Metropolitan company's depot at Portland Avenue which served the other Stamford Hill lines. The Bruce Grove line opened on 20 August 1904 with a local electric service between Tottenham and Wood Green.

A further 120 yards of line from Brantwood Road to the Tottenham—Edmonton boundary was brought into use on or about Saturday 29 October 1904. On 25 October A. L. Barber asked the Board of Trade to inspect it, but Major Pringle recommended on 28 October that the MET should be allowed to open this short section without formality, with a licence to use it until the time came to inspect the section beyond. The licence was issued on 3 November, by which time the line was already in use. The reason for opening it separately is not recorded, but may have been to allow a line of cars to await the end of matches at the nearby Tottenham Hotspurs' football ground.

Further widening was necessary on the portion through Edmonton. The horse tramway was a single line with passing loops, but during 1903 Edmonton UDC had offered to forego their right to buy the line in 1930 in return for widening from the Tottenham boundary to Tramway Avenue to 50 ft., with a further widening to 60 ft. within ten years, plus the reconstruction and widening by the MET of Angel Bridge, a county-owned bridge over the River Angel, better known today as Pymmes Brook. The UDC would supply the land free of charge. This was agreed between the parties, and the county council undertook to bear the extra cost, which amounted eventually to £27,000. The section included at its southern end a third track, at the east side of the road and bisected by the Tottenham—Edmonton boundary, for use by cars awaiting the end of matches at White Hart Lane.

The 0.437 miles of line from Brantwood Road to Angel Bridge, Edmonton (just north of Silver Street) was inspected by Major Pringle on 22 March 1905, and was approved except that the paving outside the tracks had not been completed. This was expected to take two more weeks, and the Board's certificate was issued on 10 April.

Public service with electric cars to Angel Bridge began on 12 April 1905, with through cars from both Finsbury Park and Stamford Hill, the car indicators being set at 'Edmonton' and the side boards displaying 'Angel Bridge'. A postcard issued at this time shows car 19 at Stamford Hill on this service, and since this was a Wood Green depot car, it suggests that Edmonton depot's cars (36-70) were still prevented from entering service by the line being incomplete from Angel Bridge to Tramway Avenue. Cars from Wood Green depot could reach Stamford Hill without reversing, by means of the triangular junctions at the Manor House and Seven Sisters Corner.

On 5 July 1905, Major Pringle inspected the 1.625 miles of line from Angel Bridge to Tramway Avenue, and this date probably marks the start of operation by Edmonton depot, though the cars would have run empty to and from Angel Bridge. Much more extensive widening had been necessary on this section, and Major Pringle found road widening still incomplete at five points, where powers were still awaited for compulsory purchase. At these places double line had been laid but only one track would be used, but he decided that the single line section near Bury Street was so short that the double track could be used if the footway was given temporary kerbing. The Board's certificate was issued on 19 July.

The line from Angel Bridge to Tramway Avenue was opened to the public, without ceremony, on 19 July 1905, with the last horse car probably running on the previous day. When horse operation through Tottenham ceased in 1904, the surplus cars and horses were resold to the North Metropolitan tramways for use on its London lines, but the eight Edmonton cars were probably sold off locally, for one of them survived for 77 years alongside the railway

The tramway in High Road, Tottenham was built with centre poles having extended bases to accommodate street lighting switches. No 14 is standing at an "All Cars" stop in Tottenham.
(Courtesy D. W. K. Jones

No. 19 stands at the original MET Stamford Hill terminus in the early summer of 1905. At this time the line was open only as far as Angel Bridge, Edmonton. In 1907 the LCC conduit tracks were extended across the junction to reach a new depot and the MET terminus was moved slightly further north. (C. Martin, courtesy J. H. Price)

at Lower Edmonton and was then bought by the Tramway Museum Society and taken to the Society's Clay Cross store in Derbyshire.

The MET/MCC lines in Tottenham were completed on 6 April 1906, when Major Pringle inspected the track under Bruce Grove GER station bridge that linked the Lordship Lane route with that in High Road, Tottenham. He required the wires to be repositioned under the bridge before double deck cars could run there, and when the line opened on 11 April 1906 the service was provided by single deck cars working through from Alexandra Palace East. They were replaced later in 1906 (an exact date has not been traced) by a service of double-deck cars from Finsbury Park via Wood Green and Bruce Grove to Stamford Hill, displaying a 'via Wood Green' board below the destination boxes. The main route through Tottenham now carried frequent services from Finsbury Park and Stamford Hill to Edmonton (Tramway Avenue).

The horse trams from Edmonton had charged 1d. to Angel Bridge, 2d. to Bruce Grove, 3d. to Seven Sisters Corner, 4d. to Manor House or Stamford Hill and 5d. to Finsbury Park. When electric services began the fare from Edmonton to Finsbury Park was reduced to 3d., with consequent reductions in the intermediate fares. Competition with the cheap trains of the GER was provided by a workmen's single fare (before 8 a.m.) of one penny for any journey between Edmonton and Finsbury Park, at 5.5 miles the best bargain on the MET system; it survived until after 1918. The same fare was charged between Tramway Avenue and Stamford Hill, and the low fares may have been a factor in later years in delaying the onset of bus competition on this route.

The 1905 MET terminus at Stamford Hill remained in use for less than two years. In connection with the electrification of its line from Stamford Hill to Shoreditch, the LCC bought land for a depot in Rookwood Road, Stamford Hill. To reach it, a conduit line would have to be laid along Egerton Road and the southernmost part of the MET line, and an agreement was signed on 19 December 1906 between the MET and LCC under which the MET would lay a temporary crossover north of Egerton Road and reverse their cars there while the LCC's conduit line was being built. The agreement allowed the MET to return to their original terminus when the work was finished, but these powers were not exercised. The temporary crossover became permanent, and the MET cars reversed just north of Egerton Road until arrangements were made for through running to start in 1920, after which the line was worked by LCC cars.

In 1908 the bridge taking the tramway over the railway at Lower Edmonton was reconstructed, and a 175 ft. tramway siding was added for cars turning back at Edmonton Town Hall. No. 25 waits in the siding while No. 105 continues northwards along the main line to Waltham Cross, about 1910.   (Commercial postcard, courtesy A. D. Packer

At Lower Edmonton, the tramway in New Road was carried over the GER's low level railway and Barrowfield Lane by bridges with cast iron girders. The GER thought that these should be replaced with wrought iron or steel girders to carry the trams, and until this was done the MET was not to allow two cars to be on either bridge or their approaches at any one time, and to cross at not more than 5 miles/h. An agreement was signed between the companies on 20 October 1908, and the work was done subsequently. Under a June 1904 agreement with Edmonton council, the MET also provided a waiting room with lavatories at the junction of New Road and Hertford Road, just north of the bridge.

The MET-owned tramway ended at Tramway Avenue, and the line beyond this point was a light railway built and owned by Middlesex County Council. The Metropolitan Tramways and Omnibus Company had applied in November 1898 for a Waltham Cross and Enfield Light Railways Order that would extend the line from Tramway Avenue along Hertford Road through Ponders End, Enfield Highway, Enfield Wash and Freezywater to Waltham Cross, with a branch along Southbury Road from Ponders End to Enfield GER station. The Light Railway Commissioners in February 1899 recommended approval, but the Order was held up to await details of other proposals in Middlesex.

Under the subsequent agreement with Middlesex County Council, these lines became part of the county's light railways and were authorised in the County of Middlesex (Waltham Cross and Enfield) Light Railways Order 1906. The county also proposed a line from Ponders End eastwards to the Middlesex-Essex county boundary, crossing the GER on the level at Ponders End station, and (under a 1902 proposal) continuing to Queen Elizabeth's Lodge, Chingford, but no further action was taken on this.

The section north of the Middlesex-Hertford county boundary at Freezywater was transferred by agreement to the county council of Hertfordshire, who sought to extend it to Cheshunt. The HCC were aware that for it to be a financial success Cheshunt UDC would have to moderate their demands for road widenings, but Cheshunt proved intractable and as a result it was decided to end the line eighty yards south of the Eleanor Cross. The section in Hertfordshire would be built by the HCC and leased to the MET for 42 years, as described in Appendix 5.

On 12 July 1906, the MCC awarded a £67,000 contract to Dick, Kerr & Co. Ltd. to build the 3.415-mile section from Tramway Avenue to the county boundary at Freezywater. It was inspected by Major Pringle on 26 November 1907 and found to be in good order; the certificate was issued on 28 November, and the line opened on 11 December 1907.

On 29 November 1907, Hertfordshire County Council placed a £4,176 contract with Dick, Kerr & Co. Ltd. to build the final 0.187-mile section from the county boundary to Waltham Cross. It actually cost less than estimated, the contractor's bill being £3,454. This short section was inspected by Major Pringle on 15 April 1908 and approved, the first car running on 17 April. There was little ceremony, but contemporary reports say that a car bearing Hertfordshire lettering was used at the opening. One or more Type C cars with this wording were transferred from Finchley to Edmonton depot to share in the service.

This left only the branch along Southbury Road to be completed. Construction of this line had been deferred while discussion continued on the possibility of joining it at the Enfield end with the line from Winchmore Hill, but as described in the previous chapter the link was never made. The contract for Southbury Road as far as Enfield GER station was awarded to Dick, Kerr & Co. Ltd. in July 1909 for £45,000 and the line opened on 20 February 1911, after inspection on 6 February. Two single deck cars worked the branch at first, but were replaced by double-deckers from 3 June 1911.

In April 1908 the MET applied to the Board of Trade for permission to run top covered cars on the Wood Green—Finsbury Park, Edmonton—Finsbury Park and Edmonton—Stamford Hill sections, to which Edmonton—Waltham Cross was evidently soon added. Permission was granted, and later in 1908 the Tottenham routes were among the first to receive some top-covered cars. It does

The extension along the Hertford Road from Edmonton to the county boundary at Freezywater was opened on 11 December 1907. This 1909 picture of No. 87 at Enfield Wash en route for Waltham Cross also includes a cart, a railway delivery van, a coster's barrow, a milk perambulator with shining brass churn, ornate gas lamps, and the three brass balls of a pawnbroker's shop.   (Commercial postcard, H&G Series, Author's collection)

Type C car No. 159 at Waltham Cross terminus about 1908, with "County Council of Hertfordshire" lettering on the waist panels. This terminus, 80 yards south of the mediaeval Eleanor Cross, was the most northerly point on the MET. The line was not continued further owing to the excessive demands for widenings by Cheshunt UDC.

(Commercial postcard, H&G Series, courtesy J. H. Price

not seem that they were initially allowed to run to Stamford Hill, for permission for this and Bruce Grove—Lordship Lane was given separately in February 1910.

As early as 1908 there were complaints from other road users about the centre poles in High Road, Tottenham. The East Middlesex Coroner wrote pointing out that they had caused a fatal accident, when a cyclist who had collided with one of them in Tottenham had been thrown under a motor van. Another fatal accident in Tottenham in 1909 brought renewed pressure from the Royal Automobile Club and in 1912 it was decided to replace them with side poles and span wires. The work was completed in 1914, at a cost of £2,590.

1908 also saw the construction of a 175-ft. single track siding in Lower Fore Street, a short way north of Edmonton Town Hall. This may have been laid in anticipation of some interruption to the through service during the reconstruction of Barrowfield Lane bridge but it became permanent and was authorised retrospectively in the MET's 1911 Act.

Service numbers were adopted by the MET during 1913, those for the Tottenham and Edmonton routes being 10 Stamford Hill—Edmonton Town Hall, 16 Stamford Hill—Waltham Cross, 18 Stamford Hill—Finsbury Park via Bruce Grove, 24 Finsbury Park—Waltham Cross and 26 Ponders End—Enfield. The numbers 12 and 14 were not used, but may have been kept vacant in case through running with the LCC via Finsbury Park was delayed. However, through running began on 1 March 1913 with services 27 and 59, followed by 79 on 23 June 1913, as described in Chapter 10. The LCC had a particular interest in improving services to Tottenham, as it was developing its own housing estate at White Hart Lane, which eventually had a population of 40,000.

The later history of these routes, bound up with the requirements of the armaments factories along the Hertford Road, is described in Chapter 13 on the MET in wartime. No other tramways were built in the area; but not for want of trying, as will now be described.

Type H car No. 240 standing at Waltham Cross in the early 1920s, ready for the long journey to Smithfield Market by way of Finsbury Park and the LCC conduit lines. The letter "T" after the route number was adopted as a result of the merger with the Underground group, presumably to avoid any confusion with bus services.

Tottenham—Walthamstow

In May 1901 the Metropolitan Tramways and Omnibus Company, backed by the BET, applied for a Tottenham, Walthamstow and Epping Forest Light Railways Order covering ten miles of line in the Lee Valley and Epping Forest area. The first 1.5 miles, from High Road, Tottenham along Chesnut Road, The Hale and Ferry Lane, with a second line along Broad Lane, would be in Middlesex; the rest, from the Essex county boundary at the Ferry Bridge to Woodford, with a branch to Leytonstone, would be in Walthamstow and Essex, with a depot in Forest Road east of Wood Street. Walthamstow UDC objected on the grounds that they intended to promote their own lines, and no Order was made.

Walthamstow's application for similar powers and additional routes was considered in January and March, 1902, and was granted except for the portion in Tottenham, to which Middlesex objected. Meanwhile, the MTOC had applied for the short portions in Middlesex and this time was successful, though a proposed Harringay—Tottenham link along West Green Road and Philip Lane, and a line in St. Ann's Road, were withdrawn. This left the MTOC empowered to build two lines between High Road, Tottenham and the county boundary in Ferry Lane, one along Broad Lane which would need extensive widening, and one along Chesnut Road which would be built later. The two lines totalled 0.99 miles and would meet in a triangular junction allowing a local circular route to be operated in Tottenham Hale.

Middlesex County Council sought to take over these powers, but withdrew in March 1903 because of the cost and left them to the MET. The powers were eventually granted as the Tottenham Walthamstow Light Railways Order 1906, but the company did not start acquiring land for widening until 1908 and then had to apply for an extension of time. Meanwhile, the MET had contributed £3,000 in 1906 towards the GER widening their bridge at Tottenham Hale station.

The existing bridge over the river Lee in Ferry Lane was in no state to carry trams, and the 1906 Order provided for a new bridge to be built by Walthamstow and the MET, with the company's share limited to £5,000. Plans for the bridge were approved, but Walthamstow then tried to get contributions from Middlesex and Essex county councils. Essex County Council accused the MET of postponing the work in the hope that Essex would be forced to build the bridge themselves. Eventually it was agreed on 8 July 1909 that Essex would build the bridge, and that the MET's contribution would go to them.

The MET acquired further property for road widening, and a draft agreement was drawn up and sent to the Board of Trade covering mutual through running between the MET and the Walthamstow UDC Light Railways, but unfortunately Essex and Walthamstow were in dispute about the bridge costs, and there was no sign of work being started.

In their 1911 Bill, the MET clarified their position by seeking an extension of time and applying for specific powers to take their line over the proposed new bridge and connect it with Walthamstow's line at the Ferry Boat Inn. Essex would build the bridge, at a cost now estimated at £8,000, and the MET would pay half, up to a maximum of £4,000. The cost of the line from High Road, Tottenham to the county boundary at the bridge was now estimated at £53,975. The MET told Middlesex that they were so sure the line would pay that they were prepared to pay 4½% (instead of 4%) on the capital outlay if the county built the line. Middlesex agreed to this, and were prepared to spend up to £65,000 to build it.

However, the MET changed its mind in 1912 and on 25 October announced that it now intended to make the line on the Railless principle, as part of a through route from Harringay (Green Lanes) via West Green Road and Broad Lane, terminating at the Middlesex side of the bridge. The county raised no objections and the necessary powers were obtained in the Metropolitan Electric Tramways (Railless Traction) Act 1913. Its provisions are outlined in the Appendix on trolleybuses.

The contract for the new bridge was awarded by Essex at £8,300 to W. & C. French Ltd., who began work in the summer of 1914. It was of single span reinforced concrete construction, 50 feet wide, with a 36 ft. carriageway. It was opened on 30 March 1915 by the chairman of Essex County Council, and replaced the old bridge immediately to the north, Ferry Lane having been diverted and widened. However, the war prevented a start being made on the Railless project and the MET applied for an extension of time.

After the war, since the Railless line had not been built and the MET was financially unable to do any more about it, Middlesex sought fresh powers to build the Tottenham—Walthamstow link as a light railway. In June 1923 they resolved to apply for a Light Railway Order, subject to the MET accepting a lease of the line at £4,000 per year, to Walthamstow improving the connecting tramway, and to the line being opened on or before 1 January 1926. Walthamstow doubled its line in Ferry Lane during 1925, but the discussions on the Middlesex line were inconclusive, and the matter was again shelved.

The scheme was revived in 1927 and authorised in the Middlesex Light Railways (Extension) Order 1929, but the anticipated cost of widening and of diverting a water main was now so high that the MCC in 1929 applied for an amendment to take the line along High Cross Road and thence by a new road emerging at the eastern end of Broad Lane. This variant was authorised on 13 January 1932, but the proposed formation of the London Passenger Transport Board led to its being deferred yet again. In the end, the link was made by a new LPTB trolleybus route via Broad Lane which opened on 18 October 1936.

In all the MET and MCC correspondence about this line, and about the coal wharf at Brimsdown power station, the two waterways are always referred to as the River Lee and the Lee Navigation. The author has found no contemporary example of the alternative spelling (Lea) sometimes used today, and the earlier form is therefore used throughout this book.

MET Type E car No. 142 on the reserved sleeper track on the Alexandra Palace West route, with the Palace in the background. (Tramway Museum Society

The reserved track section in later days, with No. 148 in the ownership of the London Passenger Transport Board but still in MET livery, though with the company insignia removed.

(B. Y. Williams

CHAPTER SIX

ALEXANDRA PALACE

The Alexandra Palace stands at the top of a 300 ft. hill and dominates the North London landscape for some miles around. The park in which it stands, partly in the Urban District of Wood Green and partly in the Borough of Hornsey, was formerly the Tottenham Wood Farm, owned by Thomas Rhodes, great uncle of Cecil Rhodes, who founded the African colony of Rhodesia. When he died in 1856 the estate was inherited by his grandchildren, who had a vision of a People's Park as a more worthy use of the estate than dairy farming. The inspiration was, of course, the Crystal Palace which had been built in Hyde Park for the Great Exhibition of 1851 and was afterwards rebuilt at Sydenham as a vast recreational centre, visible for miles around.

Despite selling part of the land for residential development as a means of raising funds, Thomas Rhodes' descendants had difficulty in financing their scheme and more than one grandiose design was abandoned on this count. By 1860 the grounds had been opened as a public park, and in 1862 another company was formed to use 250 acres for high class residential development and the remaining 150 acres as a recreational park with a People's Palace as the central features. The grounds were laid out as a pleasure garden in 1863 and a formal opening took place on 23 July 1863, the park being opened by, and named after, Princess Alexandra of Denmark who had arrived in England to marry the Prince of Wales, later King Edward VII.

The Alexandra Palace Company Ltd. was formed in 1866 to erect a large exhibition building to be known as the Alexandra Palace. The shell of the building was completed in that year but the money ran out and work came to a stop for several years. The building was completed in 1873 and opened on 24 May, but sixteen days later, on 9 June, it was destroyed by fire, only the walls remaining.

Money was found to rebuild the Palace, and it reopened on 1 May 1875, without the large dome but with a fine organ, a concert hall capable of seating 3,500, and a theatre seating 3,000. A contemporary account described it as of no architectural distinction, inspired probably by exhibition buildings in Paris and Vienna, its chief merit being its size and the brickwork, which as an example of solid enduring construction left nothing to be desired. Some Swiss-chalet style pavilions were built in the grounds.

The Palace company failed soon afterwards, and the London Financial Association acquired the property for £390,000 early in 1877. They obtained an Act allowing building to take place on part of the land, the remainder to be kept as an open space. The Palace and grounds were used intermittently for shows and exhibitions, and a racecourse was opened in 1888. A lessee tried to popularise the place in 1887-9, but became bankrupt, and apart from the racecourse and occasional exhibitions the Palace and grounds were closed from 1890 to 1897. A first attempt by the local authorities to buy the Palace and its grounds failed in 1891.

In October 1897 the London Financial Association granted a lease to Thomas John Hawkins, who planned to re-open the Palace and park from Easter, 1898 as a centre of public entertainment. Although there was a railway to the Palace from Highgate via Muswell Hill, Hawkins saw a need for a better means of access from the Wood Green side and a short electric tramway was built and opened on 13 May 1898 from the east gates up to the Palace. This interesting little line, the first electric tramway in the London area, is described in Appendix 1.

Hawkins' venture ended in bankruptcy, and the Palace and tramway closed on 30 September 1899. Wood Green UDC, a creditor for rates, took possession of the tramway and sold the line and its equipment. The property passed into the hands of London and Middlesex Freehold Estates Ltd., who proposed to use the park for housing. It seemed that the days of the famous North London landmark were numbered.

However, at a special meeting of Hornsey council on 28 February 1900 the chairman, Mr. C. F. Cory-Wright, announced that the new owners had given the council the chance to buy the property for £100,000. A deposit of £5,000 had already been found by seven local people, and the option had to be taken up within 12 months. The men who provided the deposit included Cory-Wright himself and Henry Burt, both members of the Middlesex County Council and highly respected public figures, and both of them were also to play central parts in the creation of the County of Middlesex Light Railways.

The purchase campaign succeeded and the Palace and park became public property on 1 February 1901 for £138,000; additional land, legal and Parliamentary costs brought the outlay to £150,000. Middlesex County Council provided £49,000, Hornsey £37,000, Wood Green £36,500 and the rest came in varying amounts from the district councils of Friern Barnet, Tottenham, Finchley and the Metropolitan Borough of Islington. The LCC offered £7,000 if the racecourse were closed down and no liquor licence applied for, but this offer was politely declined. The Alexandra Park and Palace (Public Purposes) Act 1900 set up a governing body (the Alexandra Park Trustees) to which the subscribing authorities were entitled to appoint one representative for each £7,000 contributed. The Palace and park reopened on 18 May 1901.

With C. F. Cory-Wright in the dominant position of chairman of the MCC's Light Railways and Tramways Committee and Hornsey Council and an Alexandra Park trustee, and Henry Burt, chairman of the trustees being a member of the Light Railways and Tramways Committee, there was little doubt that the question of tram services to the Palace would be pursued, and they were discussed at the very first meeting of the Light Railways and Tramways Committee on 16 April 1901. As a result, two applications were lodged with the Light Railway Commissioners in the following month.

One of these was for a through route between Highgate and Wood Green via Muswell Hill, passing just to the north of the Palace. It would commence at the junction of Archway Road and Muswell Hill Road, and follow Muswell Hill Road and Dukes Avenue to the Alexandra Palace, pass through the northeast part of the grounds and continue along Palace Gates Road to cross the GNR at Wood Green station, then following Station Road to the Wood Green junction. The other line would run from Green Lanes along Turnpike Lane, High Street Hornsey and Priory Road to the foot of Muswell Hill, then into Park Road to the Broadway, Crouch End and back along Tottenham Lane and Church Lane, Hornsey to form a circular route. Both lines appear on the map on page 30.

The applications were heard at Wood Green Town Hall on 10 November 1901, and were strongly opposed by the residents and frontagers of Muswell Hill, who claimed that their peace and quiet would be disturbed. Despite support from the Mayor of Islington, whose council had contributed £14,000 towards the Palace acquisition, the Light Railway Commissioners refused the lines through Muswell Hill and Crouch End and would only sanction the portions from Wood Green to the Palace Gates and from Green Lanes along Turnpike Lane and Priory Road to the foot of Muswell Hill. The failure of the Wood Green Station—Muswell Hill—Archway Road application was particularly unfortunate for the

MET, as it removed the possibility of serving the Alexandra Palace economically by placing it on a through route between two established traffic centres.

Discussions now took place between the MCC, the Alexandra Park Trustees and Wood Green and Hornsey councils on how to serve the Palace, and two new applications for light railway powers were made by the MCC in May, 1902. One was for 0.487 miles from the south entrance in Priory Road, Muswell Hill across private lands to the south-western door of the Palace, the other was for 0.493 miles from Palace Gates Road at the GNR bridge along Bedford Road and the eastern approach road to the north-eastern door of the Palace. The Trustees and the MCC had wanted the two lines to be linked at the Palace, but due to opposition this idea, of running trams along the South Terrace, had been dropped. The MCC offered the Trustees a wayleave rent (later fixed at £300 per year) for the right to run trams in the park, and this was accepted. At the hearing, at Wood Green Town Hall on 10 November 1902, there was no further opposition and the scheme was quickly approved. An earlier plan to build a small generating station near the northwest tower had previously been withdrawn.

In January 1903 the Trustees made further demands on the county council. They wanted control over fares, proper lighting along the tracks, facilities for their staff to board trams at the gates and collect admission fees (presumably for special events, since entry to the park was usually free), special cars to convey heavy goods, and the facility to hitch goods trailers to the cars. The MCC rejected these and especially 'the suggestion that the Trustees should convert the County Council to a sort of Pickfords.' Despite this, the Order when issued in 1903 did give the Trustees the right to hitch a van or trailer with goods, merchandise, coal or coke to any tram in the park for a change of not more than two shillings per vehicle, but there is no record that they ever took advantage of it.

The decision to build the two lines was taken by the MCC in February 1904, and the contracts were let on 13 October. Clift Ford tendered successfully at £17,266 for the line from Wood Green to the Palace Gates, and for the two sections within Alexandra Park. The 1.36 miles in Turnpike Lane and Priory Road was awarded at £39,246 to J. G. White & Co. Ltd., but this firm then withdrew as a result of the Edgware Road arbitration and at the next meeting it was transferred to Dick, Kerr & Co. Ltd. at £40,906.

The opening car, No. 145, arriving at Alexandra Palace East on 9 April 1906.
(Commercial postcard, J. H. Price collection

67

As recounted in chapter eleven, the original plan was to use double deck cars, but the MET and the county council were forced late in 1904 to reconsider this. The Board of Trade considered the lines too steep for double-deckers, and there was a low bridge in Station Road, Wood Green beneath which the road would have to be lowered by 3 ft. 6 in., involving demolition of property. James Devonshire offered to work the lines with single deck cars 'and to attach trailers at busy times', and this was accepted by the council on 12 January 1905. No trailers were ever used, and it is unlikely that they would have been sanctioned.

By March 1905 the Brush company had submitted drawings of a 36-seat four-wheel single deck car, with six windows per side and bearing many similarities to a batch of 65 cars which were being built for Shanghai. The council approved the design, and at short notice the MET asked the builders to substitute 20 single-deck cars for the last 20 double-deckers of the initial order. The single-deckers were numbered 131-150, and were fitted with the same electrical equipment as double-deckers 1-130, plus the Spencer mechanical track brake on account of the gradients. Dimensional and other details of these cars will be found in the rolling stock section of Volume 2.

The first cars of the batch were inspected at the Brush works in July 1905, and the county representatives found fault with their seating, ventilation, curtains and paint scheme. They wanted the same velvet upholstery as in the Type A cars, but Pott said that the MET had found that these cushions had quickly become dirty and insanitary, and had had to be burned. The council's sub-committee accepted this and agreed to rattan seats, but insisted on better ventilation.

The Turnpike Lane—Alexandra Palace West line was completed first, and was inspected by Major Pringle on 22 November 1905. It consisted of double street track from Green Lanes along Turnpike Lane and Priory Road to the Victoria Hotel at the foot of Muswell Hill, where the tracks turned right for the final 0.487-mile climb to the west side of the Alexandra Palace. Of this, a 467-yard section was laid on private right-of-way with 85 lb./yd. dwarf grooved rail on wooden sleepers, and included a gradient of 1 in 12. Track brakes would be required, and were to be applied in descending gradients of more than 1 in 15, with a compulsory stop for downhill cars opposite the entrance to the Nursery Gardens and at the foot of the hill before entering the curve into Priory Road. The certificate was issued on 24 November.

The line opened on 6 December 1905, with a service of single-deck cars from The Wellington (the junction of Green Lanes and Turnpike Lane) to the foot of Muswell Hill, extended to Alexandra Palace West when the park was open. The opening was marked by a lunch at the Palace, when Sir Francis Cory-Wright said that the opening of the two Alexandra Palace lines had been delayed through difficulties with the GNR, but that he hoped to have the other line open by Boxing Day or early in the New Year.

In February 1906 the MET told the county council that they proposed to work double-deck cars from Green Lanes as far as Muswell Hill, as there was sufficient clearance for them under the GNR bridge at Hornsey station. The clearance beneath this bridge was determined by the fact that the roadway crossed over the New River a few yards away. Their engineer was arranging with the railway company to place notices on both sides of the bridge warning upper deck passengers to remain seated. The county engineer thought that the cars should be fitted with top covers, and declined to accept any responsibility unless this were done.

Here things rested until October, when the MET took the matter to the Board of Trade and obtained their approval to run double-deck cars as far as the Priory Road entrance to the Palace, subject to the warning notices and to a speed limit of 4 miles/h under the bridge. The MET now introduced a through service of double-deck cars between Muswell Hill and Finsbury Park via Green Lanes, serving the residential areas of Muswell Hill and Hornsey and leaving the single-deck cars to deal with the traffic through to the Palace.

The MET rule-book included an instruction that double-deck cars must not pass on a curve on the sleeper track. So far as is known, double-deck cars

Tram Terminus, Muswell Hill.

From October 1906 a service of double-deck cars was operated between Finsbury Park and Priory Road, Muswell Hill, where passengers changed for single deck cars to the west side of Alexandra Palace. In the lower photograph the conductor of No. 79 is turning the trolley pole from the upper deck.   (Courtesy A. D. Packer and D. W. K. Jones

never worked regularly to the Palace, for they would have required to be fitted with mechanical track brakes and this brake was never fitted to any MET bogie cars. The brake could have been fitted to the four-wheel Type D cars, but in 1921 the space where it would have been mounted was used instead for a plough carrier. A picture is known of one double-decker (No. 191) on the line, in a convoy of single-deck cars used during the 1914-18 war to take either Belgian refugees or German prisoners-of-war to the Palace.

Alexandra Palace Gates, Wood Green.

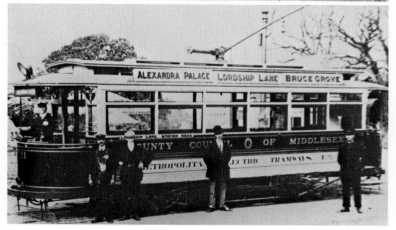

The other line, from Wood Green junction to the east side of the Alexandra Palace, was inspected by Major Pringle on 6 April 1906, and was the subject of a lengthy report to the Board of Trade on account of its gradients, the steepest on the system. There was a 1 in 17 gradient in Station Road, and severe gradients of up to 1 in 10 on the Eastern Approach Road; when the 1898-99 tramway was in operation on the same route this had been quoted as 1 in 9.75, with an average of 1 in 13. There was a 70ft. radius curve on a gradient of 1 in 15½ at the entrance to the park.

Major Pringle imposed a 4 mile/h speed limit on the downward journey within the park and on various curves, with compulsory stops at the top of Eastern Approach Road and before the curve at the park gates. The mechanical track brake had to be applied before commencing the descent from the Palace, and no traffic stops were permitted on the ascent. The certificate was issued on 7 April.

The new line was formally opened on Monday 9 April 1906, when Sir Francis Cory-Wright drove a single-deck car from Bruce Castle to the eastern terminus of the Palace. Public service began on 11 April, with a service of single-deck cars between Alexandra Palace East and Bruce Grove, Tottenham. This was of short duration, the Bruce Grove section being taken over by double-deck cars, with single-deckers working a local service between Wood Green and the Palace when the park was open, and at other times between Wood Green and the GNR station.

In January 1908, the Alexandra Park Trustees tried to get the two lines in the park connected. The county council was not against the idea, but the MET saw no justification for it in view of the poor traffic returns. It was discussed again on 12 March and at intervals until 22 June 1909, when the MCC told the Trustees that they were not prepared to do anything.

In the attempt to improve receipts, a through service of single-deck cars was introduced between Alexandra Palace East and Finsbury Park during 1908 or 1909, though the exact date is not known. No photographic evidence of these cars working south of Turnpike Lane has yet come to light, and it is not known whether it was a regular operation or one operated in conjunction with special events at the Palace. It may even have been connected with the formation of the MET Band, which gave its first public concert at the Alexandra Palace on 13 May 1909, but whilst the band prospered the through cars did not.

Because of the disappointing receipts, the MET told the council on 9 December 1909 that the company proposed to convert the penny fare between Alexandra Palace and Wood Green into two end-on halfpenny stages meeting at Wood Green station. On the Turnpike Lane route they proposed to charge a halfpenny fare between the palace gates at Priory Road and the west terminus at the Palace. The MET and MCC were generally opposed to halfpenny fares, but the chronically low receipts and peculiar traffic conditions of these routes were good reasons to give them a trial, which was agreed as an experiment.

At the same meeting, the council were told that the service of single-deck cars then working between Alexandra Palace East and Finsbury Park would be withdrawn, the single deck cars being confined to the two routes between the Palace and Wood Green. The company would issue transfer tickets enabling passengers to continue to travel for one penny between Alexandra Palace East and Turnpike Lane or between Wood Green station and Harringay (The Salisbury).

ALEXANDRA PALACE EAST

The two MET routes to the Alexandra Palace each passed through the park gates, where admission was charged for special events; tram passengers were sold combined tickets. The top picture opposite shows No. 139 at the Wood Green Gate in 1906 on the service to Bruce Grove; the centre one shows No. 145 ascending the 1 in 10 gradient of the Eastern Approach Road, the steepest on the MET, and the lower picture is of No. 131 at the East terminus in 1906 before the Bruce Grove service was cut back to Wood Green.

(Commercial postcards, courtesy Arthur Hall, J. H. Price, Author's collection

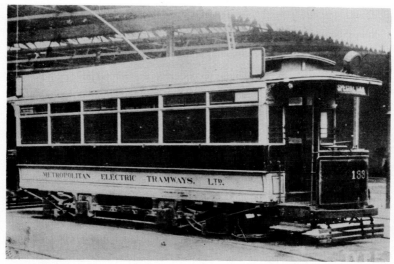

At an early date several of the single-deck cars of the Palace routes were surplus to traffic requirements. Some, like No. 133 in this c.1917 view were assigned to various departmental duties.
(The late V. Whitbread

The two local services now required only a maximum of ten single-deck cars. The service to the west side was operated when the park was open with six single-deck cars, and the east side route ran daily, with a shuttle service in the mornings by two single-deckers from Wood Green junction to Wood Green station, extended in the afternoon and evening to the east door of the Palace, running every six minutes and using four cars.

Several single-deck cars had always been surplus to requirements, though some had been used from 26 November 1906 to about April 1908 on the route from Wood Green to Bounds Green Road and its later extension to New Southgate, and several years later some of them worked between Ponders End and Enfield. On 19 April 1907 the MET board learned from James Devonshire that four of the cars had been sold to another BET company, Auckland Electric Tramways, at the original cost less 10%. This amounted to £2,881, the cars concerned being Nos. 135, 136, 143 and 144.

The MET board approved the sale, by which time the cars were already being dismantled and prepared for shipping at Wood Green depot; an ex-MET staff member told the author that the work was done in some secrecy. They became Nos. 66 to 69 at Auckland, where they were at once placed in service, still in their MET livery and with MET tickets littering the floors! Their red livery caused them to be nicknamed 'Lobsters' in contrast with the green of Auckland's own cars.

There was a sequel to this in the following year, when the MCC committee learned of the sale and took exception to not being consulted. The MET replied that as well as these four cars, many others of the class were not needed. In later years some of the surplus single-deckers were used as breakdown cars or as punch and ticket vans to work between Manor House offices and the various depots. One, sometimes two of them could regularly be seen on the single line siding from Green Lanes alongside the Manor House buildings.

The line to Alexandra Palace East had only been open six months when on 20 October 1906 a single-deck car three-quarters of the way up the hill went out of control and ran back as far as the Wood Green gates, where it was halted just before the sharp curves outside the gates. There were probably other such incidents, and the MET installed a sand bin half way down the east hill from which staff could sand the tracks in wet or icy weather.

Late in 1908, Hornsey Council put up a scheme of their own for a line from the Turnpike Lane route in Hornsey High Street along Middle Lane to the Clock Tower at Crouch End. However, the proposal was opposed by various local interests and the January 1909 meeting of the MCC committee decided to take no action.

When route numbers were allocated to the local MET services in July 1913, the Finsbury Park—Muswell Hill service became 28, the single-deck service from The Wellington to Alexandra Palace West (at that time operating in the afternoons and evenings only) was given the number 30, and the East side route took the number 32. The single-deck cars carried no route number boxes, but the number appeared on the side destination boards when carried. On 15 August 1914 route 28 was replaced by through-running route 51 from Muswell Hill to Bloomsbury, and its later history is given in the chapter on MET-LCC through running.

When war was declared in 1914, the Government immediately requisitioned the Palace and its grounds. From 8 to 16 August a reserve regiment of cavalry was quartered there; many of their 500 horses had been removed on 4 August from between the shafts of horse buses, bakers' vans and other vehicles where they stood in the street. The park became a training ground for the men and horses, but after a stampede of horses across the grounds one night the unit was moved elsewhere. The park and palace reopened on 17 August and tramway services were resumed, only to close again for the duration on 11 September when park and palace were requisitioned to house Belgian refugees. For a time there were a few special tram workings to convey parties of inmates, but then service was suspended for the rest of the war. Service 30 was withdrawn completely, and service 32 limited to a daily shuttle service between Wood Green and the GNR station.

From 1920 to 1923 two of the single-deckers, Nos. 145 and 150, were hired out to the South Metropolitan Electric Tramways and Lighting Company. No. 145 is seen in this view at Penge Depot with the Middlesex lettering crudely painted out following objections by the Middlesex County Council.   (The late Walter Gratwicke

Later in the war, some thousands of German nationals were interned there, and were employed laying out and beautifying the grounds. The park reopened on 27 March 1920, but the Palace itself remained closed, being used until 1922 by Government departments clearing up matters relating to the war. In 1921 the War Losses Commission awarded the MET £7,247 in respect of losses and damage on the Alexandra Park lines from 10 September 1914 to 30 March 1920.

The two lines in Alexandra Park reopened on 30 March 1920 in time for the Easter holiday. The weather on the opening day turned hot unexpectedly, and after the first car had reached the Palace West terminus it was found that some of the rails on the sleeper track reservation had lifted, due, it was thought to the accumulation of debris in the rail joints having been compressed by the passage of the first car, causing distortion of the rails when they expanded in the heat of the sun. It being the Easter holiday, the permanent way staff were not on duty and the breakdown gang came from Wood Green depot, armed mainly with sledgehammers. They made emergency repairs, and cars ran at reduced speed over the section pending attention from the permanent way gang. On the same day, a car ran back down the gradient on the East line and struck a stationary tram near the Wood Green gate, but luckily there were no serious injuries.

Early in 1920 two of the single-deck cars, 145 and 150, were hired out to the South Metropolitan Electric Tramways and Lighting Company, who used them mainly on short workings and football duties. A member of Middlesex County Council saw one of them working on the SMET and told the committee, who demanded that the cars return to Wood Green, but the MET refused. The 'County Council of Middlesex' lettering and arms on these two cars were hastily obliterated, and on 6 October 1920 the MCC grudgingly agreed to the hiring arrangements, but demanded that the Southmet should pay 15% per annum of their capital cost (instead of 10%) because they were not working in Middlesex. Their hire continued to the end of 1923, at £180 per year (£205 in 1921) after which they were returned to the MET and overhauled.

Another of the single-deck cars, No. 132, was converted in 1921 to a one-man car. No. 132 had been in collision with a steam wagon near Wood Green, and during reconstruction was shortened to five window bays and a length of 21 feet. The platforms were extended and fully enclosed, and arranged so that passengers could board and alight at the front. A hand-operated door electrically interlocked with the control circuit was provided on each platform, and automatic ticket-issuing machines were fitted at each end, together with a moving travel indicator ('Road Guide'). The car was fitted with Spencer-Dawson oil-operated track brakes suitable for the Alexandra Palace hills and was tried out on

No. 149 at the Muswell Hill gate. (D. W. K. Jones

The two Alexandra Palace routes continued unchanged until closure on 23 February 1938. This 1935 photograph of car 2307 (ex-139) was taken on Wood Green station bridge. (C. Carter

these routes late in 1921, but it seems likely that the Ministry of Transport would not agree to one-man vehicles operating on these gradients, since there would be no conductor present to apply the brakes in an emergency. The car was sold later in 1922 to the London United Tramways for £703.

By this time the MET had a new manager, Christopher John Spencer, who during his 20 years at Bradford had devised (with his father) the Spencer Slipper Brake and later (with J. W. Dawson) the Spencer-Dawson oil brake. During 1924, this oil-pressure brake already tried on 132 was fitted to six more of the MET single-deck cars, Nos. 134, 139, 140, 142, 146 and 150, which were then used on the Alexandra Palace East route in preference to the other cars.

A hitherto unknown experiment was carried out during 1922 on another of the single-deck cars by fitting it with wooden wheel centres; the boss of the wheel was, of course, of steel as were the rim and tyre. The wheel centre was composed of specially laminated wood, treated against warping and shrinkage, and the earth return to the rail was effected by four copper strips which bridged the wheel centres. The car worked on the Alexandra Palace lines, and gave an improvement in riding quality accompanied by a reduction of noise. However, whilst in service on the sleeper track route one of the wheels collapsed and the car had to be brought back to Wood Green on three wheels (the breakdown gang did this by placing all their heavy gear in the car's other end). It transpired that a member of the night staff at the depot had noticed that a portion of the laminated wood wheel centre had 'worked' and had simply nailed the loose section in position, without reporting the matter. The experiment was abandoned forthwith.

The later 1920s saw many improvements on the MET system, described in Volume 2, but the Alexandra Park lines, and their single deck cars took no part in this. The company suggested in January 1930 that they should be closed, but the county side wanted to keep them, and the Trustees again asked that the termini be linked up. The company tried to get Ministry of Transport consent to run double deck cars to Alexandra Palace West, but the Ministry required special brakes because of the gradient in the park. Another MCC plan discussed in April 1930 was to build a line along Mayes Road, Wood Green, to avoid the low bridge in Station Road, and the MET proposed that the two lines be linked by a new line in the park along the racecourse road, with an escalator up to the Palace.

Nothing came of any of these ideas, and the two routes survived, virtually unchanged, until replaced by London Transport motor buses on 23 February 1938.

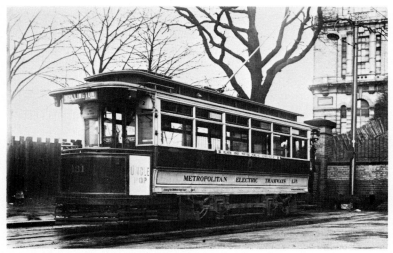

Alexandra Palace West terminus in the late 1920s, with No. 131 laying over. (D. W. K. Jones

Extract from MET Rule Book, January 1928 edition.

ALEXANDRA PALACE HILL

With regard to the operation of cars at this point, Motormen must comply with the following and any subsequent instructions which may be issued.

Ascending East Side

When car reaches the last Compulsory Stop before ascending the Hill, Conductors are instructed to intimate to passengers to alight for the Dance Hall, and notify them that the car will not stop again until it reaches the top, and that passengers will not be allowed to alight while car is in motion.

The platform chain to be put up when the car leaves the stop.

Cars running on the above routes are fitted with a pedal by means of which sand can be applied to the rear of the cars from the driving platform, and also with an arrangement whereby in the 'off' position of the controller, WITH THE REVERSING KEY FORWARD, one pair of wheels is automatically braked if the car runs back.

On these cars, if the power goes off when ascending the hill or the wheels skid so as to render the car liable to run back, the controller must at once be brought to the 'off' position and left there, the reverse key being left in the forward position, at the same time, operating the rear sand pedal and applying the hand brake, or where fitted, the oil brake to hold the car at a standstill. The controller must be left in the 'off' position until the car has stopped.

Descending East Side

The car to leave the terminus empty, no passengers being allowed to board until car is at end of curve. A row of setts is laid across the track near the cross over and also at the end of the curve. After coming over the crossover, the car must be stopped with the front of the car level with these setts. The track brake is then to be fully applied, and a touch of power given, so that the car is moved a foot or so, in order to allow the blocks to take up their position. The Inspector must then examine each block to ensure that neither is riding on top of the check rail.

If all is in order, the car will then move off with power (the track brake still being fully applied) and stop at the end of the curve with the front end of the car level with the second row of setts. If it be necessary to apply any extra braking power in addition to the track brake for this stop, the hand brake must be used.

When starting away, give one notch of power, then place controller handle on the 2nd or 3rd notch of rheostatic brake and control speed of car down the hill by the use of the hand brake, throwing as much weight as possible on the track brakes. When approaching a B.O.T. stop on the hill, the hand brake must be further applied so as to stop the car, leaving the rheostatic brake on the 2nd or 3rd notch; on no account must the stop be made by bringing the controller round towards the last brake notches.

The main principle is that the bulk of the braking for preventing the car from gathering speed should be the track brake, and the car to be kept strictly to the B.O.T. speed; at this speed practically no current will be generated on the rheostatic brake, but, if either of the brake chains break, then rheostatic will come into operation on a slight increase of speed.

Descending West Side

The car will take up passengers at the Palace terminus in the usual manner.

After coming over the crossover and before reaching the compulsory stop at Pole 92, the magnetic brake must be tested.

The car must be started from Pole 92 by releasing the hand brake with the controller handle on the last brake notch, the handle being gradually moved back to the 5th, 4th or 3rd brake notch as may be necessary to control the speed to the B.O.T. limit of 4 m.p.h. The same procedure to be followed for all subsequent stops.

All stops will be made by means of the magnetic brake and the hand brake applied to hold the car. The slack on the hand brake should at all times be kept up.

In the event of the failure of the magnetic brake prior to reaching the compulsory stop at Pole 79, the car should be stopped by means of the hand brake, and all passengers asked to alight. The conductor will then proceed up the hill and hold up any on-coming cars. When the track is clear, the car should be taken back to the Palace terminus and the depot notified.

Car Out of Control

In the event of the Motorman losing control of the car, the Conductor must immediately without signal from the Motorman put track brake hard on. Leave hand brake alone.

If car is running backwards apply sand and track brake. Leave hand brake alone.

The hand brake must never in either instance be applied by the Conductor unless he receives the recognised signal (four bells) from the Motorman.

The trial run over the route between Highgate Archway and Whetstone on 19 May 1905. Type A car No. 125 in High Street, North Finchley carrying members of the MET engineering staff.
(Commercial view, Author's collection

No. 125 stands at Totteridge Lane, Whetstone, on a staff training duty prior to the opening of the line to Highgate Archway on 7 June 1905.
(Commercial view by C. F. Haynes, Author's collection

CHAPTER SEVEN
FINCHLEY AND BARNET

As recorded in Chapter Two, one of the first applications for light railway powers by the Metropolitan Tramways and Omnibus Co. Ltd. (in May 1898) was for a line from Highgate along the Great North Road through Finchley and Whetstone to Barnet. This was not granted, but a later application for Highgate to Whetstone was successful, after agreement had been reached between the company and the Middlesex County Council. The County of Middlesex Light Railways Order 1901 gave the MCC powers to build a line from the London—Middlesex boundary at the Highgate Archway to Totteridge Lane, Whetstone, with a short branch to the site of a proposed depot and power station in East End Road, East Finchley.

The Highgate—Whetstone line would clearly be a trunk route, with good traffic prospects, and was intended to be one of the first lines to be built, though various circumstances combined to delay it. The construction contract was awarded in October 1902 to Wm. Griffiths & Co. Ltd. at £50,225, and to meet the requirements of Finchley UDC the entire roadway from the Hornsey—Finchley boundary to Whetstone was widened to 60ft. at the same time, partly to allow space for centre poles. Much of the road was at that time still in open country.

As constructed, the line began at the Highgate Archway, at the London—Middlesex county boundary which was six feet north of the south side of the bridge. The Archway, which carries Hornsey Lane high above Archway Road, is one of North London's most notable features and was built in 1897 to replace a narrow masonry arch which would have been an obstacle to tramways. However, this starting-point left a gap of three-eighths of a mile between the new MET terminus and that of the horse trams at the Archway Tavern, Highgate.

The London County Council objected to any invasion of their territory by districts outside the County, and had also expressed their dislike of using the Light Railways Act to obtain powers for street tramways. They did lodge a light railway application for this line in November 1899, but withdrew it and instead obtained the powers in their Tramways and Improvements Act 1901.

The LCC were preparing to reconstruct and electrify the North London horse tramways which they had been acquiring since 1895, and were using the conduit system, but work had not begun on their lines at the Archway Tavern when in February 1903 Middlesex asked the LCC to build this section on the overhead trolley system. In March 1904 the LCC agreed, and also agreed to lease the line to the MET for three years. The two councils met on 16 February 1905 to discuss terms, and these were later agreed as a rent of £1,500, £2,000 and £2,500 for the first, second and third years, which the MET reckoned was too high. Power would be supplied by the MET, who would also maintain the track.

As recounted in Chapter Fifteen, there were delays in finding a site for a depot at Finchley, and in laying cables, and although the contractor had begun work on the Archway—Whetstone line quite soon after work began on the Wood Green routes, it took nearly a year longer. The first trial run from Highgate Archway to Totteridge Lane, Whetstone took place on 19 May 1905, using car 125, and the Board of Trade inspection was carried out by Major Pringle on 30 May. He reported favourably, and the Board of Trade sanctioned the line on 5 June.

The opening was fixed for 7 June 1905, and the opening car, No. 125 again, was drawn up outside Highgate Police Court where Sir Francis Cory-Wright (Chairman of the MCC Light Railways and Tramways Committee) was sitting as a magistrate. Others present were his vice chairman Herbert Nield, several other committee members, Finchley UDC chairman A. E. Woodrow and other Finchley councillors, their electrical engineer E. Calvert, representatives of other councils, the chairman of the Alexandra Park Trustees (Henry Burt), and James Devonshire, W. E. Hammond and A. H. Pott of the MET. The car moved off with Sir Francis at the controls, ran non-stop to The Cricketers, North Finchley where the party disembarked and inspected the depot, then continued to Totteridge Lane and back to Highgate Archway. This time there were no speeches.

As soon as the special car had left the Archway again, the public tram service commenced. Local people were pleasantly surprised at the low fares; Whetstone— Archway (4½ miles) was 3d., North Finchley—Archway was 2d., and there were long penny stages. Workmen's cars commenced at 5 a.m. and charged 1d. single, 2d. return for the whole route. Within a week the horse buses had reduced their fares by 50%, but the trams offered a service that the omnibuses could not hope to match.

The first Highgate terminus was beneath Highgate Archway, the county boundary running across the road below the arch. This photograph was taken at the commencement of operations on the Great North Road, with No. 112 about to reverse for the return to Whetstone.

(Lens of Sutton

Meanwhile, on 16 May 1905 the LCC placed a contract with Dick, Kerr & Co. Ltd. to build the short line between Highgate Archway and the Archway Tavern, for £4,588. At the same time a £600 contract was placed with the MET to supply and erect the overhead, followed by another contract for feeder pillars at £415. Although the line was in the LCC's area, the MET used their standard poles and equipment. The line was completed in August 1905, but Islington council objected to the position of some traction poles and span wires, and the line was not inspected until 21 December 1905, the certificate being issued the same day and imposing a compulsory stop at the arch, and a 6 miles/h limit for southbound cars. Because the section was isolated from the LCC electric tramways, an MET car was used for the inspection. Public service began on the following day, 22 December 1905.

80

On 22 December 1905 the MET cars were extended down Archway Road to a new terminus at the Archway Tavern. On the left a cable tram waits to ascend Highgate Hill, and next to MET car 127 a horse tram commences a journey to Euston.

(Commercial view, Author's collection

Traffic on the Great North Road route developed quickly, especially at summer weekends, when the cars carried capacity loads and there were sometimes queues at Whetstone 500 strong waiting for trams to Highgate. The twenty-seven Type A cars allocated to Finchley depot were soon insufficient, and six more were transferred from Hendon, as the Edgware Road traffic had not developed to anything like the same extent. Transporting these cars (presumably on horse-drawn lorries) must have been a major operation, as the Great North Road was a self-contained route isolated until 1909 from the rest of the MET system.

When the line opened in June 1905 the cars were fitted with hand and rheostatic brakes only. Despite the existence in East Finchley of gradients of 1 in 18 near Huntingdon Road and 1 in 20 near St. Pancras Cemetery, Major Pringle had not required track brakes. However, no doubt with the forthcoming steeply graded extension to the Archway Tavern in mind, A. H. Pott asked the MET board later that month for £60 per car to fit Westinghouse magnetic track brakes, which was agreed. The cars were soon fitted, but despite this there was a runaway in March 1906 in Archway Road, though since it did not result in damage or injury it was not reported.

However, a serious accident occurred in Archway Road on 23 June 1906, when car 115 went out of control while descending the 1 in 22 gradient south of the Highgate Archway. About 100 yards from the arch the car struck a funeral hearse, then a horse-drawn pantechnicon, both of which were wrecked. Immediately before the tram struck the pantechnicon the motorman jumped off, and the car continued down Archway Road driverless and at an increasing speed. Near the bottom of the hill it struck a Vanguard motor bus, forcing it across the pavement into a jobmaster's premises and a restaurant; then it struck and upset a four-wheeled cab. No. 115's career was halted when it struck another MET car standing at the terminus at the foot of the hill, and both cars continued a further 40 yards off the end of the track into Holloway Road, demolishing an electric light standard and a refuge post before finally coming to rest against the kerb. Three men who were believed to be crossing the street were killed at the point where the runaway car struck the bus.

The June 1906 accident in which Type A car No. 115 ran out of control down Archway Road was the worst of the few involving the MET. Car 115 (right) struck a Whetstone-bound car at the terminus and pushed it off the end of the track. The two cars came to rest in Holloway Road.

(Courtesy D. W. K. Jones)

The accident was the subject of a report by Col. H. A. Yorke of the Board of Trade, issued in November 1906. Motorman Cone said in evidence that his first journey to Highgate was accomplished safely, but on the return journey at 2.33 p.m. to Whetstone an application of the handbrake near Muswell Hill Road had caused the wheels to lock. On the next southward journey the same happened near Shepherds Hill, Highgate, but the car was stopped on the level track at the Winchester Hotel.

Beyond this point was a falling gradient of 1 in 65, and at Highgate Archway this becomes 1 in 22, decreasing to 1 in 23 near the terminus. At the Board of Trade compulsory stop at the Archway, motormen were under orders to place the controller handle on the second brake notch before starting the descent and keep it there for the entire descent to the Archway Tavern. In this position the speed of the car was limited to 6 miles/h, the maximum allowed for downhill journeys beyond Highgate Archway.

Cone told Col. Yorke that on the approach to the Archway the rails were greasy and that when he applied the handbrake for the compulsory stop the wheels locked. The car passed on to the 1 in 22 gradient with its speed increasing, and out of control. Cone put the reversing key of the controller into the 'reverse' position and moved the controller handle to the power notches, which blew the circuit breaker. After seeing the pantechnicon on the track ahead, Cone put the controller on the sixth braking notch and jumped from the car. His controller movements, although correct, were quite futile because with the wheels locked, the motors were not generating any current to operate the rheostatic or magnetic brakes.

Col. Yorke was critical of Cone for having deserted his post, and noted that the hand and magnetic brakes were found to be in working order after the accident, and that the car was driven back to the depot (from the other end) after the accident, with no difficulty. Evidence was given that the brakes

82

had been adjusted before the car entered service to give $1/16$th of an inch clearance from the wheel treads with the brake released, which he thought was too close; with so little clearance, any handbrake application would tend to lock the wheels. He concluded that despite having received eleven one-hour lessons on the road, more instruction in how to deal with emergencies might have helped Motorman Cone in this case.

Of the 25 passengers on the car when it ran away, four or five had jumped off near the top of the hill; some of these were injured, and some of those who stayed on were slightly hurt and shocked. Conductor Griffith Davies and a passenger named Taylor were commended for persuading others not to jump off, and probably saved many from injury or worse.

Col. Yorke was critical of tramcar brakes generally, and suggested that the whole question of brakes should be taken up by the Municipal Tramways Association and the Tramways and Light Railways Association. An MTA/T&LRA standing joint committee was later formed to carry out brake trials and circulate technical advice. He considered that the magnetic brake should be in regular use and not kept mainly in reserve for emergency use; in this way, motormen would be well versed in its operation. Later the magnetic brakes on the cars were replaced by an improved version similar to the standard brake of the LCC tramways, and magnetic brakes became the service brake on almost all MET routes.

Highgate Archway, London

A later view, c.1913, of No. 77 approaching Highgate Archway from the Middlesex side. The arch was built in 1897 jointly by Middlesex and London County Councils.

(Commercial postcard

At its November 1905 meeting, the MCC decided to go ahead with the extension from Totteridge Lane, Whetstone to the Middlesex-Hertford boundary at Walfield Bank, south of Lyonsdown Road, New Barnet. This was the second attempt, for in January 1904 the MCC had tried to get this section built as an extension of the Highgate—Whetstone contract, but the contractor would not agree to the terms. This line had been applied for by Hertfordshire County Council in 1901, but in January 1902 Hertfordshire agreed to transfer the powers for this portion to Middlesex County Council, without charge. The contract was placed with Dick, Kerr & Co. Ltd., and this section was built with span wires instead of the centre poles used elsewhere on the Great North Road in Finchley. The Light Railway Order had specified a 50ft. road, but Finchley wanted 60ft. roads and gave way on the centre pole issue in return.

On 26 July 1906 Major Pringle inspected the 0.688 miles of line from Totteridge Lane to the county boundary and found everything in order, except that the last 150 yards had not yet been widened; he asked that the east track north of the crossover should not be used until this was done. The Board of Trade issued its certificate on 1 August, and the line opened without ceremony on Saturday 4 August 1906, in time for the Bank Holiday traffic. During the holiday weekend the Great North Road trams carried 38,614 passengers.

As described in Appendix 5, Hertfordshire County Council had concluded an arrangement with the MET generally similar to that between the MET and Middlesex, and the first line to be built under this agreement was the continuation of the Great North Road tramway from the county boundary to Barnet Church. Hertfordshire's 1901 application had also included powers to acquire land for a generating station, depot and offices on the west side of the road just south of the GNR bridge, but this was not built. The contract for this 1.287-miles line was awarded on 26 May 1906 to Dick, Kerr & Co. Ltd. at £21,652.

It was hoped (optimistically) that the line would be ready within three months of the start of work, but this soon proved unrealistic, as it was necessary to lower the road under the GNR at Underhill, Barnet, and East Barnet Valley UDC proved obstructive, though Chipping Barnet UDC in whose area the line ended was very co-operative. East Barnet Valley raised objections on countless minor points, wanting traction pole positions moved by a few inches, poles on Barnet Hill set back from the highway, and wood block paving for the full width of the road. The Board of Trade were called in to settle these matters, and whilst most of the poles were set back against the fencing, the MET objected strongly to wood block paving, and granite setts were used.

The first trial run took place on 16 March 1907, when car 162 of the nearly-new Type C traversed the new line carrying A. H. Pott and other members of the MET engineering staff. The HCC's powers for the line had expired on 26 February 1907 and they had asked the Board of Trade for an extension until

THE FIRST ELECTRIC TRAM IN BARNET

The first trial journey over the extension from the County Boundary at Whetstone to Barnet Church was made on 16 March 1907 by No. 162, seen here leaving the Barnet terminus for Finchley depot. The car was almost certainly one of the five lettered "County Council of Hertfordshire". (Author's collection

An early view at Barnet Church terminus, with Type A car No. 123 ready to leave for Highgate. Note the waterproof seat-covers draped over the top-deck railings.   (Tramway Museum Society

September, but by the time the Board agreed to this the line had been opened. It was inspected by Major Pringle on 26 March and was opened for traffic on 28 March 1907, the certificate having been issued by the Board of Trade on the same day at the company's request. The steepest gradient was 1 in 19.8, and Major Pringle had imposed a speed limit of 8 miles/h under the GNR bridge and 12 or 16 miles/h elsewhere. There was no opening ceremony, and the line carried record crowds during the Easter holiday.

With the start of inter-running between the two counties' light railways, a complicated system of dividing the revenue was introduced. It was divided in proportion to the mileage in each county; Barnet—Whetstone fares were divided 73% to Hertfordshire and 27% to Middlesex, Barnet—Finchley fares 30% to Hertfordshire and 27% to Middlesex, and Barnet—Highgate 18% to Hertfordshire and 82% to Middlesex. Fares for journeys wholly within one or other county were credited to that county, and special tickets were introduced for stages partly or wholly in Hertfordshire.

Barnet was at that time surrounded by some very pleasant countryside, including the popular Hadley Woods, and the trams were at their busiest on Sundays. During the week the cars ran every four minutes from Highgate to North Finchley (Tally Ho Corner) with alternate cars continuing to Barnet, but on Sundays these headways were shortened to three and six minutes respectively, with extra cars to Barnet in summer and during Barnet Fair in September.

Under the original proposals for the area, the original Whetstone terminus at Totteridge Lane would have become a junction, for a line was proposed from New Southgate along Oakleigh Road South and Oakleigh Road North. This was not built, and would have involved very considerable highway construction, for even as late as 1924, well within the author's memory, Oakleigh Road, Whetstone was little more than a straggling country lane with open fields, smallholdings and a few cottages. About 1924 a private operator started a bus service, using one small vehicle bought secondhand and running three or four times per day.

The Oakleigh Road line was one of two proposed links between the Wood Green routes and the Great North Road, one or both of which would be necessary if the MET/MCC system was not to remain in two separate halves. The choice fell on the other route, from New Southgate to North Finchley, by

Top: No. 164 of Type C at Squires Lane, East Finchley. The centre poles were replaced by side poles in 1913-14. (Courtesy D. W. K. Jones

Centre: Tally Ho Corner, North Finchley, probably in winter 1907, with Type A cars on the Highgate-Whetstone service. At this time the tracks to the right served only the depot in Woodberry Grove, off Ballards Lane. (Commercial view, Author's collection

Bottom: The rural character of many MET routes can be judged from the view of Woodhouse Road, North Finchley, soon after the line from New Southgate opened on 8 April 1909. No. 77 is bound for North Finchley from Finsbury Park. (Commercial view, Author's collection

extending the line which had been opened from the Wood Green direction as far as New Southgate station on 1 August 1907. The extension was to follow Friern Barnet Road and Woodhouse Road, but Finchley council had first to widen Woodhouse Road, with a £10,000 grant from the county council.

Friern Barnet UDC wanted the county council to widen the rather narrow bridge that carried Friern Barnet Road over the Great Northern Railway near New Southgate station. The county offered to pay one-third if Friern Barnet paid the rest, but Friern Barnet held out for 50%. As a result, the bridge was not widened until some years later, for the MCC, concerned at the mounting expenditure, took the matter to the Board of Trade, who decided that widening before the tramway was laid was unnecessary and that the line could cross the bridge with single track. This was done, and the bridge was not widened and double track laid until the autumn of 1913.

The narrow bridge over the Great Northern Railway at New Southgate was widened to allow double track working in 1913. This view with car No. 311 in Friern Barnet Road, New Southgate was taken while the work was in progress.
(Commercial postcard by E. J. & H. Clarke, J. H. Price collection

There was also a major dispute over paving. Finchley and Friern Barnet in July 1907 refused to approve the plans because the county proposed to pave the new line in granite setts; they wanted wood blocks. In December the county asked the Board of Trade to appoint a referee to settle the matter. The Board appointed Mr. R. O. Wynne-Roberts, MICE, who allowed Finchley's request for wood blocks between the tracks but ruled that the rest of the road could remain in macadam, and this was done.

The disputes over paving, road-widening and bridge works had delayed the placing of contracts to a point where in 1907 an extension of time had to be sought. This was granted and extended the period to 31 December 1908. The paving disputes having been settled by arbitration in April 1908, a contract was placed on 11 June 1908 with Dick, Kerr & Co. Ltd. at £31,437 to build the 1.525 miles from Station Road, New Southgate along Friern Barnet Road and Woodhouse Road to the Great North Road at North Finchley.

This line was inspected by Major Pringle on 7 April 1909. He found it in good order, and the line opened next day, Thursday 8 April, with a service from North Finchley (Woodhouse Road) to Finsbury Park at a through fare of 3d. The first car was driven by Henry Burt, then vice-chairman of the MCC Light Railways and Tramways Committee, but its number is not recorded.

One more line remained to be opened in Finchley, to Golders Green and Cricklewood. This had been similarly delayed by paving disputes, the councils involved being Finchley and Hendon. Hendon had sent the Board of Trade a petition signed by 325 residents of Cricklewood Lane asking for wood blocks instead of granite setts, but the Board rejected this, though allowing Hendon's own request for wood blocks on other sections.

The contract for the 3.838 miles of line from Woodberry Grove, North Finchley (the entry to Finchley depot) along Ballards Lane and through Church End, Temple Fortune and Golders Green to Childs Hill and Cricklewood was awarded on 9 July 1908 to Dick, Kerr & Co. Ltd. at £116,978, the price including road widening (mostly to 60ft.) and some expensive alterations to the road levels to reduce the gradients. The contract included the short branch at Childs Hill, from The Castle to the Middlesex-London boundary, which was built in anticipation of an LCC plan to build a tramway along Finchley Road and Adelaide Road to meet its Euston—Hampstead route at Chalk Farm.

The section from North Finchley to Golders Green crossroads was ready first, and was inspected by Major Pringle on 10 December 1909. The certificate was issued on 13 December, and an official opening took place on Thursday 16 December with the inaugural car leaving Golders Green at 12.15 p.m. in the practised hands of County Alderman Henry Burt. Public service began next day, with an eight-minute service from North Finchley to Golders Green using cars of the new Type G (217-236).

At the same time, the Charing Cross, Euston and Hampstead Railway doubled the number of peak hour trains between Golders Green and Charing Cross, with 235 trains daily in each direction, providing a train every three minutes, something unprecedented in the London suburbs at this time. The MET line between North Finchley and Golders Green became one of the most heavily trafficked routes in the London suburbs.

GOLDERS GREEN.

---1904.---

PRESENT DAY.

This view illustrates the rapid development of Golders Green. In 1904 the area was farmland as far as the eye could see. By 1907 the Hampstead Tube had reached Golders Green, followed by the trams in 1910. The lower view shows Type G cars 224 and 228, about 1911.
(Commercial postcard by E. W. Schröder, courtesy M. E. Mawson

An early view of Golders Green crossroads, looking south, with Type G car No. 236 en route for Cricklewood.   (Commercial view, Author's collection

The long-awaited link-up of the northern and western halves of the MET system became a reality on Monday 21 February 1910, when public service began on the extension from Golders Green to Cricklewood Broadway, described in the next chapter. Until this line was ready, cars from other depots could not reach Hendon Car Works and each depot had to be self-sufficient in repairs and maintenance, though Harrow Road cars had been able to reach Hendon since 23 December 1907, when the line through Willesden opened.

The spur from Childs Hill (The Castle) to the Hampstead boundary was not included in the opening ceremony and this line was very little used, as the proposed LCC line southwards into London was never constructed. In later years it was sometimes used for reversing short-working cars when traffic conditions at Golders Green became difficult, but eventually it became the second section of the MET system to be abandoned, the first having been the spur at Cricklewood facing towards London.

The British Electric Traction group in 1909 was introducing a fare structure which they called the 'Fair Fares' system. It was based on a large number of short stages of which three were given for a penny, with farthing graduations up

"Fair Fares" tickets with numbered stages used on the Finchley-Cricklewood route in 1910.
(Courtesy London Transport

to 2½d. and halfpenny stages beyond (the fare from North Finchley to Cricklewood was 3d.). The MET proposed to try this out on the new North Finchley—Cricklewood route, and the county committee agreed on 9 December 1909. Discs bearing fare stage numbers were fitted to traction poles at the appropriate points, and the system was introduced on 21 February 1910, with thirteen fare stages in place of four. The farthing graduations were expected to pose problems of change-giving, and this was avoided by issuing books of one-farthing tickets which could be bought by regular passengers. Conductors also gave these tickets as change. However, the system was found to be unworkable, and on 12 May 1910 the MCC were told that it had been abandoned.

At the same time as the 'Fair Fares' were introduced, penny transfers were introduced at each end of the route, from Long Lane (Ballards Lane) to Totteridge Lane, Whetstone and from Childs Hill (The Castle) to Dollis Hill Lane or Willesden Green Station. These were among the first of many transfers introduced later in various parts of the system, always at one penny. There were no through cars from the new line to places beyond Cricklewood Broadway, though the cars from Finchley and Golders Green turned the corner to use the spur outside the Crown public house as their terminus.

No. 203 approaches Church End, Finchley station bridge en route from Cricklewood to North Finchley, c.1912.   (Courtesy D. W. K. Jones

In 1912 some of the four-wheel Type D cars were transferred to Finchley depot to work between North Finchley and Golders Green. This caused an immediate outcry from local residents, which resulted in the four-wheelers being returned to whence they had come. By 1914, through fares had been introduced from points on the route to many stations on the Underground via Golders Green.

The link between the two halves of the MET system at Tally Ho Corner was not a direct one, as it involved a reversal on the crossover in High Street, North Finchley. Consequently there was no passenger service between the two halves, but special hired cars made the journey on numerous occasions. Football specials were also worked over the route, especially when Tottenham Hotspur had an important match.

The lease of the LCC-owned Archway Road tramway, which had expired on 20 December 1908, was extended to 31 December 1913 at an annual rent of £2,500, with the MET providing the power and maintaining the track. When 1913 came it was extended on the same terms first to 31 March 1914 and then to 30 September 1914, these being short-term arrangements in anticipation of through running.

By 1913, the LCC had numbered all its routes and the MET decided to follow suit, using even numbers to avoid any duplication with the odd numbers used by the LCC northern division. The service from North Finchley via Wood Green to Finsbury Park became 34, the Great North Road services became 36 Highgate—North Finchley and 38 Highgate—Barnet, and the Golders Green route was allocated four numbers, 40 Cricklewood—North Finchley (daily), 42 Cricklewood—Whetstone (weekdays), 44 Cricklewood—Barnet (Sundays) and 46 Golders Green—Tally Ho Corner which ran only at busy times.

The success of the LCC-MET through running on the Enfield route from August 1912 soon led to its extension and during 1914 the LCC Tramways installed a conduit/overhead change pit at the Archway Tavern, with the MET sharing the cost. Through running commenced on 24 September 1914 with services 9 and 19, as described in Chapter Ten, and the rent paid by the MET for the Archway Road tramway ceased to be payable. From 1 August 1915 the LCC supplied the power on this section, but the nearest feeder was 220ft. north of the boundary and the MET thereafter paid the LCC £20 per year to supply this piece of line. For part of 1927 the LCC also supplied power for the next section as far as Muswell Hill Road.

When Board of Trade sanction was being sought in 1912 for the extended use of top-covered cars on the MET, A. H. Pott had evidently agreed not to use them on Archway Road, probably as a result of the earlier runaways. From 24 September 1914 LCC top-covered cars regularly worked along this section, and on 2 October the Board of Trade agreed that the MET could do the same.

The later history of the Finchley routes will be dealt with in Volume 2, but it is convenient to deal here with two suggested lines that were not built. In October 1901 Finchley UDC asked the county council to build a line along East End Road to link the Great North Road line with Church End, and late in 1908 some residents of Friern Barnet and Muswell Hill asked the MCC to build a line from the 'Orange Tree' in Friern Barnet Road along Colney Hatch Lane and Muswell Hill Road to Archway Road. However, most Muswell Hill residents were still opposed to having tramways there, and the January 1909 meeting of the MCC committee decided to take no action.

Type B/1 car No. 60 at the Tally Ho Corner terminus of route 40 at North Finchley, probably in 1919. The car has just traversed the facing crossover, which was later replaced by a trailing one and an automatic trolley reverser.
(Courtesy D. A. Thompson)

CHAPTER EIGHT

EDGWARE TO WILLESDEN

One of the earliest proposals for tramways in the area covered by this book was that of the Common Road Conveyance Company, who, as already mentioned in 1871 obtained a Provisional Order (confirmed by the Metropolitan Tramways Orders Confirmation Act 1873) to build a 12.25-mile 'tram railway' from the Essex Arms in Watford via Sparrowherne toll gate, Bushey, Bushey Heath, Great and Little Stanmore, the Edgware toll gate, the Hyde, Cricklewood, the Slade and Shoot-up Hill to the Edgware Road (now Brondesbury) station of the Hampstead Junction Railway at Kilburn. The company was short-lived and was wound up in February 1875 without having built any tramways.

From 1871 to 1901, the population of Watford increased from 12,071 to 32,559 and that of Willesden from 15,869 to 114,811. Middlesex County Council later claimed that Parliament, in sanctioning this line over thirty years earlier, had recognised the need for tramway communication between Watford and London, and that a scheme granted as far back as 1873 to a company but not built should therefore now be granted to a public authority, who would provide facilities for a vastly increased population.

In their joint application of May, 1899, Middlesex County Council and the MTOC sought powers for a light railway from The Crown at Cricklewood along the Edgware Road through Hendon and Edgware to the Queens Head in Great Stanmore, following the same route as that granted in 1871. This was granted as far as Church Lane, Edgware but not beyond.

Meanwhile, two rival sets of proposals had been made for tramways in Watford, one by a company, the other by Hertfordshire County Council. As described in Appendix 5, the lines authorised to Hertfordshire included one to the Middlesex boundary at Bushey Heath.

In November 1899, the BET had reached an understanding with Hertfordshire County Council similar to its later agreement with Middlesex, and would therefore operate Hertfordshire's lines on the county's behalf. To render this practicable, it would be essential to connect the HCC line at Bushey Heath with the MET at Edgware. The distance to be covered was not great—about 3½ miles—and the Watford proposal caused the MCC and MET to include the Cricklewood— Edgware line among the first lines they built, even though it would run partly through open country and would for some years be isolated from the main system.

This line was authorised by the County of Middlesex Light Railways Order of December 1901, as 4.85 miles of double track line from The Crown at Cricklewood to a terminus 150 yards north of Church Lane, Edgware. The contract to build it was awarded by the MCC on 23 October 1902 to J. G. White & Co. Ltd., and the line was expected to open in July 1904. A site for a depot and generating station was obtained north of Annesley Avenue, in the part of West Hendon known as Colindale, and although the generating station was not built this site also housed the MET company's training school and tramcar overhaul works.

The MCC applied again in 1902 for a line from Edgware through Stanmore to the Middlesex-Hertford county boundary at Bushey Heath, where it would join the HCC's Watford line. As on the previous occasion, Hendon Rural District

The original tram terminus south of Cricklewood Broadway near the Middlesex-London county boundary; this early view shows No. 100 ready for departure to Edgware. This short section fell into disuse after plans to extend towards Kilburn failed to materialise.

(Commercial view, Author's collection

Council, Stanmore and Harrow Weald Parish Councils and the local residents and landowners all opposed it, making it quite clear that Stanmore's population of some 2,000 wished to remain a secluded rural community. The Light Railway Commissioners rejected the scheme on the grounds of local opposition, insufficient demand and excessive cost, but they did sanction the 0.962 miles from Edgware to Canons Park.

Construction of the Cricklewood—Edgware line was delayed by the newly-laid track subsiding in May 1904 at Hendon, near the Welsh Harp bridge over the Silk Stream. Contractors J. G. White told the MCC that they were not liable, and suggested arbitration. Sir Douglas Fox, a famous civil engineer, was chosen and ruled that the council should pay £4,000 of the estimated £5,276 repair cost, with interest to date. J. G. White, whose men had also been observed trying to obliterate a foreign manufacturer's name from the steel girders used in the Silk Stream bridge, took no further part in constructing the MET/MCC system.

The line from Cricklewood to Hendon depot was ready first, and was inspected on 15 November 1904 by Major Pringle. He found the permanent way and electrical equipment satisfactory, but asked for some modification to the lifeguards of the cars. This delayed the opening, and after he inspected and approved on 30 November the 1.525-mile section from the car shed to the Edgware terminus, the entire Cricklewood—Edgware line opened without ceremony on Saturday 3 December 1904.

The cars allocated to the line at the start were 27 of Type A, probably Nos. 84-110. Six of them, possibly 99-104, were transferred to Finchley in time for the June 1905 opening of the Highgate—Whetstone route, and a further six followed later in that year, which would leave only fifteen at Hendon. Fifteen cars for 5½ miles of line implies that service was rather sparse, but the area beyond Hendon was quite undeveloped and traffic did not develop to anything like the extent of that on the Great North Road. The first six months of the Highgate—Whetstone route produced more traffic than a whole year on Cricklewood—Edgware.

WAITING FOR THE TRAMS. EDGWARE. 16.4.06.

94

Top left: No. 98 passes the "Old Welsh Harp", a well-known landmark at West Hendon, about 1905. (Courtesy A. D. Packer

Centre left: No. 109 passes "The Old George Inn" a short way before reaching Edgware terminus, early in 1905. Some months later this car was transferred (with others) to Finchley depot for the Highgate-Whetstone route. (Commercial postcard

Lower left: A busy scene at Edgware terminus on Easter Monday, 1906. Occasional busy days contrasted with long periods when traffic beyond Hendon was disappointing. (S. G. Allpress

---

One factor may have been that the fares were distinctly higher than on the other MET routes. Only three stages were given for one penny, six for twopence and nine for threepence, against four, eight and twelve on the Edmonton route, so the fare from Cricklewood to Edgware was threepence. Except in summer, it seems that at least one car in two turned back at Hendon depot, and in 1913 only one car in three ran beyond this point. The MCC soon decided that the Edgware route would not generate profitable traffic unless it went on to Watford, and decided to make another attempt to obtain powers.

In November, 1905 the MCC therefore applied again to the Light Railway Commissioners for a line from the Hertfordshire boundary at Bushey Heath via Watford Road and Stanmore Hill to the Edgware Road at the foot of Brockley Hill, the point to which a line from Edgware had already been authorised in 1903. The application included an alternative route from the Queens Head, Great Stanmore along Dennis Lane and across Little Common and some fields to rejoin the first line near Canons Park, but this alternative was later withdrawn.

The inquiry was held at the Middlesex Guildhall on 9 February 1906, and once again the proposal was fiercely contested by the Rural District Council and the Stanmore residents. They accused the county of sending a man to sit in a cart at Stanmore to obtain signatures to a petition in favour of the scheme, but it emerged that the man was a builder from Alperton, a Mr. Haynes, who had canvassed the area on his own initiative! Stanmore residents were alarmed at the prospect of excursionists being dumped on them, but MCC chairman Sir Ralph Littler said that the best way to avoid this was to take the line through to Bushey, because the excursionists would probably then go on to Watford.

A surprise witness for the opposition was Mr. J. B. Hamilton, general manager of Leeds City Tramways, who came firmly on the side of the Stanmore residents. He said the costs were too high, and there was not the slightest chance of the line paying, as it would never be a working class area. Speaking for the residents, the Rev. Stewart Bernays, Rector of Stanmore, revealed that the MCC committee had told him that one scheme or another would be forced on them whether they liked it or not, and he closed a lengthy diatribe against the MCC by saying that the spiritual welfare of Stanmore was at stake. The Commissioners, after retiring, decided that there was not a strong enough public need for the line, and that the application failed. The decision, received with applause, nevertheless surprised many in the room.

Counsel for the Stanmore residents had openly accused the builders of wanting the tramway built for their own ends, and their opposition was undoubtedly due more to dislike of building development than trams. Speculation in building land is also the most likely explanation for the several attempts by Harry G. Assiter, a member of Harrow Weald Parish Council, to interest the MCC in building lines west of Edgware. On 31 July 1903 he sent the MCC a scheme to link the Edgware and Sudbury termini by a line mainly across open fields, claiming to represent local owners and residents. The MCC sent an officer to inspect the alignment with James Devonshire of the MET, and found only 33 houses. Assiter tried again in 1904, 1906, 1907 and 1909, claiming

95

the support of Wealdstone council, and in 1905 he also suggested a route from Canons Park via Brockley Hill and Aldenham Reservoir to Bushey, avoiding Stanmore. The MCC considered all his proposals undersirable, and took no action.

On 1 March 1906 the MCC decided to appeal to the Board of Trade against the Stanmore decision. This failed, and its rejection rendered the authorised Hertfordshire Light Railways practically valueless. Following the short extension of the Ponders End line into Hertfordshire at Waltham Cross in 1908, Hertfordshire built no more tramways and relinquished its remaining powers in 1914. Trams therefore never ran in Watford, and the link with Edgware was eventually made in 1913 by an LGOC motor bus service, which ran through to Kilburn.

The MCC had deferred confirming a contract with Dick, Kerr & Co. Ltd. to build the authorised line from Edgware to Canons Park, but at their April 1906 meeting they decided to build the line, partly in the hope of a successful appeal but also because the Canons Park estate was now in the hands of developers and other estates would soon follow. Canons, as the great house was called, was built in 1712 by the Duke of Chandos (Georg Frederic Handel was his *Kappelmeister,* and composed some of his best-known works there) but was pulled down in 1744. The property had changed hands several times, and was expected to be used for housing.

The contract to build the 0.962 mile line from Edgware terminus to Stone Grove, Canons Park was awarded on 5 April 1906 to Dick, Kerr & Co. Ltd. for £7,843. The start of work was probably delayed in hopes of a successful outcome to the appeal, which would enable the line to go further, but even without this it was hoped the extension would feed additional traffic to the main route. It was built during 1907 and inspected by Major Pringle on 5 October; the certificate was issued two days later and the line opened on 31 October 1907 with an infrequent service to Willesden Green which improved later as more houses were built. However, much of Canons Park estate became a golf course and a further part became a public open space. A full survey of housing development in and around Edgware will be found in Alan A. Jackson's book *Semi-Detached London,* published by George Allen & Unwin in 1973, and shows that development was slow until the arrival of the electric railway from Golders Green in the 1920s.

On three occasions, attempts had been made to obtain light railway powers for a route from Hendon to Golders Green, without success. For convenience, these are dealt with in the appendix on Trolleybuses, since the proposed MET trolleybus scheme of 1909-10 covered the same route. Several attempts were made to bring the Edgware Road tramway further into London, but these form a separate story, the subject of Appendix 7.

The remainder of this chapter deals mainly with the lines from Childs Hill and Cricklewood through Willesden to join the Harrow Road line at Craven Park, which had to be built if the MET system was to become a physical entity. A first application of 1899 had failed because the promoters had not properly notified the property owners affected, but Willesden Council and other local bodies were generally in favour provided that the narrow streets along the route were widened at MCC expense.

The MCC therefore re-applied in 1902 for a line from the Edgware Road at Cricklewood along Chichele Road, Walm Lane, High Road Willesden, Church Road Willesden and Craven Park, where it would join the Harrow Road line. The Metropolitan Railway objected on the grounds that it would have to alter the bridge at Willesden Green station, and there were many problems of road widths beyond this point, but the whole line was authorised in the MCC's 1903 Light Railway Order, and in October 1904 it was decided to build the first half-mile from Cricklewood to Willesden Green station, which would bring extra traffic to the Edgware Road trams by acting as a feeder to the Metropolitan Railway, whose line through Willesden Green was being electrified. The electric trains commenced on 1 January 1905.

Although the section from Cricklewood Broadway to Willesden Green Station was only 0.618 miles in length, there was a full turnout by the Middlesex County Council's Light Railways and Tramways Committee for the formal opening on 30 March 1906, when No. 92 was driven by County Alderman Herbert Nield. In this scene at Cricklewood Broadway cars 90 and 92 have headlamps on both the dash and the canopy panel; those on the dash were later removed.

(Greater London Record Office

The contract to build this 0.618-mile line along Chichele Road was given to Dick, Kerr & Co. Ltd. on 26 October 1905 at £15,160, and was laid as a double track except for the curve at Cricklewood Broadway, which was single. The line was inspected by Major Pringle on 20 March 1906 and sanctioned three days later. Despite its short length, there was a ceremonial opening on Friday 30 March 1906, when County Alderman Herbert Nield drove the first car, No. 90, and No. 92 followed behind. Public service began on the following day, 31 March, with through cars from Edgware and Hendon to Willesden Green, reversing at a crossover on the bridge outside Willesden Green Metropolitan Railway station.

The section of line from Willesden Green station to Dudden Hill Lane, Willesden was to be built along narrow, winding streets with shops and other small businesses on either side, though there were large houses with business and professional owners in Walm Lane. Up to 2½ acres would be needed for widening if a double line were to be laid, even though a width of 32ft. had been agreed as sufficient. Much correspondence had taken place between the MCC, the Board of Trade, and the frontagers on widenings and clearances, and at the time construction began the MCC had not been able to secure all the necessary land.

The contract to build this line was awarded to Dick, Kerr & Co. Ltd. at the same time as the Chichele Road section and on the same scale of prices as for Harlesden—Stonebridge Park, an exact cost figure having to await the outcome

97

Tram Terminus, Willesden Green.

No. 108 stands at Willesden Green Station shortly after the opening from Cricklewood in March 1906, about to depart for Edgware. Cars reversed at a crossover on the bridge.

(Commercial postcard

of the road widening negotiations, which could affect the track layout. At several points an acceptable pavement width could only be obtained by taking private forecourts, and negotiations became so protracted that the MCC decided to lay two sections of interlaced track, one about 30 yards long near Willesden Green station, the other 160 yards long in High Road, Willesden near the Spotted Dog public house. These were to be temporary; Willesden UDC had agreed to them, and the county went ahead without submitting revised plans to the Board of Trade, though it had asked them for, and obtained, an extension of time.

On 5 January 1907, 114 occupiers of premises in High Road, Willesden had sent a petition to David Lloyd-George, President of the Board of Trade, protesting against the action of Willesden UDC in approving the two sections of interlaced track. Most of them had been holding out for higher sums in compensation than the county was prepared to pay, but it seems that the Board declined to intervene.

By June, 1907, the line was ready from Willesden Green station along Walm Lane and High Road as far as 'The Case is Altered' public house near the junction with Dudden Hill Lane. This 0.823-mile section included the two interlaced portions, and when Major Pringle arrived to inspect the line on 25 June he was not clear as to whether they were temporary or permanent, and reported that before issuing a certificate the Board of Trade should ask the MCC what was intended. This was the first and only case in which the Board withheld their sanction of a new line anywhere on the MET system, and in July the county engineer and solicitor visited the Board and gave an assurance that the interlaced lines were temporary.

Meanwhile, the third contract, for the 1.697 miles of double line from Dudden Hill Lane along High Road, Church Road and Craven Park to join the Harrow Road line was awarded on 8 November 1906 to Dick, Kerr & Co. Ltd. at £25,000. Building this line took about a year, and on 20 December 1907 Major Pringle arrived to inspect it. He found that while the roadway had been widened to the required 32ft., the council had been unable to come to terms with the owners of some private forecourts in Church Road. Some of them took the view that the county council should buy the whole of their property when all that was required was a narrow strip of land to provide the necessary 50ft. between fences. In the circumstances, Major Pringle was only prepared to recommend a six-month certificate, pending settlement of the dispute.

The Board issued its certificate for the Willesden Green—Dudden Hill Lane section on 5 December 1907, subject to the interlaced portions being doubled within two years, and since there had been much disquiet in Willesden over the delays, the whole line from Willesden Green to Craven Park opened hurriedly and without ceremony on Monday 23 December 1907 with only verbal permission for the final part, the certificate being issued next day. It was now possible, in theory, to run right through from Canons Park to Lock Bridge, but for the time being the service from both directions terminated at Willesden Green station, where through passengers had to change.

Despite frequent requests by the Board of Trade, the main section of interlaced track was not doubled until the spring of 1911, when High Road Willesden had been widened to 32ft. throughout. Dick, Kerr had tried to start work in late 1910, but occupiers of premises between 49 and 63 High Road had physically obstructed them, and when work was resumed in January the police were in attendance. The short interlaced section near Willesden Green station remained throughout the life of the tramways. It also became necessary to relay the west side of the curve in High Road at Pound Lane, for Major Pringle found that the tracks on this curve had been laid too close together to allow 15in. between passing cars. Until this was done, he imposed a compulsory stop before the curve and a condition that cars should not pass there.

A second service, from Willesden Green to Willesden Junction station, was added to the Lock Bridge service on 3 June 1908, and when the line in Horn Lane opened on 7 October 1909 this was extended to Acton. Willesden Green remained the terminus from both directions until 21 March 1911, after which some cars ran through to Cricklewood or Hendon.

Only two more lines now remained to be built, but one would form the vital link between the two halves of the MET system. This was from North Finchley to Cricklewood via Golders Green, the contract for which was awarded in July 1908 to Dick, Kerr & Co. Ltd. for £116,978, including the spur to the Hampstead boundary at Childs Hill. The construction of the line north of Golders Green is described in Chapter Seven, but its opening on 16 December 1909 still left a 1.568-mile gap from Golders Green to Cricklewood via Childs Hill and Cricklewood Lane.

One of the few sections of interlaced track on the MET system was in High Road, Willesden. This 160-yard length near the "Spotted Dog" was doubled in the spring of 1911.
(London Borough of Newham Libraries

99

Two views of Type D four-wheel cars shortly after the introduction of a through service from Hendon to Willesden Junction and Acton on 22 March 1911. The upper picture shows No. 172 in The Broadway, West Hendon; the lower picture shows No. 174 in the busy Church Road, Willesden. The white band on the pole instructs drivers to coast through the overhead feeder.
(Courtesy A. D. Packer and London Borough of Brent, Grange Museum of Local History

The unusual post-1923 track layout at Cricklewood Broadway, viewed from Chichele Road. The route from Willesden to Edgware turned to the left, and the short piece of straight track in the centre carried cars on the Paddington-North Finchley service (from 1923) in both directions across Edgware Road. Part of the former single line curve from the old terminus in Edgware Road can be seen, but the track from the London-Middlesex county boundary to the junction had by this time been removed.   (D. W. K. Jones

Various widenings were necessary, and Hendon Council had sent the Board of Trade a petition signed by 325 residents of Cricklewood Lane asking for wood block paving instead of granite setts. The Board had rejected this, and the line was paved in dressed granite setts instead of the type used on earlier lines. It was inspected by Major Pringle on 14 February 1910, and was sanctioned subject to suitable speed limits and one compulsory stop. Cricklewood Lane included a gradient of 1 in 14, and there were sharp curves at each end. The certificate was issued on 18 February.

The long-awaited link-up of the northern and western halves of the MET was realised on Monday morning, 21 February 1910, when Henry Burt drove the first car from Golders Green Crossroads to Cricklewood, accompanied by the usual MCC and MET contingents and representatives of Hendon UDC. Speeches were few, and there was little celebration, but the opening of this line meant that the MET system was now fully integrated, and full use could at last be made of Hendon works. From this date, all overhauls, repairs and repainting were carried out there, and new cars were erected there.

A through service from North Finchley to Cricklewood commenced on the same day, 21 February 1910. At Cricklewood Broadway, after observing the compulsory stop, the cars turned left to use as their terminus the spur at the Crown, which had been used by Hendon and Edgware cars until their diversion to Willesden Green station 30 March 1906. This arrangement continued until 1915, after which the cars reversed at the end of Cricklewood Lane in order to save unnecessary mileage. After this, the spur at The Crown, which had been built in hopes of an extension to Kilburn, was little used and was eventually removed.

During 1910, the Willesden and Edgware services still turned back at Willesden Green station, so any passengers going through from Golders Green to Willesden had to change cars twice in half a mile. On 22 March 1911 this was changed and through cars began to run from Acton to Hendon and from Paddington to Cricklewood. When route numbers were allocated in 1913, the routes became 54 Willesden Green—Hendon depot, 56 Willesden Green—Canons Park, 60 Paddington—Cricklewood, 66 Acton—Hendon Depot, 40 Cricklewood—North Finchley and 44 Barnet—Cricklewood.

There was no connection across Cricklewood Broadway from Cricklewood Lane to Chichele Road until summer 1923, when a single track connection was laid and route 60 extended to run through from Paddington to North Finchley. On Sundays it was extended to Barnet, becoming at 14½ miles the longest route on the MET system.

By 1913, traffic had risen sufficiently to justify a four-minute joint service between Willesden Green and Hendon depot by routes 54, 56 and 66, with a twelve-minute service beyond Hendon to Edgware and Canons Park. The three services were still operating in this form in 1919, and had carried heavy traffic to and from the several aircraft construction plants established in the Colindale area during the war. There were several changes in the services from 1921 onwards, and these will be described in Volume 2.

One of the best-known landmarks on the MET system, the Jubilee Clock at Harlesden, erected to commemmorate the Diamond Jubilee of Queen Victoria in 1897 still stands at the junction of High Street and Station Road, though it has lost its weather vane and the four ornate gas lanterns. Until 1927 the left-hand side of the triangular tramway junction was a single track used by the Hendon-Willesden-Acton cars in both directions. (Commercial view, courtesy J. H. Price

CHAPTER NINE

HARROW ROAD AND ACTON

Although the horse tramway of the Harrow Road and Paddington Tramways Company, described in Chapter One, became a part of the MET system in 1904, there had previously been some disagreement between the London United Tramways and the Middlesex County Council as to who would build and operate electric tramways in this part of London.

The London United Tramways' main route between Shepherds Bush and Uxbridge was opened on 4 April 1901 as far as Acton Hill and was extended to Southall on 10 July. The LUT was therefore well established in the Acton area before the MET arrived, and was contemplating extensions to the north of the Uxbridge Road.

The LUT company's Bill in the 1901 Session included three such lines; one from Hammersmith Broadway to Willesden (Harrow Road) via Shepherds Bush and Wood Lane, one from Acton to Willesden via Horn Lane and Old Oak Lane, and one from the Askew Arms to Old Oak Lane via Friars Gate Lane. These coincided in date with the MCC's May 1901 applications for lines from Harlesden (Jubilee Clock) via Horn Lane to Acton and onward to Mill Hill Park station, and the circular route in Chiswick and Bedford Park. The first LUT line would have met the Harrow Road horse tramway at College Park, and the LUT had also applied for a line from Shepherds Bush to Camden Town which would cross the horse tramway at Porchester Road.

When the LUT Bill came before Parliament, all the lines in the county of London were struck out due to opposition from the LCC. When the MCC applications were heard by the Light Railway Commissioners on 6 November 1901, agreement was reached that the MCC would withdraw its proposed lines south of the Uxbridge Road, and the LUT would withdraw its proposed line from Acton to Willesden, leaving this route to the MCC. A formal agreement was signed on 28 November under which the LUT undertook not to acquire any interest in the Harrow Road and Paddington Tramways Company and not to promote any tramway north of a line from Uxbridge to Willesden Junction. The MCC undertook not to promote any route south of this line, with the exception of that from Willesden Junction to Acton via Horn Lane. As soon as the MET's application for this line was granted, the LUT withdrew from the area.

As related in Chapter Two, the Middlesex County Council obtained a Light Railway Order in December 1901 to extend the Harrow Road tramway through Harlesden and Craven Park to the Iron Bridge at Stonebridge Park, where a depot and generating station would be built on an eight-acre site alongside the LNWR. Negotiations then began between the Harrow Road and Paddington company and the MET, culminating in a decision by the MET board on 2 November 1902 to buy a majority stake in the HR&P company at £6 10s. for each HR&P £10 share.

Under the guidance of the MET, the Harrow Road company promoted a Bill in the Spring 1903 Session of Parliament for powers to electrify the line between Harlesden and Lock Bridge. The Chippenham Road line was not mentioned, except as a dotted line on the plans, for the MET had other plans for the area. They applied on 22 May 1903 for a Light Railway Order for a line

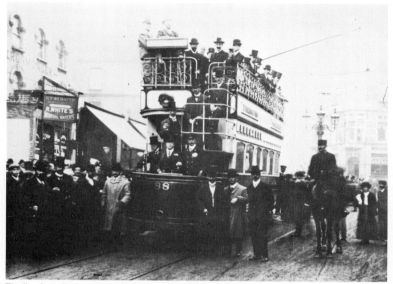

The line from Harlesden (Royal Oak) to Stonebridge Park was opened on 10 October 1906, with Sir Francis Cory-Wright driving No. 88. The scene is at the Jubilee Clock.
(Greater London Record Office

from Harrow Road via Walterton Road, Malvern Road, Cambridge Road, Cambridge Gardens and Cambridge Avenue to the Edgware Road at High Road, Kilburn, but this was withdrawn in October after the Cricklewood—Kilburn line with which it would have connected failed to gain authorisation.

The Harrow Road company's Bill became law on 11 August 1903, by which time agreement had been reached (on 13 June 1903) for the horse tramway to be sold to the MET. The transfer was sanctioned by another HR&P Act, of 22 July 1904. The 1903 Act included an obligation to double the lines in the borough of Paddington, using wood block paving, and to widen parts of Harrow Road in Willesden Urban District and the Metropolitan Boroughs of Hammersmith and Paddington. In return for the widening, Willesden would defer its right of purchase until 31 December 1930, but the LCC could buy the London portion in 1907.

On 13 October 1904, the MCC awarded a £36,338 contract to Dick, Kerr & Co. Ltd. to build the 1.437 miles of line from the horse tram terminus at the Royal Oak, Harlesden, to the Iron Bridge at Stonebridge Park. This short line took a considerable time to build and equip, being delayed early in 1906 by the flooding of the River Brent at Stonebridge Park. It was inspected on 10 August 1906 by Lt.-Col. P. G. Von Donop, RE, and the Board of Trade certificate was issued on 15 August, but opening was delayed for two months because the Metropolitan Water Board were laying new water mains. The line opened on 10 October 1906, immediately after Sir Francis Cory-Wright drove the first car, and was worked by ten cars transferred to Stonebridge Park from Hendon.

The Harrow Road and Paddington company was left in possession of its horse tramway until 16 August 1906, when in return for £36,921 the MET took over the track, properties, horses, cars and loose plant of the HR&P and became the operator (for a few days) of the horse tramway. The contract to reconstruct and electrify the line was given by the MET to Dick, Kerr & Co. Ltd. on

6 April 1906 at a contract price of £31,790, and work had to begin by 11 August in order to avoid a penalty of £4 per day to the borough of Paddington prescribed under the HR&P Act of 1903. On 16 August the MET board was told that attempts to work the horse tram service during the reconstruction was delaying the work, and the board decided that the service should cease on 1 September. Part of it seems to have closed slightly earlier, on 26 August, and the horses, cars and harness were sold at auction on 6 September, realising £1,477, except for one car retained to work the statutory journeys over the Chippenham Road branch.

By October 1906 work was well advanced, but Willesden UDC had asked for a contribution of £2,500 towards the cost of widening the bridge over the North London line at Kensal Green, in return for consenting to the tramway being opened before completion of road widening. The council also wanted a bond to ensure that the other widenings were done within 18 months, but later relented. Widening of the railway bridge had not begun when the tramway opened, and this section was worked as a single line until November 1908.

On 17 December 1906 Major Pringle inspected the reconstructed Harlesden—Lock Bridge line and found it in order, though some footways had still to be widened, and there were two temporary sections of single line, one at the railway bridge, the other between Greyhound Road and Felixstowe Road, where an 8 mile/h speed limit was imposed until widening was completed. A similar restriction applied between First Avenue and Portnall Road, where double track was laid in the as yet unwidened road. Service between Lock Bridge and Harlesden began on Saturday 22 December 1906, apparently without ceremony, and the cars worked through to Stonebridge Park.

The Harrow Road and Paddington tramway had its own allocation of cars, initially five Type C bogie cars of series 151-165 and 15 Type D four-wheelers of series 166-190. Plans of them were sent to the Board of Trade, where someone noticed that they were an inch wider than the specified 6ft. 9in. The cars were altered, as described elsewhere, and this requirement plus the separate accounting kept the Harrow Road cars apart from the rest of the MET fleet for many years.

Type A car No. 92 at Craven Park during the period from 10 October to 21 December 1906, when electric cars worked only between Stonebridge Park and Harlesden. They were extended to Lock Bridge (Harrow Road) on 22 December 1906 and to Wembley on 15 April 1908.

(Courtesy A. D. Packer

The Lock Bridge at Westbourne Park was not a natural terminus, and it had always been the intention (even in horse tram days) to extend the line towards Paddington. The problem was two bridges over the Grand Junction Canal, particularly the one at Paddington Basin, described as being of antique design and in ramshackle condition. This bridge would have to be reconstructed if trams were to reach Paddington.

A further difficulty was that the proposed extension lay wholly in the county of London, in the Metropolitan Borough of Paddington, and the LCC had a policy of owning all tramways in its area. Moreover, the LCC was empowered to purchase the rest of the Harrow Road line in its area as from the end of 1907. The MET could only build the extension if granted guaranteed security of tenure for both lines, or alternatively the LCC might be willing to build the line and grant the MET running powers.

These discussions lasted for more than a year, and by the end of 1907 the LCC had decided that it should own the whole line in its area and allow through running by MET cars in return for a percentage of receipts. The MET would build the extension, and sell it to the LCC on completion.

The constructional details were agreed between the MET and Paddington borough council on 17 June 1908. The company was to widen Harrow Road where necessary, pay £4,500 towards the council's recent widening of Harrow Road at Pickford's Corner, and build a new single-span girder bridge 48ft. wide and 30ft. long over the Grand Junction Canal at Paddington Basin, the bridge to become the property of the Borough Council.

A further agreement between the MET and the Company of Proprietors of the Grand Junction Canal was signed on 11 July, to protect the latter's interests during the rebuilding of the bridge. In return for their consent, the canal company were relieved of the liability for the old bridge and gained the benefit of the new one, including increased headroom, all at the expense of the MET. Meanwhile, the necessary Bill had completed its passage through Parliament and became law as the Metropolitan Electric Tramways Act of 1 August 1908.

The contract to build the Paddington extension was awarded to Dick, Kerr & Co. Ltd. on 28 January 1909, together with the new bridge. No contract price is recorded in the minutes, and the LCC, who were to buy the line on completion, arranged instead for Dick, Kerr to accept a price based on their tender for the LCC's Hammersmith—Putney Bridge line. The cost of the bridge was £6,049.

Agreement was reached in February 1909 on the terms of sale to the LCC of the 1.473 miles of reconstructed tramway in Harrow Road from Lock Bridge to Plough Lane (the present Kilburn Lane), the price being £40,000 including £14,250 for the cost of widenings in Paddington and £1,500 for the Chippenham Road line. Since the MET company's property formed the security for the MET 4½% debentures, it was first necessary to substitute 5,000 Ordinary £10 shares in the North Metropolitan power company for the Harrow Road tramway in order to arrive at a similar figure. This done, the Harrow Road and Chippenham Road lines became LCC property on 18 October 1909, though it was still separated from the LCC's Hammersmith lines by a section of purely MET tramway between Scrubs Lane and Plough Lane. The MET operated the line under a temporary LCC-MET agreement of 16 July 1909, and had to complete the road widening, including the purchase of No. 530 Harrow Road.

The permanent agreement between LCC and MET, signed on 18 October 1909, was a complicated document. The MET was to pay a rent based on ¹/₂₅th of the LCC's purchase price, with a different allowance for widening costs, plus £500 per single track mile for renewals, and twopence per mile for all car miles run in excess of 234,000 per year, a figure calculated from the existing service. If traffic receipts exceeded one shilling per car mile the LCC could ask for more cars to be put on, but if in succeeding months earnings fell below this figure the MET could take them off again. The agreement could be terminated after seven and fourteen years, with provision for subsequent through running.

Other conditions in the agreement covered fares, with workmen's single and two-journey tickets to remain on issue at the fares charged on 21 December 1907, the date on which the LCC gave notice to purchase the line. The cars were to be kept in good condition, with tarpaulins to be provided on upper deck seats, the company was to repair and maintain the tramway, and must not discontinue working the line. Perhaps more significant was the proviso that the staff should be employed under conditions not less favourable than those on the LCC tramways, and could not be discharged for joining a trade union, a clause which had the effect of tying wages and conditions on the entire MET system to those of the LCC.

Provision was also made for the line to be used by cars of the LCC, whose line along Scrubs Lane, opened on 30 May 1908, met the Harrow Road line at College Park, and was the first complete LCC route to be worked on the overhead system. The LCC could run one car to each three run by the company, and if they did so, the company would supply the power and certain MET-LCC payments would be reduced. Each party would retain the fares taken on its own cars, and pay its own accident claims.

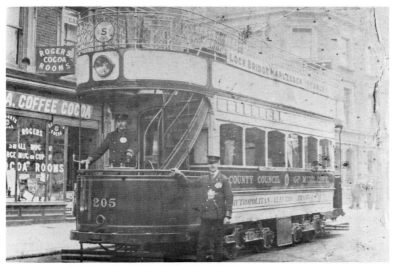

Type C/1 car No. 205, delivered in 1908, seen at the first Harrow Road terminus at Lock Bridge on the service to Wembley.   (Courtesy L. A. Thomson

The Paddington extension was opened in two sections. First to be inspected was the 0.612-mile portion from Lock Bridge to Warwick Crescent, by Major Pringle on 13 July 1910. It opened next day, on verbal authority, and was the subject of another temporary agreement with the MET. The final 0.562 miles were inspected by Major Pringle on 30 November 1910 in the presence of representatives of the LCC and the canal company; all were satisfied, and the inspecting officer wrote that the new bridge would be of immense advantage to all kinds of traffic. The certificate was issued three days later and public service began on 6 December 1910, with through cars from Paddington to Sudbury and Willesden Green. A reference in the minutes of Acton UDC for June 1911 indicates that there had also been a through service (perhaps experimental) from Acton to Paddington; the council protested at its withdrawal.

The only known photograph of one of the Type Z cars of the London United Tramways on hire to the MET to work the Harrow Road route between May 1910 and July 1911. This one, LUT No. 77, became No. 477 during its stay with the MET, the additional numeral "4" being added to the original number. (London Borough of Newham Libraries

To enable LCC cars to work through to Paddington, a junction was put in by the MET at College Park in April or May 1910, the MET's share of the cost being £877. However, the first cars to use it probably belonged neither to the MET nor the LCC, but to the London United. The MET had ordered further cars for the Harrow Road line, but pending their arrival had hired ten cars from the LUT. Because of the 80-yard gap then separating the MET and LUT tracks at Acton Market Place, the LUT cars most probably went via Shepherds Bush and were presumably slewed round from the LUT to the LCC tracks where they crossed at Goldhawk Road. They were of LUT Type Z (1-100), and while the fleet numbers of the whole batch are not known, a photograph exists of one at Harlesden, No. 77, to which has been added a larger 4, making the car number 477. All ten cars were hired from May to December 1910, at a cost of £1,093, and six were retained until 22 July 1911 at a further cost of £349.

The junction was in regular use from 3 June to 31 August 1911, during the Coronation Exhibition at the White City, when LCC cars ran a through service between Hammersmith and Paddington. This raises the question of clearances between passing cars, since the LCC E/1 cars were 7ft. 1in. wide against the prescribed MET width of 6ft. 9in., but the service was short-lived. The LCC at this time was also planning a shorter route from the Harrow Road to White City, diverging at Porchester Road and traversing the Ladbroke Grove area, but this line was not built.

When the second seven-year period of the through running agreement expired in 1923, the 1909 agreement was not renewed and the Harrow Road line was treated as a through-running route on the same basis as those in North London, balanced by additional LCC car-miles between Finsbury Park and Enfield. LCC cars never again worked to Paddington, but from 1924 they worked regularly to Craven Park and beyond, the College Park junction having been altered in 1923 to allow this.

WEMBLEY AND SUDBURY

The original intention, as described in Chapter Two and Appendix 6, had been to extend the Harrow Road tramway from Stonebridge Park to Wembley and then north to Harrow and Harrow Weald. Attempts to reach Harrow had been defeated by the strong objections from Harrow School, but Wembley UDC, on the other hand, had objected to any scheme which left the tram terminus in their district.

By early in 1906, the MCC had come to an understanding with Wembley on this point, and had decided to take the line through Wembley to The Swan at Sudbury, a few yards from the Harrow boundary, and no further. This 1.030-mile extension was the subject of an inquiry on 9 February 1906, and was authorised in the County of Middlesex Light Railways (Extensions and Lands) Order of 7 February 1907.

The MET and MCC were in no hurry to build this line, as much of the route beyond Stonebridge Park was undeveloped. The contract for the 1.312 miles from Stonebridge Park to Wembley LNWR station was awarded to Clift Ford at £25,735 on 7 February 1907, and the line was inspected by Major Pringle on 7 April 1908. The footpaths had not yet been widened throughout, but since there were open fields on either side of the road this was not an objection. The certificate was issued on 9 April and the Lock Bridge—Stonebridge Park service was extended to Wembley & Sudbury LNWR station from 15 April 1908.

After the MCC had obtained an extension of time from the Board of Trade, the final contract taking the line on from Wembley station to The Swan at Sudbury was awarded on 28 January 1910 to George Wimpey & Co. Ltd. at £27,132. There were the usual arguments over paving, and dressed granite setts were adopted. The work was delayed by bad weather and unstable terrain, and Wembley council claimed for damage to side turnings caused by heavy traffic diverted from the main road during construction. The 1.030-mile line was inspected on 10 September 1910 by Lt.-Col. P. G. Von Donop and opened with verbal permission on 24 September, the certificate being issued three days

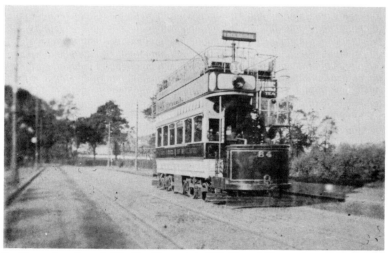

No. 84 near the outer end of the Wembley route in 1908. Most of this route beyond Stonebridge Park depot was in open country and remained so until after the 1914-18 war, when rapid development took place. (Courtesy A. D. Packer

Few early photographs exist of Sudbury terminus. This one, taken in the early 1920s, shows the terminus at "The Swan" with a Type H car about to return to Paddington.

(Commercial postcard

later. The service provided ran from Sudbury to Warwick Crescent, pending completion through to Paddington on 6 December 1910. The MCC agreed to pay the contractor an extra £6,335 because of the difficulties encountered.

THE ACTON BRANCH

The next line in the area to be taken in hand was the link between Harlesden and Acton, the south-western extremity of the MET system. In its original form, under an MCC application of May, 1901, this would have run from Harlesden (Jubilee Clock) along Station Road, Old Oak Lane, alongside a footpath to Horn Lane, then along Horn Lane and across High Street, Acton into Mill Hill Road to finish at the District Railway's Mill Hill Park station, later renamed Acton Town. On 28 November 1901 the MTOC had signed a territorial agreement with the LUT, as a result of which the line was cut back to finish at the south end of Horn Lane, near Acton Market Place.

In April 1902, it was decided that from Old Oak Lane to Horn Lane in North Acton the line would follow Victoria Road, at that time a narrow private road. This would be taken over by the MCC and widened to 50ft., including the 13ft. hump-backed bridge over the Grand Junction Canal, which would have its approach gradients eased. The bridges taking Victoria Road under the Midland Railway and over the Great Western near Acton Wells junction would both be widened to 50ft., with the road lowered under the Midland bridge to allow for double deck cars.

The chairman of the MCC, Sir Ralph Littler, asked that a branch be built along Acton Lane to the Royal Agricultural Society's showground at Twyford (Park Royal), which had opened in 1901. The MET board advised against it, and the showground itself was closed a few years later, becoming part of Park Royal industrial estate.

Because of the civil engineering involved, construction did not begin until 1906, after agreement had been reached for the Midland Railway to widen their bridge at a cost of £6,409. On 8 November 1906 a £5,000 contract was awarded to Dick, Kerr & Co. Ltd. for the 0.250-mile section from the Jubilee Clock along Station Road to the north end of the LNWR railway bridge at Willesden Junction station, and on 7 February 1907 the main contract was placed with R. W. Blackwell & Co. Ltd. for the 2.208 miles from Willesden Junction to the south end of Horn Lane, Acton.

The quarter-mile section from the Jubilee Clock to Willesden Junction was inspected by Major Pringle on 7 April 1908 and approved; it was double track apart from 50 yards of interlaced track in Station Road. At the same time he noted that the MCC had laid a single line curve at the Jubilee Clock from High Street, Harlesden into Station Road, to give a direct route towards Stonebridge Park depot; this had been omitted from the plans, and was therefore laid without any specific authority, but he did not object and sanctioned its use at 4 miles/h with a compulsory stop at each end. The certificate was issued on 9 April, but the line did not come into use until 3 June 1908.

The rest of the line, from Willesden Junction to Acton, took longer than expected and at one point the MCC threatened the contractor with legal action. However, when he inspected it on 23 September 1909 Major Pringle found no fault with the construction, and sanctioned the line subject to some speed limits on curves and a compulsory stop before entering Old Oak Lane from Victoria Road. The certificate was issued on 27 September.

The Acton branch marked the completion of the lines in the area, and a formal opening took place on 7 October 1909. County Alderman Herbert Nield, MP, drove the first car (No. 92) from Horn Lane terminus to Willesden Junction, and County Alderman Charles Pinkham, vice-chairman of the MCC Light Railways and Tramways Committee, drove it back to Acton.

The Acton line opened on the following day, 8 October 1909, with a service from Acton to Willesden Green, using in both directions the single line forming the west side of the junction at the Jubilee Clock, with appropriate crossovers. No service was provided over the third side of the junction, though one must have been envisaged when the layout was planned. Acton UDC asked for a through service to Hendon, but the company replied that Willesden Green station was a convenient transfer point. When the first MET map and guide appeared late in 1910, the services were shown as Warwick Crescent—Wembley, Warwick Crescent—Willesden Green and Acton—Willesden Green, but by 1913 they had been given route numbers and were 58 Paddington—Craven Park, 60 Paddington—Cricklewood, 62 Paddington—Sudbury, 64 Acton—Harlesden and 66 Acton—Hendon. An Acton—Paddington service had been tried briefly in 1911.

In its 1913 Act, the MET obtained powers to lay a second curve at the Jubilee Clock to complete a double track triangle junction, these powers being needed to overcome the opposition of a frontager. The MET then sold these

Type D car No. 182 in Horn Lane, Acton, on 9 October 1909, the second day of service on this branch.   (London Borough of Ealing Libraries

Type A car No. 92 at Acton terminus at the start of the inaugural run between Acton and Willesden Junction on 7 October 1909, with County Alderman Herbert Nield, MP, at the controls.   (Greater London Record Office

powers for £500 to the county council in 1914, but the war prevented further progress. The scheme was revived about 1924, but the MCC had now decided on further widening here and in Station Road, and obtained fresh powers in its 1925 Act. The corner was widened and the curve laid late in 1927.

Only one other tramway was built in Acton, but its story is more involved than anything so far described. The tracks of the MET and LUT came quite close to each other at Acton Market Place, but were not connected. About 80 yards separated the MET terminus in Horn Lane from the London United's Shepherds Bush—Uxbridge line in the High Street.

After the two companies had come together in the London & Suburban Traction group, described in Chapter Twelve, the MET proposed to the MCC on 4 June 1913 that a single line connection should be made from the MET tracks in Horn Lane along King Street to make a westerly connection with the LUT line in High Street, which would create a useful route for through cars to Hampton Court and other places. The MCC sent the plans to Acton UDC and asked their consent.

On 30 July county engineer H. T. Wakelam visited Acton, where the course of the proposed line had been chalked out on the road surface, and examined the route with Henry Burt, A. H. Pott and a member of Acton council, the Rev. G. S. de Sausmarez. De Sausmarez was also Rector of St. Mary's Parish Church in King Street, and straightaway objected on the grounds of alleged 'noise and disturbing influences' which passing trams would cause to worshippers in his church. Since a tram going round a sharp bend often emits a loud ringing tone that can rival the high notes of a church choir, his fears may have been justified.

The Reverend Councillor carried a great deal of influence within Acton council, and the party inspected some possible alternative routes. One was along The Steyne from Horn Lane to High Street, another was via Rectory Road and The

Cars allocated for accounting purposes to the line which the MET had purchased from the Harrow Road and Paddington Tramway Company did not bear the "County Council of Middlesex" wording on their side panels. The original allocation included fifteen Type D four-wheel cars, two of which are seen above at Craven Park junction on the Willesden Green-Acton service. In 1910 they were joined by ten new top-covered cars of Type H (series 242-266) one of which is shown below at Harlesden. The motorman is the late William Whitbread.

(Courtesy D. W. K. Jones; the late Victor Whitbread

Steyne. The MCC and MET representatives concluded that these would cost too much, because of the amount of property that would have to be acquired for road widening, and the MCC decided to ask Acton UDC for a definite decision on the King Street route.

This took several months, and on 17 December 1913 Acton replied still objecting to King Street and suggesting a line from Horn Lane through Acton Market Place, which the county would have to widen, together with part of High Street to make room for the turnouts. This was based on laying a double line, and would involve the acquisition of expensive commercial property.

The MCC and MET each produced alternative suggestions. The county engineer in February 1914 proposed two one-way single lines, northward through the Market Place to Horn Lane, and southward turning east from Horn Lane into Churchfield Road West and reaching the High Street by way of Grove Road. The MET suggested a single line through the Market Place, with no widenings, to be used only during limited hours for the purpose of moving cars between depots. Instead of forwarding these plans, the MCC told Acton that the cost of widening the Market Place would be prohibitive, and asked them to reconsider the original King Street route. Nothing came of this, and on 14 May 1914 the MCC decided to take no further action.

Just over a year later, the matter was raised again, this time in a new form. A. H. Pott, as manager of both MET and LUT, had suggested to the Metropolitan Munitions Committee that the London United repair works at Chiswick could be given over to munitions production if the LUT cars could be maintained at Hendon. The King Street link, or something like it, was essential for this, and Pott asked Acton UDC to reconsider the line, saying that the company was willing to consider any reasonable restrictions on the use of the line put forward by the church authorities. He had sent a copy of his letter to the Board of Trade, who on 29 June asked Acton Council for their observations.

Acton council met on 6 July 1915 and invited comments from Mr. A. W. Mackenzie, a churchwarden of St. Mary's Church, who said that the inconvenience and noise to the Church would be considerable, and doubted 'whether a few tools used in the engine-room of a tramways company' would help materially in increasing the output of munitions. The Reverend de Sausmarez asked that the line should not be used during Divine Service, and Councillor Arney wanted this ban applied during Matins and Evensong only. Both amendments were lost, and Acton council agreed to the line being built, subject to it not being used for passenger traffic.

Work began at once, and at the end of July 1915 Pott wrote to the Board of Trade to say that the line was ready and asked if an inspection was necessary. The Board considered inspection unnecessary, and the line was put into immediate use, Chiswick LUT works being turned over to munitions production and London United cars making the journey to Hendon Works for repairs and overhaul. The line in Horn Lane was cut back by 40ft. to allow for the curve into King Street, and the new line was laid in the dwarf rail also used on the Alexandra Palace sleeper track. Only a single line was laid, as the special work necessary for a double line junction with the LUT could not be obtained at short notice. The cost of the connection was a munitions expense, which was ultimately recovered (by the London United Tramways) from the national exchequer.

On 9 July 1915 Pott asked if Acton council would agree to workmen's or special cars using the line, as the MET was now carrying considerable munition workers traffic to and from the shell-filling factories at Park Royal, but the council on 20 July declined to change the terms of their consent. Early in 1916 the MET applied without success for powers to use trailer cars between Acton and Willesden (see Chapter Thirteen) and after this was rejected, because of police objections, an arrangement was made between the companies for London United cars, presumably based at the LUT's Acton depot, to work (with LUT motormen) between Acton and Paddington and between Acton and Hendon. No record has been traced of the number of LUT cars involved or the terms of operation, though a charge was made for each LUT car running over the MET system to reach Hendon works.

The legality of the King Street line was not allowed to pass unchallenged. On 10 August 1915 the Commissioner of Police wrote to MET secretary A. L. Barber asking under what Act the line had been constructed. Barber replied that it had been laid with the approval of Acton UDC and the Board of Trade. The Commissioner then wrote to the Home Office to say that had the proposal come before Parliament in the usual way, the Police would have objected to the line from a traffic point of view.

Acton terminus a few days before the end of tramway operation in 1936, showing in the foreground the wartime curve from Horn Lane into King Street, connecting the MET and LUT tracks.
(M. N. A. Walker

There followed some interesting correspondence within the Board of Trade which came to light during research for this book. The chief inspecting officer, Col. P. G. Von Donop, saw no objection to the line despite the tight curve, and the other senior officers upheld the view that since Acton UDC had agreed, the Board was correct in allowing the line to be laid without statutory authority as the need for it was urgent. If the companies wished to maintain the connection after it had served its wartime purpose, then they should obtain statutory authority for it. The Home Office agreed, and the Police did not raise the matter again.

In November 1919, Acton UDC asked the MET to build a line from the Gipsy Corner junction of Horn Lane and Willesden Lane past the Central Middlesex Hospital to rejoin the main route at some other unspecified point and serve some factories which were nearly a mile from any tramway. The MET told the MCC that there would only be traffic at peak hours and that the time was not opportune for such expenditure. The LGOC was persuaded to put on a bus service.

Although the LUT Chiswick Works was fully operational again in June 1919 and LUT cars no longer needed to visit Hendon, the King Street line at Acton remained in place until the end of tramway operation, and its later uses will be described in Volume 2. In 1919 the London Traffic Advisory Committee suggested that a through passenger service should be run from Ealing to Willesden for factory workers, and the MET included in their 1925 Bill an application for powers to widen Rectory Road and The Steyne and lay a double line connection from Horn Lane to High Street. The Bill became law on 7 August 1925, but although the road works were carried out, the tramway was not laid.

The Harrow Road and Acton lines were worked entirely by open top cars until 1910, when ten new top-covered Type H cars of the 242-266 batch were allocated to Stonebridge Park depot, and entered service on Harrow Road on 16 May. These and the four-wheelers were sent away in 1920 to be fitted with plough carriers and used on the MET-LCC through routes in North London, and Stonebridge Park received in exchange about half the original 1-70 series of 1904, including some that had been fitted with open-balcony top covers in 1912-14. This established a tradition that the Harrow Road line would be worked by the oldest cars on the system, a practice which continued to the end.

At least one Type H car of the 1911 batch, No. 293, was used on the Harrow Road line when new. One of the advertisements is for the affiliated North Metropolitan Electric Power Supply Company.   (Courtesy the late V. Whitbread

No. 25 of Type B, transferred in 1920 from the northern MET routes to Stonebridge Park, stands at Paddington terminus about 1927, ready to return to Sudbury. No. 25's Brush trucks had been turned round with driving wheels leading.

(The late Dr. H. A. Whitcombe, courtesy Science Museum

CHAPTER TEN

MET-LCC THROUGH RUNNING

In describing this aspect of MET operations, which commenced in 1912, it is first necessary to go back to 1902 and explain the peculiar status of the 0.54-mile section of tramway between Finsbury Park and the Manor House, which was to have an important influence on the question of through running between the Metropolitan Electric and London County Council tramways.

Until 1900 both sides of this tramway were in Middlesex, but when on 15 May 1900 the Urban District of South Hornsey was abolished and its area incorporated in the Metropolitan Borough of Stoke Newington, this brought the London—Middlesex boundary down the centre of Seven Sisters Road, leaving one side of the tramway in Hornsey (part of Middlesex) and the other in London.

The London County Council had a policy of owning all tramways in the county, in some instances (including the North Metropolitan) leasing them back to the companies to operate until electrification began. They therefore objected to the sale to the MET in 1902 of four pieces of North Metropolitan track which lay within the county of London, and these were initially excluded from the sale.

These lines were operationally part of the MET system. One was the 0.346 miles in Green Lanes from the Manor House northwards to the county boundary at Hermitage Road, another was 0.55 miles in Seven Sisters Road from the Manor House to Amhurst Park Road, and a third was the southernmost 0.126 miles of the Stamford Hill tramway. The first two of these were in Stoke Newington, the third in Hackney. The fourth was 'so much of the Boundary Tramway as is situate in the County of London', i.e. one track between the Manor House and Finsbury Park. The Board of Trade upheld their sale, and the four lines were transferred to the MET for £10,000 on 30 December 1903. The LCC agreed not to exercise powers of purchase for the boundary tramway until 10 April 1910 (this being the expiry date of the new lease granted to the North Metropolitan for its London lines) and for the other lines until 31 December 1930.

There was a legal dispute over the electrification of the boundary tramway and three other short sections in London, the LCC claiming that the North Metropolitan's 1897 powers to electrify them had expired. This was resolved and the line opened for electric traction on the overhead system on 22 July 1904, with the MET electric cars turning back at the corner of Blackstock Road, Finsbury Park, where passengers had to change to horse tram, horse bus or train to continue towards London.

The position changed again on 1 April 1906, after the North Metropolitan had surrendered the residue of its lease to enable the LCC to start electrifying the lines in North London. The North Metropolitan Tramways (Winding Up) Act 1906 included provision for the MET to sell the boundary tramway to the LCC after 10 August 1910, subject to Hornsey's consent. This made the line an exception to the rule that each county would keep to its own territory, since the LCC would become the owner of the track on the Hornsey (Middlesex) side of the boundary. However, Middlesex County Council raised no objections.

LCC conduit electric cars reached Finsbury Park from Holloway (Nags Head) on 9 July 1908, and the LCC's intention was to run a through service on the conduit system from Holloway to Moorgate via Finsbury Park, Manor House, Green Lanes, Southgate Road, East Road and City Road. Most LCC cars in North London were not fitted with trolley poles, and it would therefore be necessary to equip the boundary tramway on the conduit system. However, parts of this route were not yet electrified and Shoreditch borough council were carrying out major road works which seemed likely to delay completion until at least 1913.

As early as 1901, talks had taken place between the two county councils on possible mutual running powers and also on through fares, but no agreement had been reached. The subject had not been raised again except in respect of the southernmost section of the Archway Road line, which the LCC built for the MET to operate. However, a first step towards closer co-operation was taken in May 1909 when the LCC decided to advertise the connecting MET services on its cars working in North London, and placed orders with Hurst Nelson for 420 sets of route boards and brackets, worded as follows:

—190 sets 'Change cars at Stamford Hill for Tottenham, Edmonton, Ponders End, Enfield and Waltham Cross';

—70 sets 'Change at Finsbury Park for Wood Green, Alexandra Palace, Winchmore Hill, Bush Hill Park, New Southgate, Edmonton and Ponders End';

—84 sets 'Change cars at Highgate for East Finchley, Whetstone, Totteridge and Barnet';

—50 sets 'Change cars at Harrow Road for Paddington, Willesden and Wembley';

—26 sets 'Change cars at Bow Bridge for Stratford, Forest Gate, Manor Park, Leytonstone, Wanstead and Epping Forest' (in this case the neighbouring tramway was West Ham).

On 14 June 1910, the LCC served notice on the MET and Hornsey Borough Council of their intention to purchase the Finsbury Park to Manor House tramway under the terms of the Tramways Act 1870. The MET (and some district councils) were concerned lest passengers for Finsbury Park might be compelled to change at the Manor House after the sale of this section to the LCC. In February 1911 the MET board learned that the LCC intended to reconstruct the line on the conduit system and put in a change pit at the Manor House to enable MET cars to run through, and the LCC's 1910 Bill had sought powers for a terminal loop at Finsbury Park with tracks in Fonthill Road, Evershot Street, Hanley Road, Regina Road and Tollington Park, but this had been rejected.

In its 1911 Bill, the LCC included an alternative loop line at Finsbury Park that would have provided an off-street terminus for the MET. It would consist of a track in Blackstock Road, turning on to land to be acquired between Blackstock Road and Finsbury Park Road, and returning along Finsbury Park Road to rejoin Seven Sisters Road. The part on private land would be double track, the rest single.

The Blackstock Road loop was struck out of the LCC Bill, and the local authorities in the MET area were becoming restive over the continued uncertainty surrounding access by MET cars to Finsbury Park after the boundary tramway was sold to the LCC. On 13 October 1911 the MET directors resolved to promote a Bill in Parliament to give the company compulsory running powers to Finsbury Park.

In case this failed, the MET also prepared a Bill for the 1912 session of Parliament for a private tramroad inside Finsbury Park, at the suggestion of Hornsey Borough Council. It would start just inside the southwest entrance and run inside the park to the Manor House entrance, where it would join the lines in Green Lanes and Seven Sisters Road. The idea was supported initially by Middlesex, Islington and Stoke Newington, and support also came from an unexpected quarter (the Commissioner of Police). The LCC was hostile, and petitioned against the Bill, but despite this it passed the Standing Orders Committee of the House of Commons and passed a Second Reading.

At this point, the LCC offered to modify its stance and offer a workable arrangement for through running, including retention of the overhead to Finsbury Park to enable MET cars without plough gear to run through, and the MET's Bill was withdrawn. The LCC chief officer of tramways, Aubrey Llewellyn Coventry Fell, met James Devonshire in March 1912 to draft an agreement, and the LCC Highways Committee on 2 April 1912 agreed to the principle of mutual through running. In the same month an arbitrator, Mr. R. Elliott-Cooper, MICE, settled the price to be paid by the LCC for the boundary tramway at £7,350.

The start of competition. In 1911 the LGOC introduced bus route 29 from Palmers Green to Victoria, which paralleled the tramways and avoided the change at Finsbury Park. These two photographs were taken in Seven Sisters Road near the MET's terminus, the upper one probably in 1912, the lower one probably in 1914, with car 86 on route 28 to Muswell Hill.

(M. N. A. Walker, D. W. K. Jones

The reason for the LCC's change of heart was probably the onset of motor bus competition. The summer of 1911 had seen the start of a regular motor bus service between central London and Palmers Green (Aldermans Hill), and the LGOC was building a garage at Palmers Green from which to work it. This service paralleled the tramways all the way from Euston Road, and was gaining traffic from both tramway operators by avoiding the need to change at Finsbury Park. The MET, not yet associated with the LGOC (this was some months away) was planning to retaliate by introducing its own fleet of buses, some of which would be based at a proposed garage near Wood Green.

The agreement drafted by A. L. C. Fell and James Devonshire was for a through tram service between Euston Road and Enfield. Each party's car mileage would be proportional to the length of track in its area, the MET to run six cars to each four run by London, and there would be additional cars from Euston Road to Palmers Green. Receipts from through running cars would be divided in proportion to the receipts per car mile on the corresponding routes, which were 13.032 pence in London and 11.387 pence in Middlesex, the Finsbury Park—Manor House section being regarded as part of the LCC's portion.

Under this agreement, the LCC would install a temporary change pit at Finsbury Park, and would reconstruct the Finsbury Park—Manor House line on the conduit system within two years with a change pit at the Manor House, but retaining the

Left: LCC car No. 1602, at Wood Green Depot, one of the 15 LCC cars hired by the MET in 1912 and the first car to run through. Posters on the canopy read "The First Electric Car from Euston Road to Palmers Green and Enfield". The driver is the late Philip Pugh.

(Courtesy the late Philip Pugh)

Right: The notice issued by the MET giving fares on the first through route between Enfield and Euston Road. First and last times appeared on the reverse. (Courtesy London Transport

overhead to Finsbury Park, to which Islington borough council had agreed. The MET would pay the LCC 6½d. per car mile for its short-working cars on this section, and the MET undertook not to run its own buses on any part of a through running tram route without the LCC's consent. The arrangements would be for successive periods of twelve months, subject to three months notice. The MET and LCC would share equally the cost of the change pits at Finsbury Park and Manor House. The MET would fit its cars with plough gear, top covers and 40hp motors, and would hire fifteen cars from the LCC to work its agreed mileage until there were enough MET cars with plough carriers to work the company's share of the mileage.

The MET board agreed to the terms and the agreement was signed on 30 May 1912, followed on 17 July by the sale of the boundary tramway to the LCC. The 20 type H cars ordered in January from Brush would now be delivered with plough carriers, and the county committee had agreed to the proposed fares and stages. A new junction was ordered from Hadfields for the Manor House, replacing the north-to-east curve and reinstating a direct north-south connection at a cost of £799; this was completed in 1913. The MET's share of the Finsbury Park change pit cost was £759.

Although this aspect will be fully covered in the rolling stock schedule, it is worth restating here that commencing with Nos. 192-216, all MET cars ordered from February 1908 were fitted with LCC-type trucks by Mountain & Gibson or Brush, of which one truck had an extension at the inner end designed to accept a plough carrier. The LCC were rather less prepared for through running, for in 1911 none of its North London cars had trolley poles. The first LCC cars to be ordered with trolley bases (other than 25 for Hammersmith) were Nos. 1227-1426 of 1910, most of which ran without poles when new, and the LCC had to take other cars into works and fit trolley poles and cabling retrospectively. Many North London cars never received this treatment.

The fifteen LCC cars hired by the MET were E/1 Class cars 1590-1604, delivered by Brush about December 1911. They were in the standard LCC livery of chocolate and primrose, and bore the initials 'MCC' in gold letters on the waist panels, with the company's name in small letters on the solebar. They were stationed at Wood Green depot, together with most of the plough-fitted MET Type H cars 297-316.

The earliest known view of through running operations at Finsbury Park. LCC car No. 1060 leaves its plough at the temporary change pit opposite Blackstock Road preparatory to continuing on the overhead system to Palmers Green. Note the three-track layout, at this time the centre track was a stub end. (Commercial view, courtesy J. H. Price

The opening of the through service from Enfield to central London took place on the morning of Thursday, 1 August 1912. The first car to run through from Euston Road to Enfield Town was hired LCC E/1 car 1602, which bore posters on the upper deck ends proclaiming it as 'The First Electric Car from Euston to Palmers Green and Enfield.' There was little ceremony, and the local press reports concentrated on the fact that there were halfpenny fares on the LCC section but not on the MET part. 70,000 people travelled on the following Bank Holiday Monday, 42,000 of them in MET cars.

In anticipation of through running with the London County Council Tramways, many Type H MET cars were fitted as new with LCC-type colour-light indicators. The top picture shows No. 242 at Waltham Cross before through running began; the lower one shows No. 306 at Wood Green on through service 31 to Palmers Green before the colour lights were replaced by route number stencils. The open-top car is on the service from Bruce Grove to Finsbury Park.
(Tramway Museum Society and D. W. K. Jones

During December 1912 talks took place between the MET and LCC about further through running, and on 17 December the parties agreed to through running services between (a) Edmonton and Holborn via Finsbury Park; (b) Edmonton and Seven Sisters Corner to Euston Road; (c) North Finchley to Holborn via Wood Green and Caledonian Road; (d) Waltham Cross to Smithfield; (e) Muswell Hill to Bloomsbury and (f) New Southgate to Aldersgate Street via Green Lanes and Essex Road. A slightly different method of sharing receipts was proposed, based on equal shares for the first four weeks, a record to be kept of each car's takings in the fourth week and used to determine the division of pooled receipts for the next three months, similar records to be taken in the thirteenth week of each subsequent quarter. After the first full year, the count would be taken only once every six months. Each party was to pay its own working expenses and any accident claims in its area, and unless the LCC agreed the company could not book passengers through to Underground railways or buses on any of the through routes.

This would require many more MET cars to be fitted with plough carriers, and this was put in hand. At the end of 1912 the MET fleet consisted of 312 cars, of which 85 had enclosed top covers and 105 could be fitted with plough gear. The 145 cars fitted with Brush Type BB reversed maximum traction trucks were not considered suitable for conversion to conduit operation, though six of them did receive plough carriers of a makeshift design in 1919 or 1920. Because the MET cars available were insufficient for the needs of several busy routes, the MET sought to extend the hire of the fifteen LCC cars, but they were required elsewhere and were transferred to Clapham in August 1915. Later, another batch was hired from 1916 until 1918.

The LCC cars in North London were all top-covered, and the LCC had proposed that after 12 months the MET should fit top covers to all cars working the through routes. In the final agreement this was left to the discretion of the two managers, and MET open-top cars continued to work on all through routes until 1929-30.

The Type H cars built from 1910 to 1912 had arrived fitted with three light route-signal boxes similar to those used by the LCC, and these had also been fitted to some earlier Type H cars and to the five Type F cars, at a cost of £104. No evidence has come to light to show whether any use was made of the boxes prior to the start of through running, but photographs show that MET cars fitted with these boxes worked on the Euston Road—Enfield through service, presumably displaying at night the code applicable to the LCC portion of the route. These signals were short-lived, for the LCC route-numbering scheme in North London began in January 1913 and by 1914 the boxes on the MET cars were converted to serve as stencil boxes for the route number. The fitting of number stencils and boxes to all MET double-deck cars was completed early in 1915, at a cost of £632.

The first through routes to start working under the new agreement commenced on 1 March 1913. They were between Seven Sisters Corner and Euston, and Edmonton Town Hall and Holborn, and they took the respective service numbers 27 and 59 in the LCC series. By this time, the original through services had received the numbers 29 (Euston—Enfield) and 31 (Euston—Palmers Green), though ten years later 31 became part of 29. These four were joined on 23 June 1913 by service 79, Smithfield Market to Waltham Cross.

The original one-year agreement of 12 August 1912 for the Euston—Enfield route was now nearing its end, and was renewed on the same basis as the other routes, with equal shares to each operator. This 24 July 1913 agreement also provided for through running on the Archway Road route, and for the permanent retention of the overhead between Finsbury Park and the Manor House. The MET with its large number of cars not fitted for dual operation had said that it would have cost them £250 per car to fit plough carriers to the fifty or so cars that only ran to Finsbury Park for football, holiday or other special traffic.

MET cars ran through to Holborn terminus from 1 March 1913. In this post-war view at Holborn, Type F car No. 213 stands ready to leave on a rush-hour working to Albany Road, Enfield Highway. (Courtesy London Transport

By this time the MET company had become associated with the Underground railways, and although the second MET-MCC agreement ruled out through bookings with the Underground at Finsbury Park, the MET maintained that there was a continuing need for a local service north of Finsbury Park by cars going no further south. This was opposed by the LCC, who wanted all cars to run through, and by the Metropolitan Police, who disliked cars reversing there because of the congestion, rather unjustly since the MET in 1905 had paid £1,500 towards widening Seven Sisters Road at this point. The subject was raised on many subsequent occasions, but nothing was done until 1915.

It had been intended that the next through route would be one from New Southgate to Aldersgate Street via Mildmay Park, but delay in putting in the necessary change pit brought a change of plan, and on 23 November 1913 an LCC/MET joint service using LCC cars and numbered 21 was introduced from Holborn (Grays Inn Road) to North Finchley via Kings Cross, Finsbury Park and Wood Green. MET cars continued to work locally between Wood Green and North Finchley as service 34.

The December 1912 agreement for the other routes required the MET to pay half the cost of two change pits at the Manor House, one in Green Lanes south of the junction and one in Seven Sisters Road. The former was built first, allowing the introduction on 15 August 1914 of a new route 51 from Muswell Hill to Bloomsbury. The MET cars which worked this service had to be open topped, because the first MET top-covered cars could not pass under the GNR bridge in Turnpike Lane. Route 51 broke new ground for MET cars, as it ran via Green Lanes, Mildmay Park, Essex Road, Angel and Rosebery Avenue, terminating in Theobalds Road near Southampton Row. It was unique in sharing tracks with single deck cars at both ends, the Alexandra Palace cars along Turnpike Lane and the LCC Kingsway Subway single-deckers between Islington Green and Bloomsbury.

The reconstruction of the Finsbury Park to Manor House tramway for conduit operation began in the summer of 1914 and took nearly a year. It was completed

THE METROPOLITAN ELECTRIC TRAMWAYS, Ltd.

NOTICE.

On and after SUNDAY, 16th AUGUST, 1914

the service of Cars now run between

Muswell Hill & Finsbury Park

will be withdrawn,

AND A

NEW SERVICE SUBSTITUTED BETWEEN

Muswell Hill & Southampton Row,

BLOOMSBURY

Via Green Lanes, Essex Road, "Angel,"

Rosebery Avenue, Theobald...

DEPART.			Week Days	Sundays
Muswell Hill to Southampton Row	First Car	,,	6.18	8.42
The "Wellington" to	,,	,,	4.9	8.51
"Manor House" to	,,	,,	4.18	9.0
Southampton Row to Muswell Hill	,,	,,	5.29	9.29
Muswell Hill to Southampton Row	Last Car	,,	11.48	11.50
The "Wellington" to	,,	,,	11.57	11.59
"Manor House" to	,,	,,	12.6	11.48
Southampton Row to Muswell Hill	,,	,,	11.45	11.17
,, ,,	Wood Green	,,	12.35	12.17

Manor House Offices,
Seven Sisters Road,
FINSBURY PARK, N.

By Order,
W. R. HAMMOND,
Traffic Manager.

P.T.O.

Muswell Hill & Bloomsbury Route

(fare stage tables — Courtesy London Transport)

The notice issued by the MET on the inauguration of through service No. 51 between Muswell Hill and Southampton Row (Bloomsbury) on 16 August 1914.   (Courtesy London Transport)

by 30 April 1915, from which date through cars to London changed from overhead to conduit at a new change pit in Seven Sisters Road near the Manor House junction. Short-working MET cars turning back at Finsbury Park continued to use the overhead. The temporary change pit at Finsbury Park opposite Blackstock Road was then removed, and the LCC's three-track layout, on which its cars had since 1912 reversed on the centre track, was altered to give a through double track with a third track on the north side. This third track formed a loop, approached through crossovers and turnouts at each end, and was long enough to allow three cars to stand there.

Through running into London via Highgate began on 24 September 1914, using a new change pit at the foot of Archway Road. MET services 36 and 38 were replaced by the extension of two LCC routes which hitherto had terminated at Highgate; route 9 from Moorgate was extended to Barnet in place of 38, and 19 from Tottenham Court Road was extended to Tally Ho Corner, replacing 36. Route 9 was worked by LCC Class E/1 cars, whilst route 19 was worked by MET bogie cars from Finchley depot. These were at first open-topped, but covered top MET cars were soon introduced, as already recounted. On 1 December 1914 route 19 was extended to Barnet and 9 curtailed at North Finchley.

Three scenes on the Great North Road route after through running began on 24 September 1914. The top picture shows LCC E/1 car No. 1612 at Tally Ho Corner, about 1924; the centre picture shows cars 212 and 284 beneath Highgate Archway in the 1920s on service 19, Tottenham Court Road-Barnet; the bird's eye view below is of Type C/1 car No. 208 at the Archway Road change pit soon after through running began.

(Courtesy A. G. Forsyth (1612) and D. W. K. Jones

The MET was now a full member of the Underground group of companies, and although the LCC maintained its opposition to tram/tube through bookings at Finsbury Park, it agreed to their introduction at Highgate. They commenced on 1 December 1914, and were from principal stages between Tally Ho Corner and Winchester Hotel (Archway Road) to Camden Town, Warren Street, Tottenham Court Road and Charing Cross. There were also through bookings between the tube railway and the LCC trams to Highgate Village.

On 7 May 1915 plans were agreed to spend £16,076 to equip more cars with plough carriers, top covers, and more powerful motors for through running, but by early in 1916 it became clear that war conditions would prevent this. The MET asked the LCC to extend the hire of the 15 cars until August 1916, but the LCC would not at first agree. The cars were to be returned in August 1915; they had cost the MET £3,360 in hire charges and £2,504 for wear and tear ('dilapidations'). On 5 July 1916 the LCC Highways Committee relented and agreed to lend cars for a further period.

By May 1916 the company was in arrears of car mileage over the joint routes, and the LCC was pressing for this to be worked off. James Devonshire asked the LCC to hire 20 cars for six months on the same terms as before, and this was agreed. Their numbers are not known, but they were stationed at Wood Green depot and worked on the Euston Road—Enfield route. Five were returned to the LCC in October 1916, but the hire of the other 15 continued to April 1918.

From April 1915 the boundary tramway in Seven Sisters Road was dual-equipped for conduit and overhead, with a change-pit at the Manor House. The Finsbury Park change-pit was removed and the third track extended to form a double-ended lay-by. This postwar view shows an LCC car on route 21, followed by four MET cars. (Courtesy London Transport

Most MET-LCC through routes were worked wholly by the cars of one or other operator, but service 29 was always worked by both MET and LCC cars. This view of LCC Class E/1 car No. 1052 at Enfield Town also shows the turnout leading to the never-completed spur towards Southbury Road.   (Greater London Record Office

The LCC still insisted on the hired cars being used on through services only, an MET request of January 1915 for permission to use them.on short journeys to Finsbury Park and Archway Tavern having been rejected. No photographs are known of them working on the latter route.

Because of war conditions, the MET now had a chronic shortage of plough-fitted cars, and from 1 May 1916 route 51 was split at the Manor House, each operator working its own section (in the MET's case, on longer headways). From the same date, the Palmers Green—Tottenham Court Road workings were withdrawn except at rush hours. By 1917 further cuts were unavoidable, and on 26 February 1917 service 19 was withdrawn and replaced by service 38, Barnet—Highgate. The portion south of Highgate was covered by LCC route 69, and to help out this route was extended along Archway Road to Fortis Green Road at rush hours and on Saturdays.

One further curtailment proved to be necessary, when on 2 May 1917 service 21 was divided at Finsbury Park, the MET section becoming 34. Finchley depot now had no conduit cars, and the dual-fitted cars were exchanged with some trolley-only cars from Wood Green and Edmonton until September 1918. Through services 9, 27, 29, 59 and 79 continued throughout the war, and route 19 resumed on 2 September 1918. The hired E/1 cars were returned to the LCC on 12 April 1918, having cost the MET £1,580, and it was 1920 before the other through services could be resumed, route 51 on 7 July and route 21 on 27 October.

The other point at which the MET tramways met those of the LCC in North London was Stamford Hill. Through running here, although discussed in 1914, was not possible at that time because of a length of experimental side slot conduit in Kingsland Road, Dalston which required ploughs that could not be detached from the car in the usual way, and which MET cars could not negotiate. In October 1918 the MET offered to contribute towards a change pit for a Liverpool Street—Seven Sisters Corner service, and talks were resumed in July 1919 on a more extensive scheme of through services.

Agreement was reached in January 1920, by which time the line in Kingsland Road was being reconstructed with the normal centre slot conduit. A change pit was installed at Stamford Hill, and the MET board approved an outlay of £2,000 to equip additional cars, including the ten Type H cars from Stonebridge Park depot. However, when through running began at Stamford Hill on 2 June 1920 it was worked exclusively by LCC cars on service 49 from Liverpool Street to Edmonton Town Hall, extended at rush hours and weekends to Waltham Cross. To balance the mileage, routes 59 and 79 were now entirely worked by MET cars, from Edmonton depot.

There were many subsequent changes in the through running arrangements, and these will be described in Volume 2. They include the introduction of route 53 on 1 April 1924 over new track in Amhurst Park, which the LCC had hoped could be an all-conduit section. The expensive reconstruction of the boundary tramway by the LCC on the conduit system in 1914-15 proved to be quite unnecessary, for no cars without trolleys ever ran there.

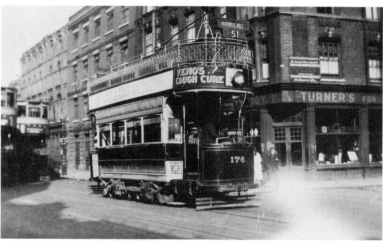

Owing to a shortage of conduit-equipped MET cars, the 26 Type D and D/1 cars were fitted with plough carriers in 1920 and were used on the Muswell Hill-Bloomsbury service until 1931. This view shows No. 176 at Bloomsbury. (N. D. W. Elston

Type A car No. 73 at Finsbury Park about 1922, en route for Tottenham Court Road from Palmers Green, passes Type H car No. 307 for Enfield Town. No. 73 was one of six Type A cars which were fitted with plough carriers in 1919-20. The motor bus is one of the Tramways (MET) Omnibus Company's vehicles of LGOC Type K.

(Courtesy London Transport

CHAPTER ELEVEN

ROLLING STOCK, 1904 to 1914

A fully detailed MET rolling stock schedule, with constructional and equipment details, will be published in Volume 2. It is necessary, however, to include in Volume 1 a chapter describing the choice of car types, the influence of the Middlesex County Council and the allocation of cars to the different routes and depots.

It is necessary first to explain that for fiscal purposes the MET passenger cars were divided into four groups:

1) The 'Tramways' cars purchased by the MET as part of the capital expenditure on the former North Metropolitan horse tramways. These cars were the sole responsibility of the MET.

2) The 'Middlesex' cars purchased by the MET to work the Middlesex County Council's light railways as a charge on the joint revenue. The design and construction of these cars had to be agreed with the council, and these cars would bear the council's name.

3) A small number of 'Hertfordshire' cars (proportional to the mileage) purchased under similar arrangements to the Middlesex cars but whose cost would be charged to the revenue due to the County Council of Hertfordshire, whose name they would bear.

4) The 'Harrow Road' cars purchased by the MET in its own right as part of the company's expenditure in buying and electrifying the Harrow Road and Paddington company's horse tramway. These were the sole responsibility of the MET.

Apart from a tendency to keep the Harrow Road cars to their own line, the different types were allocated according to traffic needs and not necessarily to the lines to whose capital they had been charged. Indeed, any attempt to do so would have prevented through running between the different sections of some major trunk routes. However, the MET usually arranged for opening ceremonies to be performed by 'Middlesex' cars when county council dignitaries were present, and a 'Hertfordshire' car (162) made the first trial run to Barnet on 16 March 1907.

It was anticipated in 1902 that the entire scheme would require 300 cars, and this proved eventually to be correct. Fortunately, in contrast with the London United, they were not all ordered at once and so later batches were able to benefit from improvements in design. The initial requirement was seen as 100 cars, soon increased to 150.

Under the agreement of 30 September 1898 between the Metropolitan Tramways and Omnibus Company, the British Electric Traction Company and the British Thomson-Houston Company, the contracts for rolling stock would be placed with BTH. Since this date, the Brush Electrical Engineering Co. Ltd. of Loughborough had joined the BET group and was now its principal supplier of rolling stock. On 24 October 1902, the MET directors accordingly decided that the rolling stock should be bought from Brush, on the understanding that Brush would, wherever possible, sub-let to BTH for electrical equipment. At their December meeting, they decided that the first contract would be for 100 double-deck open-top bogie cars.

By March 1903 the initial requirement had risen to 150 cars and a tender was received from the Brush company for 150 double-deck bogie cars at

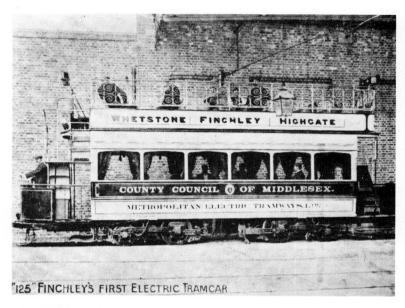

"125" FINCHLEY'S FIRST ELECTRIC TRAMCAR

"FINCHLEY BROCHURE."   [Copyright Photos, P. DENNIS.]

The Type A cars (Nos. 71-130) were all allocated to the expenditure of Middlesex County Council and bore the County title on the waist panel. No. 125, seen here at Finchley Depot when new, illustrates the two-flight staircase and the ornate and expensive internal appointments.

(P. Dennis, courtesy A. G. Forsyth

£115,557, one-third to have transverse seats inside and the rest longitudinal. However, no decisions could yet be taken as Middlesex County Council were still discussing rolling stock matters.

The County Council favoured the double-deck uncanopied type of car with Robinson divided staircases which had gone into service in 1901 on the London United Tramways system in West Middlesex. The MET had confirmed on 2 April 1902 that they would use cars similar to those of the LUT, though the Council at that time felt that they should be smaller, and asked for drawings. They may have had four-wheeled cars in mind, but this was not stated.

The company now asked the Council to finalise its requirements, and submitted a drawing of London United Tramways No. 222, a double-deck uncanopied open top bogie car with Robinson staircases and seating 69 passengers. The council agreed to the use of cars of this design on the Wood Green—Bruce Grove, Highgate—Whetstone and Cricklewood—Edgware routes, and asked James Devonshire to submit sketches showing colours and internal fittings. The result was an order for 80 cars almost indistinguishable from the LUT design except for the trucks and different electrical equipment, and seating 70.

By this time, the extended canopy introduced on the Liverpool tramways had become popular and for its own seventy 'Company' cars the MET chose an open top bogie design with full canopies and with six windows per side, of unequal sizes, with electrical equipment the same as the County Council cars. On the original drawings they are referred to as Type B and Type A respectively, though it was several years before these designations appeared on the cars themselves.

Having obtained the Council's Agreement, the company finalised details with Brush and on 9 September 1903 sealed a £119,359 contract with Brush for the supply of 150 double-deck cars with spare trucks and armatures, comprising 70 company (or 'MET') cars and 80 'MCC' cars. However, while agreement had been reached on the general design, there was to be much more discussion on points of detail, even after construction had begun. Some of these discussions will be described in the appendix on Liveries in Volume 2.

The first MET cars to enter service were Nos. 1-35 of Type B. Nos. 36-70 of Type B/1 were nearly identical, and in many respects Nos. 1-70 were similar to the Class A cars of the London County Council. No. 48 waits at Enfield Town terminus, about 1910.

(London Borough of Enfield Libraries

133

During April 1904 councillors Nield and King Baker visited the Brush works at Loughborough with James Devonshire and A. H. Pott of the MET to inspect a sample car, No. 71 of the 'County Council' class (Type A). At the next meeting the sub-committee asked for changes in the ventilators and for the saloon floors to be covered in closed fibre matting; they also asked for changes in armorial detail and lettering and for a different type of lifeguard. An attempt to replace the luxurious buttoned-velvet seats by woven rattan was defeated. The fact that these discussions were taking place as late as 27 April, with the opening of the first routes imminent, indicates the difficulties the company faced from the committee's indecision.

While the 'County Council' cars were held back at Loughborough for alteration, the 'MET' cars 1-70 were well advanced by March 1904 and Brush proposed to deliver half of them by the end of April. Nos. 1-35 were delivered to Wood Green and Nos. 36-70 to Edmonton; the last arrived in August. Nos. 71-83 arrived at Wood Green in time for the opening of the Bruce Grove line on 20 August, with Nos. 84-103 arriving at Hendon depot in time for the opening of the Cricklewood—Edgware line on 3 December. Nos. 104-130 were intended for Finchley, but the first few were delivered to Hendon as Finchley depot was not ready. Nos. 1-35 at Wood Green were the first to enter service, followed by 71-83. Nos. 74 and 75 were an exception to the above allocation, and started life at Hendon.

Up to August 1904, the MET and the council had not planned to use any single-deck cars, and the final twenty of Nos. 71-150 were intended as Type A double-deckers for use on the Alexandra Palace lines. However, Major Pringle of the Board of Trade had walked the routes before construction began and considered the gradients rather steep for double-deckers, as did his colleague Colonel Yorke, whilst Wood Green UDC opposed the necessary lowering of the roadway by 3ft. 6in. under the GER bridge in Station Road, Wood Green. Construction of the last 20 County Council cars of the first batch was deferred, and early in 1905 it was agreed to replace them with single-deckers. The result was a batch of 20 four-wheel single-deckers (Nos. 131-150, Type E) of which the first few were inspected at Loughborough in August 1905. The later story of these cars will be found in Chapter Six.

1905 arrivals included Type E, four-wheel single-deck cars Nos. 131-150 obtained for the Alexandra Park lines on which double-deck cars could not be operated. No. 139 in original condition, photographed at Muswell Hill. (Courtesy D. W. K. Jones

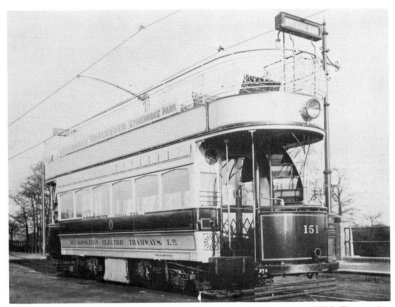

Nos. 151-165 were the third batch of MET double-deck cars and arrived in 1906. The monitor roof construction was retained, but internal appointments were simpler. In these Type C cars direct quarter-turn stairs replaced the Robinson type staircases and became standard for all future double-deck cars.   (The late Walter Gratwicke

The Type D four-wheel cars, Nos. 166-190, were obtained in 1906, mainly for use on the routes through Willesden. No. 179 is seen in original condition at Harlesden.

(The late Walter Gratwicke

In June 1905, just after the Highgate—Whetstone route had opened, A. H. Pott recommended to the MET board that the 27 Type A cars at Finchley should be fitted with Westinghouse magnetic track brakes at £60 per car. Of these, six had been transferred from Hendon, and a further six or seven were transferred from Hendon to Finchley in the last months of 1905 and also received magnetic brakes. The traffic on the Great North Road route developed healthily right from the start, but it is evident that the gradients had shown that hand and rheostatic brakes alone were insufficient. The magnetic brake was to be used in emergencies only, but some years later those on the Great North Road cars were replaced by an improved version which became the service brake.

The next rolling stock contract was placed with Brush on 9 March 1906 and comprised 40 cars of which 20 were to equip the Harrow Road line and ten were required for 'Great North Road and Edgware Road summer traffic', perhaps including replacements for those Hendon had had to send to Finchley. The order was divided into 15 open top bogie cars at £869 each and 25 open top four-wheelers at £742 each.

The allocation of individual cars between the various capital accounts is not recorded, but it is known that of the 15 bogie cars (Nos. 151-165, type C) five were allocated to the MET (ex-North Metropolitan) tramways, five to Hertfordshire County Council and five to the Harrow Road and Paddington tramways; Hertfordshire cars 159 and 163 have been identified from photographs, and the batch was probably 159 to 163. The 25 four-wheel cars (Nos. 166-190, Type D) were divided ten to the MET tramways and fifteen to the Harrow Road and Paddington. As the MET and Harrow Road cars did not carry any distinguishing lettering it is not possible to identify the allocation of the individual cars.

No additions were made to the passenger fleet in 1907 except for the transfer of second-hand car 191, described in the rolling-stock notes, but by early in 1908 the company was about to embark on a five year programme which would involve the purchase of 125 double-deck cars by 1912. Specifications were being prepared for the first 25 cars, and top covers were being considered for the first time. The London County Council's E and E/1 classes with totally-

The solitary Type D/1 car, No. 191, was a sample car built by the Brush company for Leicester and sold to the MET in 1904. It entered the passenger fleet in 1907 and is seen here at Canons Park about 1919. Soon afterwards the car was reposted to four windows per side and altered to conform with the Type D vehicles. (The late Dr. Hugh Nicol)

enclosed upper saloons had entered service in 1906 and 1907 and were proving highly successful. The MET fitted a frame of similar dimensions on an open top car and tested clearances on the Edmonton and Wood Green routes before finalising specifications.

On 15 April 1908 A. H. Pott wrote to the Board of Trade sending a drawing and asking permission to place five top-covered cars in experimental service on these routes. He estimated that the cover would weigh from 2½ to 3 tons, bringing the weight of the body with top cover to 8 tons. The inspecting officer, Major Pringle, accepted the design of the top cover but considered that the extra weight would make the cars more difficult to control. Pott replied, detailing the gradients of the Wood Green-Finsbury Park, Edmonton—Finsbury Park, Edmonton—Stamford Hill and Lordship Lane—Bruce Grove routes on which the cars would be used, adding that they would be fitted with a power track brake, and on 11 May the Board gave their approval.

By this time 25 pairs of trucks were already on order from Mountain & Gibson, ordered on 21 February 1908 at £3,912, and an £11,294 contract for the bodies was placed with Brush on 15 May. Electrical equipment was ordered from BTH at £5,988. There were 20 canopied open-top bogie cars (Nos. 192-211, Type C/1) generally similar to those of 1906 but with minor differences, and five top-covered cars, Nos. 212-216 (Type F), structurally similar to the open-toppers except that the monitor ceilings in the lower saloons had been reduced in height to allow for the fully-enclosed top decks. Photographs of these cars when new indicate that they may have been adapted at a late stage from open top while under construction. The final costs per car were £913 for the open-top trams and £1,117 for those with top covers.

Of these 25 cars, 18 were allocated to the Middlesex County Council, three to the Harrow Road and Paddington tramways, and four to the MET tramways. There was no allocation to Hertfordshire County Council, and none were made in future years, though 207 and 208 became Hertfordshire cars at a later date.

The 1908 delivery comprised 20 open-top bogie cars (Nos. 192-211, Type C/1) as shown above, and five top-covered cars (Nos. 212-216, Type F) illustrated on the cover. All 25 cars were equipped with Mountain & Gibson maximum traction trucks with provision for adding plough gear to work over the London County Council's conduit lines. This view shows No. 199 taking up the plough about 1929 at the change pit in Archway Road, Highgate.

(The late Dr. Hugh Nicol

The Board of Trade had adopted a very cautious approach to the use of top-covered cars on the MET, and their attitude was clearly influenced by the June 1906 runaway in Archway Road, Highgate, an event which cast its shadow over the operations of the MET for many years. This will explain why a similar order of 1909 for 25 cars consisted once again of 20 open top vehicles and only five with covered tops. The equipments were ordered on 22 April from BTH at £16,479, with Westinghouse magnetic track brakes at £1,500, and the trucks were ordered from Mountain & Gibson at £3,625. Due no doubt to uncertainty about top covers, the bodies were not ordered (from Brush) until 7 July; the 20 open-top bodies cost £399 each as against £603 for those with top covers.

Type G, Nos. 217-236, marked a departure from previous practice. The monitor roofs used hitherto on all cars except Nos. 1-70 were replaced by plain arch ceilings, and 40hp motors were fitted. This posed picture was taken near Winchmore Hill.　　　　　　(Courtesy A. D. Packer

These cars were built with flat ceilings in the saloons, instead of the costly monitor (clerestory) ceilings which had long since been given up by most other tramways but which the MET had been forced to use by the county council. In the five covered top cars (Nos. 237-241, Type H) the ceilings were slightly lower and resulted in an improved design which would remain unaltered for several further batches. All 25 cars had 40 hp motors; the older cars had proved to be underpowered, especially when carrying the additional 2½ tons of a top cover.

All 25 cars were lettered County Council of Middlesex, and some of the Type G cars were delivered to Finchley in readiness for the opening of the line to Golders Green and others went to Wood Green.

On 12 November 1909 the MET board approved the purchase of 15 more top-covered Type H cars in three batches of five. Later, this number was found to be insufficient and the order was increased to 25 (Nos. 242-266). The total cost of these cars was £27,462, or £1,098 each, and before they arrived in 1910 A. H. Pott obtained Board of Trade approval for their use to Stamford Hill, which had a slightly steeper gradient than the other ex-North

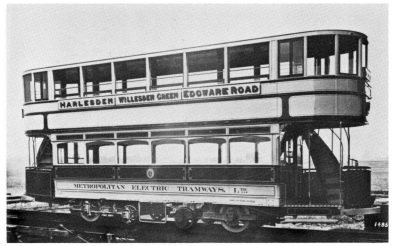

The Type H cars, Nos. 237-316, were delivered in batches from 1909 to 1912. This car of the 242-266 series stands on the works traverser at the Brush Electrical Engineering Company's works at Loughborough, builders of all pre-1912 MET cars.

(Leicestershire Museums, Brush collection

Metropolitan routes. Ten cars were allocated to (and lettered) Middlesex County Council, ten to the Harrow Road and Paddington and five to the MET Tramways.

The MET directors on 27 January 1911 agreed to order a further 30 Type H cars, again from Brush, at £31,273 with BTH electrical equipment and Westinghouse magnetic track brakes. They were entered in the company's capital ledger at £1,045 each, and entered service later in 1911 as Nos. 267-296, divided equally between the MET and MCC lines. These cars brought the company's fleet of top-covered tramcars up to sixty. A final batch of 20 Type H cars, Nos. 297-316, was ordered from Brush on 26 January 1912 and delivered later that year at £1,068 each (£21,365) complete with plough carriers for use over the LCC conduit lines. All 20 were allocated to Middlesex County Council and carried the full title.

At the MET board meeting of 31 May 1912 a request from A. H. Pott to replace the 28hp motors in 165 cars with 40hp motors was considered. The cost, including magnetic brakes, would have been £40,920 less the value of the old motors, but in July the board decided only to re-motor the double-deck cars stationed at Wood Green depot, perhaps because a rival motor bus service had just been started to Palmers Green. This plan was implemented later in 1912, but apart from 18 further cars re-motored in 1915-16 no more were done until after the end of the war.

At the same time that these 78 cars received the new motors, 31 of them received open-balcony top covers, and more would have been done but for the war. Pott had sent the Board of Trade on 2 February 1912 drawings of a top cover suitable for the various canopied open-top cars, which the board approved except for use on the Archway Road and Alexandra Palace lines. It is clear that Pott had agreed verbally to keep top-covered cars off Archway Road, undoubtedly as a result of the earlier runaways, and that the Board wished to see this arrangement continued. The cars fitted were 151-165 and sixteen of the 1-35 class, at a cost of £8,469. When new motors and magnetic brakes were added to the cost the outlay on these cars became £16,060, or £518 per car, so the top covers cost £270 each. The Board of Trade continued to press for all cars in the fleet to be fitted with magnetic brakes, and this was completed early in 1917.

METROPOLITAN ELECTRIC TRAMWAYS — CAR FLEET AS BUILT

M.E.T. Type	Car Numbers	Type (as built)	Year built	Builder	Seats	Truck(s)	Motors	Controllers
B	1-35	Open top	1904	Brush	30/38	Brush BB bogies	GE 58 2 x 28hp	BTH B18
B/1	36-70	Open top	1904	Brush	24/38	Brush BB bogies	GE 58 2 x 28hp	BTH B18
A	71-130	Open top uncanopied	1904	Brush	30/38	Brush BB bogies	GE 58 2 x 28 hp	BTH B18
E	131-150	Single deck	1905	Brush	36	Brush Conaty	GE 58 2 x 28hp	BTH B18
C	151-165	Open top	1906	Brush	32/42	Brush BB bogies	GE 58 2 x 28hp	BTH B18
D	166-190	Open top	1906	Brush	22/32	Brush Conaty	GE 58 2 x 28hp	BTH B18
D/1	191	Open top	1903	Brush	22/33	Brush AA	GE 58 2 x 28hp	BTH B18
C/1	192-211	Open top	1908	Brush	32/42	M&G 3L bogies	GE 58 2 x 28hp	BTH B18
F	212-216	Covered top	1908	Brush	32/46	M&G 3L bogies	GE58 2 x 28hp	BTH B18
G	217-236	Open top	1909	Brush	32/42	M&G 3L bogies	GE 67 2 x 40hp	BTH B49
H	237-241	Covered top	1909	Brush	32/46	M&G 3L bogies	GE 67 2 x 40hp	BTH B49
H	242-266	Covered top	1910	Brush	32/46	Brush LCC-type bogies	GE 67 2 x 40hp	BTH B49
H	267-296	Covered top	1911	Brush	32/46	Brush LCC-type bogies	GE 67 2 x 40hp	BTH B49
H	297-316	Covered top	1912	Brush	32/46	Brush LCC-type bogies	GE 67 2 x 40hp	BTH B49

Seating figures shown thus: 22/33 are for lower and upper deck respectively.
Car 191 was built as a Brush demonstrator for Leicester and was bought by MET in 1904.

The year 1912 ended with 312 cars in stock (Nos. 1-316, less four single-deckers sold to Auckland) and this total was to remain unchanged until 1927. Apart from some changes of electrical equipment, the MET fleet remained unchanged from 1912 until the end of the period covered by this volume.

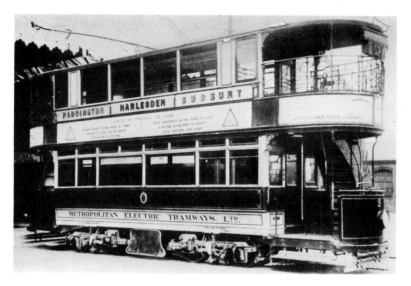

Commencing in 1913, thirteen of the Type B cars (including No. 3, photographed above at Stonebridge Park Depot) and the fifteen Type C cars (Nos. 151 to 165) were fitted with open-balcony top covers built at Hendon Works. At the same time, they received GE67 40hp motors and magnetic brakes. More cars would have been done but for the war.

(Tramway Museum Society; the late V. Whitbread

MET Type H car No. 299, B Type 'General' motor bus B2092 (registration LF 8745) and taxicab H 5481 in a posed photograph, probably in Woodhouse Road, Friern Barnet, in 1912. The trio were also photographed in line abreast, but the reason for the photographs is not known. The tram seated 78, the bus 34.

(Courtesy London Transport

CHAPTER TWELVE
BUSES AND THE COMBINE

By about 1910, the petrol-driven omnibus had become much more than the novelty these vehicles had been in the first ten years of the twentieth century. By 1906 they had already reached a stage of development which saw them as a potentially serious threat to the newly-established electric tramways, and it is likely that tramway operators would have had to take the bus competition seriously at a much earlier date than they did but for the serious accident which befell a Vanguard bus that ran out of control down Handcross Hill in Sussex on 12 July 1906 with the loss of several lives.

This disaster occurred within days of the MET runaway on Archway Road, Highgate, in which a Vanguard omnibus was also involved (its undergear collapsed when struck by the tram). It was not until about 1910 that public confidence in motor buses was restored with the introduction of more strongly built vehicles with improved brakes and transmission. During this period the motor bus had been making itself felt on tramway routes and had become a regular topic of discussion at MET board meetings. The MET had itself bought a motor-bus in 1910 for £500, probably for evaluation.

In 1911, the LGOC introduced the famous 'B' type vehicles which were proving very reliable and were being built in large numbers. These became the standard LGOC vehicle for many years, and at about the same time the Tilling-Stevens petrol-electric vehicles of Thomas Tilling Ltd. entered service on many London routes; these vehicles were also a great improvement on earlier types and like the 'General' vehicles they saw many years of service in the capital. Furthermore, the Underground company had obtained powers in 1911 to own and work buses.

Up to this time, the MET system had been reasonably profitable despite the large sum paid each year to the Middlesex County Council as the fixed rent for its lines. In 1909 the MET paid 5% dividend on the 4½% Ordinary shares, £25,000 on the 5% Preferred shares and placed £6,000 to reserve. The MET relied for its profits on the busier routes, and used them to offset the losses on the newer routes and that to Edgware, which were still unprofitable. Bus competition on the best routes would therefore pose a serious threat to the whole network.

In November 1911 the MET board set up a special committee to consider how best to meet the threat, and on 4 December considered a suggestion from James Devonshire that the company should institute its own service of motor omnibuses, to compete, specifically, with the LGOC and work in conjunction with the tramways. A separate company would be formed, and the BET (which was expanding its bus operations in the provinces) would be invited to help in financing the venture.

By 8 December the BET had offered £100,000 in support and details had been agreed. A new company would be formed with an authorised capital of £200,000 in ordinary shares and £100,000 of debentures, the trustees for the debenture holders being the Electrical and General Investment Co. Ltd., which was the financial wing of the BET group. The intention was that the ordinary shares would be subscribed for jointly by the MET and the BET, but in the event the MET subscribed for the whole of the Ordinary shares.

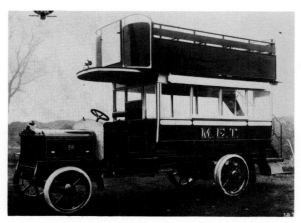

A Tramways (M.E.T.) Omnibus Company Daimler bus with Brush-built body ready for despatch from the Brush works at Loughborough in the autumn of 1912. (Brush Electrical Engineering Co. Ltd.

The proposed title of the company was Metropolitan Tramways Omnibus Company Ltd., but the Registrar refused to allow this name, perhaps because it was too similar to the MET's own original title of Metropolitan Tramways and Omnibus Co. Ltd. The amended title chosen was The Tramways (MET) Omnibus Co. Ltd., and it was registered on 13 January 1912.

The Omnibus Company's first Board meeting was held on 16 January 1912 at 1, Kingsway, by which time the LGOC had announced plans to extend its operations to a 15-mile radius in place of the previous 12 miles, and to build a garage at Palmers Green. The new company's directors were confirmed in office; they had been nominated by Emile Garcke in his capacity as chairman of both MET and BET, and were James Devonshire (chairman), Sydney E. Garcke (Emile Garcke's son), W. L. Madgen and R. J. Howley, with A. L. Barber as secretary. The directors agreed that the first service would operate between Hendon and Tower Bridge via Edgware Road, Oxford Street and Trafalgar Square.

On 14 February they approved a draft contract with the Daimler company for 100 omnibus chassis, including a three-year maintenance contract, and a contract with Christopher Dodson Ltd. for 100 34-seat bodies. The bodies were sub-contracted to the Brush company at Loughborough, members of the BET group, and in June it was decided that 20 bodies should be built by the MET at Hendon works. It is not known whether any were built there, for in July a further order for 100 bodies was placed with Brush. The chassis order was increased to cover a total of 300 vehicles.

The Board decided that its main garage would be at Colindale, on an MET-owned site at the corner of Annesley Avenue and Edgware Road, and this land was transferred to the bus company in April 1912 and contracts placed for a garage to hold 200 buses. Another garage for 50 buses would be required at or near Wood Green, and a site was found in March 1912 in Mannock Road off Westbury Avenue. However, by 30 May the MET and LCC had decided instead to compete with the LGOC buses along Green Lanes by running through trams from Euston to Enfield, and under this agreement the MET undertook not to run its own buses on any part of a through running tram route. As a result, the Wood Green site was given up in favour of one at High Cross, Tottenham.

In the autumn of 1912, as described later, the MET accepted an invitation to join the Underground group of companies, of which the LGOC was already a member, having joined at the end of 1911. The proposed MET omnibus service must have been a major reason for the offer, but since it held the promise that the LGOC would no longer compete for the MET's traffic, it was accepted. It was further agreed that the MET buses should be worked by the LGOC on behalf of the Tramways (MET) Omnibus Co. Ltd., and an agreement to this effect was signed on 20 December 1912.

As a result, when the first MET omnibuses ran on 28 January 1913 between Hendon and Tower Bridge, they worked not from the MET premises at Colindale but from the LGOC garage at Cricklewood. The Colindale premises opened on 10 February 1913, and those at Tottenham on 17 July 1913. The LGOC agreed to buy the Tottenham garage, but did not require the Colindale premises on a permanent basis, and ceased to use them on 13 March 1914. They were resold to the Aircraft Manufacturing Co. Ltd.

M.E.T. Motor Garage, Tottenham.   (A)

The Tramways (M.E.T.) Omnibus Company's garage in Tottenham was built in 1913. The MET bus is standing ahead of one owned by the Gearless Motor Omnibus Company, which became associated with the MET in October 1912.   (London Borough of Haringey Libraries)

Delivery of the MET's Daimler buses was completed in June 1913, the total reached being 225 buses and three lorries. In January it had been decided to substitute 100 'B' type chassis for the balance of the Daimler order, and the bodies for these were built by Brush to the standard LGOC design, though finished like the Daimlers in the royal blue livery adopted for the MET buses, with the initials MET in large gold characters shaded white. A Brush works photograph of about Easter 1913 shows a convoy about to leave for London, consisting of MET Daimlers 180 and 182 and MET 'B' type B2330, B2336, B2339 and B2342.

The MET buses were operated partly on routes that formed an extension of the MET tramways, such as Hendon—Tower Bridge, Kilburn—Watford, Cricklewood—Willesden—Victoria, Edmonton—Victoria Station and Tottenham—Elephant & Castle, and partly on LGOC routes elsewhere in London. Soon after the start of the 1914-18 war, the Daimlers were taken by the Government, 70 being sent to France and the remaining chassis being re-used for Army vehicles, the bodies being kept by the LGOC for re-use.

A Tramways (M.E.T.) Omnibus Company's motor-bus arriving at Reigate on service 160 from Stockwell. These vehicles had bodies to the standard LGOC pattern, built by Brush on 'B' Type chassis.   (Photomatic Ltd.)

The MET bus fleet thereafter consisted of standard LGOC types of vehicle, still in the royal blue livery and lettered M.E.T., but in November 1916 the MET board agreed to an LGOC suggestion that the initials should be changed to the word METROPOLITAN as and when vehicles came in for repainting. In later years this fleetname, with the M and N larger than the other letters (which were underlined) was also adopted for the MET tram fleet, replacing the full company name on the rocker panels.

As this book is a history of the Metropolitan tramways system, it is not proposed to go further into the historical and operational details of the Omnibus Company. The reader is strongly recommended to the excellent Omnibus Society monograph of 1977 by Mr. G. J. Robbins entitled *Metropolitan— The Story of the Tramways (MET) Omnibus Company Limited 1912-1933.*

When the MET joined the Combine at the end of 1912, a pooling agreement was reached covering fares taken on the LGOC buses and on the trams on routes common to both. It ran initially for six years, and its aim was to co-ordinate services and prevent the running of unnecessary car miles. The revenue pool consisted of the gross receipts of the trams, and LGOC receipts from passengers carried over tramway routes. After working costs were deducted the revenue was pooled and divided between the parties in agreed proportions. During the six years of the first pooling agreement (to 1918) the LGOC paid £30,000 into the joint revenue account of the MET and the Middlesex County Council.

Another result of the merger was that the MET finally gave up any idea of moving its operating headquarters to Hendon. By May 1913 the London & Suburban Traction group had also obtained control of London's other tramway company, the South Metropolitan Electric Tramways and Lighting Co. Ltd., and the MET's Manor House offices became the operating headquarters for all three tramway companies. On 1 May 1915 the three companies came under the full administrative control of the Underground group and their headquarters and registered office were transferred to Electric Railway House, Westminster, but the traffic and engineering departments remained at the Manor House.

The first hint that the company's future might lie in friendly co-operation with the principal motor bus operator was given in the chairman's address to shareholders at an Extraordinary General Meeting held on 26 July 1912, when MET shareholders agreed to a reduction of capital by £235,512, this being the directors' estimate of shares unrepresented by assets. The shareholders present expressed their confidence in the directors' conduct of the company affairs, and the company's capital was reduced to £1,078,504. The vote of thanks to Garcke and the board was proposed by Joseph Barber Glenn, secretary of the Provincial Tramways group, which had evidently retained until this time the financial interest in London trams which it had acquired in the days of the North Metropolitan horse trams.

At this date, confidential negotiations were already in progress between the directors of the MET and those of the London United Tramways, which was already associated with the Underground group. The decision to negotiate was taken by the MET board on 17 July 1912, and by the autumn it had been agreed to form a holding company, the London and Suburban Traction Company Limited. The L&ST acquired controlling interests in the MET (95%), the LUT (97%) and the Tramways (MET) Omnibus Co. Ltd. (100%), the SMET being added in May 1913. The remaining 5% holding in the MET was retained by the BET until November 1928.

The first meeting of the L&ST directors took place at Electric Railway House on 22 November 1912, two days after the company was registered. The first directors were William Acworth (LUT), A. H. Stanley (LUT), Emile Garcke (MET), James Devonshire (MET) and E. R. Soames for the MET's omnibus company. James Devonshire was appointed managing director and A. L. Barber secretary. The registered office was at the BET headquarters in Kingsway.

The formation of the Combine was soon followed by through bookings between the partners. The first tram-to-Underground bookings were those between the LUT and the Central London Railway at Shepherds Bush, but these were soon followed during 1913 by those between the MET and the Hampstead tube at Golders Green, mentioned in Chapter Seven. Similar bookings via Highgate followed in 1914, but through tram-to-tube bookings at Finsbury Park were excluded by the terms of the through running agreement with the LCC.

MET route 10, Edmonton-Stamford Hill, was paralleled along part of the route by 'General' bus service 76, one of the many instances where the 'Combine' trams and buses competed for the same traffic. The MET trams were however compensated from a revenue pool, described on the previous page. (Courtesy D. W. K. Jones

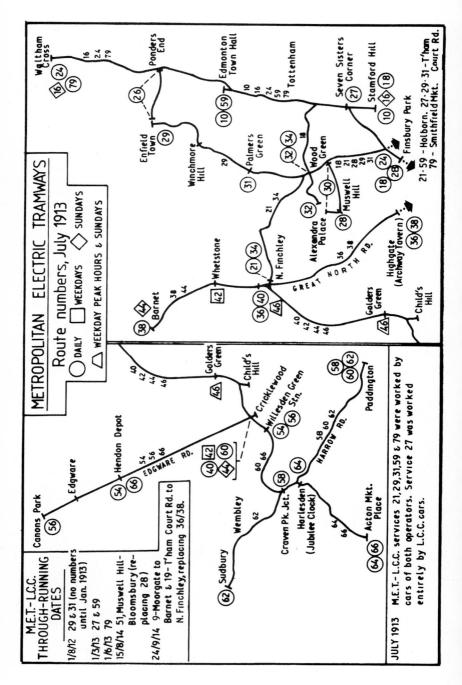

METROPOLITAN ELECTRIC TRAMWAYS
Route numbers, July 1913

○ DAILY □ WEEKDAYS ◇ SUNDAYS
△ WEEKDAY PEAK HOURS & SUNDAYS

M.E.T.-L.C.C. THROUGH-RUNNING DATES

1/8/12 29 & 31 (no numbers until Jan. 1913)
1/3/13 27 & 59
1/6/13 79
15/8/14 51, Muswell Hill-Bloomsbury (replacing 28)
24/9/14 9-Moorgate to Barnet & 19-T'ham Court Rd. to N. Finchley, replacing 36/38.

21-59 - Holborn. 27-29-31-T'ham Court Rd.
79 - Smithfield Mkt.

JULY 1913 M.E.T.-L.C.C. services 21,29,31,59 & 79 were worked by cars of both operators. Service 27 was worked entirely by L.C.C. cars.

148

The Underground group had a very active advertising department, headed from April 1912 by Frank Pick, and its influence was evident in the Tramways Map and Guide, successive issues of which have been of great assistance in compiling this history. Free maps had been issued for some years by the Underground companies and the LGOC, and the MET had followed suit in 1910, issuing its first map at a time when the Enfield—Ponders End, Wembley—Sudbury and Warwick Crescent—Paddington lines had to be shown as 'In Course of Construction.'

The London bus services had been carrying route numbers since 1908, and the London County Council had numbered its tram routes in 1912, using odd numbers in its northern division and even numbers in the southern. By January 1913 the LCC through-running routes over the MET to Palmers Green and Enfield were numbered, and the MET decided to number their local routes, using even numbers and starting at 10. A curious result of the Combine formation was the addition of a suffix letter 'T' after the MET route number, presumably to distinguish tram routes from those of the LGOC with similar numbers, and this letter appeared in the route information section on the reverse side of the Map and Guide, though not on the map itself. The suffix letter later fell into disuse, and appeared for the last time in the Map and Guide dated Summer 1922. Some while elapsed before it disappeared from the cars, but it had never appeared on the LCC cars working on the through-running routes.

Although the threat of direct LGOC competition had been removed by the merger and replaced by a contribution from LGOC profits, the MET still faced serious financial problems. Holders of the Ordinary shares received 1% in 1915 and nothing thereafter, and as operating costs increased during the war the position worsened. Holders of the 5½% Preferred shares received only 2½% in 1917, and by the end of 1918 the dividend on these shares was £40,000 in arrears. Nothing had been added to the Reconstruction and Renewals Fund since 1911, though the price of rails almost trebled between 1914 and 1918.

The London United Tramways were in even greater financial difficulties, and in June 1917 called in a Receiver, a partner in the firm of chartered accountants Price, Waterhouse & Co. This gentleman refused to authorise payment of the

As a result of the formation of the Combine, a suffix letter 'T' was added to MET route numbers, presumably to distinguish tram routes from the bus routes of the LGOC. This photograph of car 293 on service 26T at Enfield was taken in 1933.   (N. D. W. Elston

MET's account in respect of work done on LUT cars at Hendon Works during May, 1917. On hearing of this on 29 June, the MET board authorised A. L. Barber to take steps to enforce payment. These steps appear to have been effective, as the matter was not raised again and LUT cars continued to travel to Hendon Works until the LUT resumed possession of their own car works in 1919.

The overhauling of London United cars at the MET's Hendon works, which began in 1915, was not conceived as an economy made possible by the merger but rather as a wartime measure, suggested by A. H. Pott, to release the LUT works at Chiswick for the manufacture of munitions. The first essential step, recounted in Chapter Nine, was to link the two companies' lines at King Street, Acton, and the overhaul agreement of 30 June 1915 between the two companies became effective as soon as the link was completed at the end of July. The LUT cars were worked on at Hendon by LUT staff, and at least one special car was run in each direction per day to take the LUT men to and from Hendon. The MET made a small profit from the work (£1,609 in 1916) and also made a mileage charge for running the LUT cars over the MET system.

The London United's works was released by the Ministry of Munitions on 25 June 1918, but the LUT staff continued to overhaul their company's cars at Hendon until 30 May 1919, pending rehabilitation at Chiswick. Discussions took place in November 1923 on reviving the arrangement on a permanent basis, and after further new equipment had been installed at Hendon the practice was resumed in 1926.

Although the MET's registered office was transferred to the Underground group headquarters in 1915, the directors of the MET retained their positions until after the war, as did their secretary, A. L. Barber, though he had relinquished a similar appointment with the Omnibus company after the LGOC took over operation. Changes to the MET board did not follow until 14 August 1919, when two new directors were appointed; they were William Corvin Burton and William Mitchell Acworth. Burton, an American, was resident director of the Underground Electric Railway Company of London and was appointed managing director of the MET in succession to James Devonshire, but the appointment was very short-lived, for within a month he returned to America and Sir Albert Stanley was appointed in his place. Acworth was a barrister and a director of the LUT and L&ST.

WE ARE A HAPPY FAMILY—AND A BIG ONE.

Three London United Tramways Type T cars near Station Road, Barnet on the occasion of the Hounslow Depot staff children's outing in August, 1924. (Courtesy G. L. Gundry

Another link with the BET was severed in December 1919, when the board agreed that legal work carried out for the company by the successors of the late Hugh C. Godfray would from 1 January 1920 be done by the Underground Group's solicitors, Stanley & Co.

One useful result of the merger was the availability of LGOC motor bus chassis for use as MET service vehicles. Between 1920 and 1928, thirteen LGOC 'B' type chassis were acquired by the MET and rebodied for use as tower wagons, permanent way lorries, stores vehicles and a breakdown tender. The tower wagons used the bodywork of former MET horse-drawn tower wagons, and the last horses were disposed of by 1927.

A notable event with far-reaching effects took place in the autumn of 1919, when the Underground group sent four of its senior officers (including MET manager C. J. Spencer) on a study tour of urban transport systems in North America. On their return each member of the party prepared a paper describing the systems they had visited and the methods they used, with suggestions for the adoption of some of the American practices in London conditions. These papers were read at a meeting of directors and senior staff on 30 January 1920 and were later produced as an illustrated booklet. Further details will be given in Volume 2.

Although the MET and LUT systems remained operationally separate, there were occasional special staff trams for sports fixtures between the companies, and there was some sharing of works cars. LUT cars were used on the MET's Acton route during the 1914-18 war, as described elsewhere, and some LUT top-covered Type T cars were borrowed by the MET in 1924 to help serve the Wembley Exhibition. There is however no record of any MET cars having worked in passenger service on the LUT. In later years a few MET cars were sometimes stabled at the LUT's Acton depot.

The best-documented example of a passenger journey between the two systems occurred in August 1924, when the LUT Hounslow Depot staff children's outing took the form of a visit to Folly Farm, then a well-known pleasure resort near Hadley Woods, Barnet. Three LUT Type T cars, gaily decorated with bunting, flags and balloons, made the two-hour journey from Hounslow via the King Street link and over the MET system through Willesden, Cricklewood and Finchley to Station Road, New Barnet, where their occupants transferred to motor *chars-a-banc* which took them to Folly Farm. MET pilotmen travelled on the cars, which were stabled in Finchley depot until required for the return trip.

Manor House offices in 1920, during the period when they were shared by the M.E.T., the London United Tramways and the North Metropolitan Electric Supply Company (note the "Use Electricity" slogan on the gable end).   (Courtesy London Transport

151

CHAPTER THIRTEEN

THE WAR AND ITS AFTERMATH

The outbreak of war in 1914 affected the MET in various different ways, the effects becoming progressively more marked as hostilities continued. In this chapter each facet will be examined separately, save for the partial curtailment of MET-LCC through running which has already been described in Chapter Ten, and the measures taken to overhaul London United cars at Hendon which have been recounted in Chapter Twelve.

LIGHTING RESTRICTIONS

The first wartime change in tramcar lighting was made by the MET in 1914, when small wooden lamp mountings were fitted to the offside of each car's dash to carry an acetylene or calcium carbide lamp of the type then used on bicycles. The lamps were for use during power failures, and when not in use hung on the underside of the stairs.

The MET was unusual in having fitted most cars not only with an electric headlamp on the upper deck canopy but also a red electric rear light just above the coupling-slot of each fender. Under the Lights (London) Order of 26 August 1916 the headlamps were masked with translucent material (later with black paint) and each car was fitted with low-powered sidelights (two at each end) on the underside of the canopy, or in the case of the uncanopied Type A cars on correspondingly-placed rods. At the same time, the rear lights were moved towards the offside of the car. The sidelights were known as Police Lights and were retained after the war in modified form.

In September 1916 Enfield UDC, whose area contained two large Ordnance factories, wrote to the Board of Trade and the Admiralty expressing concern at sparking from the tramway overhead in Green Lanes and Hertford Road which might attract enemy airships. They were told that instructions had already been given to all tramways to prevent sparking, but were not satisfied and asked the Commander in Chief Home Forces to receive a deputation. This was at a time when night raids by German airships were at their height.

On 8 September 1916 James Devonshire told the MCC that the MET was obeying the instructions and that automatic points and frogs where flashing was likely to occur would be worked by hand at night. Further changes to car lighting to comply with wartime regulations were made, at a cost of £1,763, which the company tried unsuccessfully to claim back.

THE SEARCHLIGHT TRAMS

The 1914-18 war was the first in which powered aircraft were used as offensive weapons. From the autumn of 1915, the Germans mounted raids by Zeppelin airships, which though large and unwieldy had an almost silent approach which gave an element of surprise. They were able to approach London unseen under cover of darkness, release their bombs and make off with little chance of interception. Against this, the hydrogen gas which filled the envelope was highly inflammable and the airship could thus be destroyed by a single incendiary bullet.

In December 1915 the War Cabinet decided to establish a ring of search-lights around London, some 10-12 miles out, and the Royal Engineers were given orders to requisition any buildings or equipment which could be useful. The

No. 272 stands at Sudbury terminus in 1918, with darkened headlamp and wartime "police lights" below the canopy. The Harrow Road Type H cars were transferred away in 1919-20 and fitted with plough carriers to operate through routes over LCC conduit lines.

(The late V. Whitbread

task was given to the London and Tyne Electrical Engineers Companies RE, and some of the details which follow are taken from this unit's official history, published in 1935.

The searchlights were mounted on a wide variety of platforms, mostly mobile, including lorries, canal boats, and electric tramcars. The trams were driven by RE personnel who had been motormen with the South Shields and Tynemouth tramways. The official history *War in the Air,* published in 1931, mentions nine searchlight trams, six on the MET, two of Ilford UDC, and one of Croydon Corporation, though it is known that there was also one on the LUT at Hounslow, and one at Bexley. Known searchlight sites on the MET were at Canons Park, Barnet Church, and in Southbury Road, near Enfield Town. When the searchlight tram occupied the terminal stub at Barnet, the service cars reversed on the crossover near the Red Lion Hotel, some 150 yards further south.

The trams were equipped with 60 cm. searchlights, mounted on the open top deck towards one end, the other being occupied by a shelter for the men, made from sheet steel. The lower deck windows were boarded up, and much of the lower saloon was taken up by a generator which took its power from the overhead line supply. The cars also had meters to record current consumption, and one of the men operating the car at Southbury Road found that by reversing the terminals the meter could be made to run in reverse, thus reducing the indebtedness of the War Office to the MET! The rest of the saloon was used as a mess-room.

All these trams were of the uncanopied type, as were the MET Type A cars. This was necessary in order that the heavy equipment to go in the saloon could be hoisted over the dash and controller, which would have been much more difficult with a fully canopied car. They also had double sliding doors sufficiently wide to admit the generator, and these doors were kept locked, so the staff at the depots (to which the cars returned each day) had to carry out maintenance from the pits. The cars were painted in dark green, a colour much used by the Army on home duties in the Great War. All numerals and lettering were obliterated and a War Office number was painted in white on the inside of the dash.

On the night of 1/2 October 1916, one of the heaviest Zeppelin attacks of the war took place, using eleven airships of a new and faster type and concentrating on North London. The Zeppelins were attached to both the German Army and Navy, and Naval Zeppelin L 31, commanded by Captain Heinrich Mathy, was spotted and picked out by searchlights. As it went out of range of one light it was picked up by another, until it was over Barnet, where it was caught in the beam from the searchlight tram at Barnet Church. The Zeppelin was engaged by 2nd Lt. W. J. Tempest of the Royal Flying Corps and burst into flames, to the cheers of a crowd assembled in the centre of Barnet. L 31 fell to the ground at Potters Bar and was completely destroyed; Capt. Mathy and all his crew were killed, and lie buried in Potters Bar churchyard.

No official record has been traced which might identify any of the MET searchlight trams. The company was short of cars, but the associated London United Tramways had in store surplus cars of their Type X (Nos. 101-150). No trace of any payment to the MET for tramcars has been found in the records of the War Compensation Court, and the late Claude W. Lane, founder of the tramway at Seaton, and who during the Great War lived opposite Finchley depot, told the author that the Barnet searchlight car was LUT No. 121. Since the LUT's traffic and engineering offices in 1915 were located in the MET's premises at the Manor House, it is understandable that the RE requisitioning officer may have thought that the cars belonged to the MET.

The official history *War in the Air* (Clarendon Press, 1931) says that six cars belonging to the MET were requisitioned. Only three searchlight stations are known on the MET, but it is possible that the others were used on the LUT system, and there was probably a spare car in case one broke down or was put out of action. Two LUT Type X cars were later used as a bungalow off St. Albans Road just outside Barnet, but it is not known whether they had been searchlight trams. By the end of 1916 improved purpose-built searchlights were available and from December the trams were withdrawn, the last being those at Finchley and Hendon depots in March 1917.

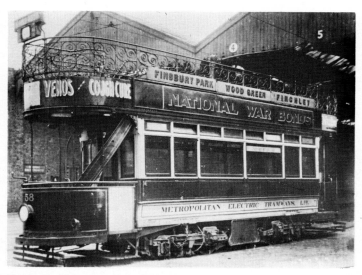

Type B/1 car No. 58, bearing a National War Bonds banner, stands at Finchley Depot during the 1914-18 war. The route board shows that the car is allocated to route 34, Finsbury Park-North Finchley, which was reintroduced on 2 May 1917 when the through service between North Finchley and Holborn was suspended. (The late V. Whitbread

154

SERVICES

During the war the MET had to carry a vast amount of extra traffic generated by the development of war work in local factories, especially at Enfield Highway, at Hendon, and around Park Royal. This coincided with shortage of staff and with maintenance difficulties created by lack of labour, spare parts and materials. Early in 1915 there was also a period of abnormal staff sickness.

The company had to balance the needs of services on residential routes with those carrying heavy industrial traffic. 1915 opened with a series of complaints from Middlesex County Council about poor services in the Enfield Highway area, to which on 4 February A. L. Barber wrote a detailed reply to Henry Burt explaining the company's difficulties. He said that the MET was in close touch with the Royal Small Arms Factory, the War Office and all other authorities concerned with wartime traffic, and the superintendents of the Royal Gunpowder and Small Arms factories had written to MET traffic manager W. E. Hammond in early February, saying that services were now sufficient for their requirements. The company had extended the shuttle service along Southbury Road to Albany Road, Enfield Highway via Ponders End, providing a direct service between Enfield Town and the factories. The Royal Small Arms factory was working on Sundays, and the MET was the only tramway system in the country issuing workmen's tickets on Sundays.

On the western lines, traffic was intensified with the establishment of shell-filling factories at Park Royal and aircraft factories along the Edgware Road at West Hendon. Services in residential areas had been cut to allow cars to be diverted to areas with war factories, and on 2 February 1915 a memorandum on rolling stock was sent to the board of London and Suburban Traction. From 1916, a number of cars, with motormen, were hired from the London United Tramways and operated on the MET, while based at the LUT's Acton depot. These cars worked between Acton and Paddington and Acton and Hendon, with some cars continuing to Edgware and Canons Park. No record has been traced of the number of cars involved or the terms of hire.

During the war, in order to provide direct transport from the Harrow Road to factories on the Acton branch which were engaged on war work, a direct service (route 64) was operated between Acton and Paddington, using the third side of the triangular junction at the Jubilee Clock. An MET letter of April 1916 refers to a loop near Park Royal, which does not appear on any map, but suggests that the MET had built, or was planning to build, a third track on which cars could wait at factory shift times.

Early in 1917, Southgate UDC, whose area included Palmers Green, Bowes Park, Winchmore Hill and Old and New Southgate joined in the barrage of complaints about bad services. A. L. Barber wrote on 12 April pointing out the company's obligations to increase services in areas with munitions factories, and that purely residential areas had to suffer. He said bluntly that he could not increase services on the Palmers Green—Enfield section. In the same month the Board of Trade called on all tramway undertakings in the south of England to reduce coal consumption by 15%, and this led to further cuts in services in residential districts.

Relatively few photographs of MET cars exist from this period, but those taken in 1919 illustrate the poor condition of the cars at that time. Many cars were off the road for long periods owing to lack of maintenance and spare parts, and as early as October 1915 the MCC complained to the company about excessive noise. Materials now had to be obtained from whatever sources presented themselves, and in 1916 two sets of truck frames were obtained from Hurst Nelson & Co. Ltd., with a further three sets in 1917, of the type supplied to the LCC.

METROPOLITAN ELECTRIC TRAMWAYS, LTD.

SERVICE 21
NORTH FINCHLEY
AND HOLBORN

WILL BE SUSPENDED

FROM MAY 2

Separate Services
will be run between
Holborn & Manor House
and between
Finsbury Pk. & Nth. Finchley

In common with many other undertakings, the MET coped with wartime staff shortages by engaging conductresses. (Courtesy D. W. K. Jones

The April 1917 poster is a very early example of Edward Johnston's sans-serif alphabet, commissioned by Frank Pick for the UERL. (Courtesy London Transport

CONDUCTRESSES

By 1917 the MET had lost large numbers of platform staff to the Services, and the remaining male conductors were almost all over military age, whilst some retired motormen had returned to the company's service for the duration. The shortage of conductors was partially offset by engaging women, and about 160 female conductors were on the staff, after earlier objections from the Metropolitan Police and the trades unions had been withdrawn. One of the MET conductresses engaged in 1917 was Mrs. Rose Jones, *née* Freer, now living at Aston Abbots, Buckinghamshire, who has described her experiences.

Mrs. Jones arrived in London in 1914 and entered domestic service at Highgate. Early in 1917 she joined the Metropolitan Electric Tramways as a trainee conductress, enlisting at the Manor House offices. Here she underwent a medical examination and on being passed fit was measured for a uniform, meanwhile commencing practical training immediately under an experienced conductress working from Wood Green depot. A few days later, her uniform was ready, and this consisted of a dark grey jacket and skirt, edged with about one inch of black leather around the cuffs and bottom hems, together with the standard collar badges. Mrs. Jones also received two uniform hats, a dark grey straw hat with a large brim and a dark grey felt hat of similar shape. The rest of the outfit comprised two white shirts, a winter topcoat in dark grey, leather trimmed, and black leather boots reaching half-way to the calf.

After a short initial period at Wood Green she was transferred to Finchley depot for the remainder of her two-month training period, and worked on the routes to Barnet, Cricklewood, Finsbury Park, and over the LCC lines to Euston. After initial training Mrs. Jones became a 'spare girl', which meant that she could be allocated to any route worked by Finchley depot.

Hours of work for conductresses were ten hours per day, and pay during training was £1.10s. per week, rising to about £2 per week after training. There were various shifts; early duties commenced with the first car from Finchley depot at 4.04 am, and this shift finished at 2.30 p.m. During a short meal break, the car was taken over by a spare crew at Tally Ho Corner up to Barnet and back. The following week, the shift would commence at 4.30 am, finishing at 3 pm, and so on until the latest duty, finishing about 1 am. A six-day week was worked, with a free day which could vary.

Through Mrs. Jones, it is learned that MET cars worked over route 9 (North Finchley to Moorgate). It has long been held that LCC cars only worked this service, but during these war years MET cars worked some of the first and last journeys on this route, presumably to eliminate unnecessary mileage between North Finchley and Holloway depot for the LCC cars. During this initial period at Finchley depot Mrs. Jones worked with various drivers on different types of car, and recalls car 13, one of the Type B/2 cars remotored and top-covered just before the war, which may have been transferred to Finchley from Stonebridge Park when relieved by the hire of LUT cars.

About the end of 1917 Mrs. Jones was allocated to route 38, which was at this time working between Barnet and Highgate. When in September 1918 route 19 was reinstated to Tottenham Court Road, she found it a particularly heavy task to hold over the conduit points at Camden Town North London Railway station for the car to turn from Camden Road into Kentish Town Road. By the time Mrs. Jones left the service in the autumn of 1919 she was earning £4 per week and was entitled to one week's holiday per year; in the last year of her service an eight-hour day was introduced. Most conductresses had left the company by this time, but a number carried on for some time afterwards, until all the regular staff had returned from military service. The company provided canvas seats for conductresses, at a cost of £24 in 1916 and £30 in 1917; the number bought is not recorded.

TRAILERS

By the spring of 1916 it seemed likely that there would soon be 14,000 people employed in the Park Royal industrial area, mainly in shell filling factories. The MET had many cars off the road due to the acute shortage of motormen and to lack of maintenance and spare parts, and was discussing with the Ministry of Munitions the possibility of using trailers.

On 13 March 1916 the Ministry wrote to the Board of Trade asking whether the Board would authorise the MET to work trailers between Acton and Willesden, and A. H. Pott wrote to the Board on the same day asking permission to use trailers on the Acton–Hendon and Acton–Paddington routes, provided that brakes and side guards were fitted to the Board's satisfaction. He also asked the Commissioner of Police for his views, and notified all the local authorities along the proposed routes together with the LCC. The cars were intended to operate at peak hours, 5 am to 9 am and 4.30 pm to 9 pm.

It was the company's intention to use some of the four-wheel open-top cars (Nos. 166-191) as trailers, with bogie cars of Types F, G and H as tractors, these groups having GE 67 40hp motors. Pott's letter to the Board of Trade said that the 'small cars' would be converted, implying that motors, controllers, trolley poles and other electrical equipment would be removed and, no doubt, used to keep other cars on the road. On 27 March Pott sent the Board a drawing showing the proposed routes and drawings of couplings, brakes and protection gates.

No objections were raised by any of the local councils. On 7 April the LCC wrote to the Board of Trade supporting the MET application in respect of the Harrow Road route, the MCC resolved on 13 April to ask the Board to approve the scheme, and the Royal Borough of Kensington was in favour. Col. Von Donop recommended on 13 March that permission should be given provided the LCC braking and guard arrangements were adopted, and that there were no severe gradients requiring track brakes.

Type H car No. 266 in wartime condition and with conductress on a Craven Park short-working of Paddington-Cricklewood route 60.   (The late V. Whitbread

On 19 April 1916 the Commissioner of Police wrote to the Board of Trade objecting to the proposal on the grounds of congestion and road safety. The Board of Trade had been at loggerheads with the police ever since the LCC first contemplated using trailers in 1905, and the LCC had only obtained trailer powers by going to Parliament. The Board sent the Commissioner's letter to Pott, who replied that reversals would be carried out only at Acton (Horn Lane), Park Royal, Station Road Harlesden (near Jubilee Clock), Hendon depot, and Edgware terminus. A proposed reversal at Cricklewood Broadway would not now be required, the trailers would be taken on to Hendon and shunted in the depot yard. If the Commissioner of Police was prepared to license female drivers, the MET would not press for trailers.

The Board of Trade were now in some difficulty, with Pott continuing to press the company's case and the police remaining implacable in their opposition. The Board were evidently able to convince Pott that they would be unable to obtain police approval, and after the MET directors considered the position Pott wrote to the Board of Trade on 5 May to withdraw the application 'owing to the views expressed by the Commissioner of Police.' He added that if the labour problem became so acute that the MET could not cope, he might have to reopen the matter.

This appeared to be an end to the matter, and the company managed to maintain services by engaging female conductors, and by much juggling with rolling stock and reducing services in residential areas. The position had worsened by early 1918, when there were numerous suspensions of service for varying periods (such as route 18, Bruce Grove—Finsbury Park, from 23 to 27 March). On 15 February the Director of Inland Transport at the Ministry of Munitions wrote to the Board of Trade about the critical position of the tramway services in Edgware Road (Hendon), serving the aircraft factories, and proposed to ask the MET to use trailers.

The MET agreed to use trailers, subject to Board of Trade and police approval, and the Ministry of Munitions was prepared to bear the cost of equipping the cars. It was proposed initially to convert six Type D cars, and to adapt twelve bogie cars as tractors. Military vehicles driven by Royal Army Service Corps men had been used to convey the workers, but with poor results. Major Pringle, the inspecting officer, recommended the Board to agree to the use of trailers at rush hours for the duration of the war between Cricklewood and Hendon, with brake and drawbar equipment similar to that of the LCC trailers. He added that he did not think this facility should any longer be prevented by police objections; the only alternative would be to employ women tram drivers.

The Commissioner of Police maintained his opposition to even this limited measure, and the proposal was dropped by all the parties. On 13 April the Director-General of the National Labour Supply Board wrote to the MET to say that it had been agreed with the trades unions that no objection would be raised to women tram drivers in London, and London operators duly lodged applications for women to be licensed as tram drivers, but the police delayed issuing them until after the Armistice, when there was no longer a pressing need for them, and none were engaged.

The employment of women drivers had previously been opposed by the Tramways Union Association, but another consideration may have been the amount of physical strength needed to apply the handbrake. This would have been lessened by the fact that during 1917 the MET at last completed the fitting of magnetic track brakes to all its bogie cars. The Board of Trade had kept up sustained pressure on the company to fit these, and but for the war all would have been fitted well before 1917. 112 cars were involved, costing £78 per car.

A NEW MANAGER

On 16 October 1918, the directors of the London and Suburban Traction Company learned that A. H. Pott, general manager and engineer of the three Combine tramway companies, had tendered his resignation from 31 October. His career is described in the biographical appendix, as is that of MET Traffic Manager W. E. Hammond, who retired two months later.

The new manager, appointed by the L&ST board on 16 October and by the MET board two days later, was Christopher John Spencer, the general manager of Bradford Corporation Tramways, who had been seconded to the Admiralty as an assistant director of its labour division. Spencer took over the managership of the MET, LUT and SMET, and SMET manager A. V. Mason became deputy manager and engineer to the three systems.

THROUGH RUNNING

As described in Chapter Ten, through running between the MET and LCC systems on routes 19, 21 and 51 had ceased at various dates during the war due to shortage of conduit-fitted MET cars. Route 19 was resumed on 2 September 1918, but in April the LCC had declined to extend the hire of fifteen LCC cars to the company, and it was 1920 before the other through services could be resumed, route 51 on 7 July and route 21 on 27 October.

The poor financial outlook of the MET after the war prevented the purchase of new cars and meant that the postwar rehabilitation of the rolling stock had to be carried out on the most economical basis. The only further cars considered suitable for the fitting of plough gear were the four wheelers, MET 166 to 191, most of which were in service on the western half of the system. Their trucks were lengthened in 1920 to allow the fitting of plough carriers, their gear ratio was changed to allow them to keep up with the faster LCC cars, field shunting apparatus was fitted to improve the performance of their ageing motors, and the sanction of the Ministry of Transport was obtained to run these cars over the LCC conduit system without magnetic brakes. Some of Wood Green's original bogie cars were sent to Stonebridge Park to replace them, and the four-wheelers took over route 51 (Muswell Hill—Bloomsbury). Despite LCC objections, they continued to work the route until 1931, by which time they had become the last open top trams to work into central London.

June 1920 saw the introduction of a through service via Stamford Hill, described in Chapter Ten. This used LCC cars only, but to balance the mileage routes 59 and 79 were now worked entirely by MET cars, from Edmonton depot. The last Type H cars still without plough carriers were transferred from the Harrow Road and equipped for through running, but this did not suffice for the football specials serving the Tottenham Hotspur football ground, and on 23 January 1920 the MET board sanctioned expenditure of £2,000 to equip further cars. Of this, £1,469 was spent on the 26 four-wheelers.

The remainder was used to equip six Type A cars, Nos. 73, 80, 88, 97, 113 and 118. Plough carriers fabricated from steel plate and sections were fitted at the driving end of one of their Brush Type BB reversed maximum traction trucks, but it was found that the extra weight at this end of the truck increased the tendency of the pony wheels to lift and derail, especially at facing points. The six cars were therefore fitted with modified compensating gear, which reduced the tendency for the pony wheels to lift, but no further cars with this type of truck were adapted for conduit operation.

FINSBURY PARK

In 1915, the London County Council made a further attempt to obtain powers for a loop line at Finsbury Park, presumably for use by short-working MET cars, but without result. Conditions outside the tube stations here and at Golders Green worsened and on Whit Monday 1919 a series of photographs was taken at these and other points. Those taken at Finsbury Park and Golders Green showed huge queues waiting at these points for trams to continue their journeys northwards from the tube stations, which at that time were the outer termini of the present-day Northern and Piccadilly lines.

The through service between Holborn and North Finchley via Finsbury Park was withdrawn on 2 May 1917 and not reinstated until 27 October 1920. It was replaced by MET service 34 between Finsbury Park and North Finchley. This Whit-Monday, 1919 photograph at Blackstock Road shows the traffic problems of the day.   (Courtesy London Transport

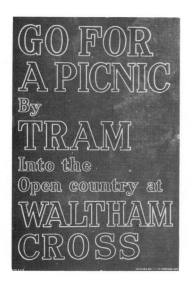

GO FOR A PICNIC By TRAM Into the Open country at WALTHAM CROSS

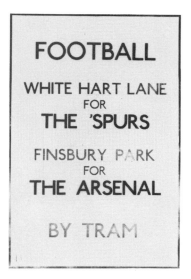

FOOTBALL

WHITE HART LANE
FOR
THE 'SPURS

FINSBURY PARK
FOR
THE ARSENAL

BY TRAM

In January 1920 the various bodies concerned at Finsbury Park agreed that the best solution might after all be a lay-by inside the park. The acting MCC engineer, W. E. Froome Crook, proposed instead that the kerb should be set back and the third track reconstructed close to the kerb, so that passengers could enter and leave the trams direct from the footway. This would have been a good solution, but the Metropolitan Police Commissioner would not agree.

MINISTRY AND LTAC

During 1919 the Government introduced a Bill to create a Ministry of Ways and Communications. The resulting department was given the less cumbersome title of Ministry of Transport, and took over from the Board of Trade the functions in respect of railways, shipping and tramways, together with responsibility for trunk roads, vehicle legislation, and general policy affecting land and water transport. The Board of Trade staff concerned were transferred to the new Ministry from 1 January 1920.

Because of the special conditions in London, the department appointed a committee to advise the Minister on all matters relating to transport in the capital. This was the London Traffic Advisory Committee, and it was to exercise considerable influence on passenger transport in London. It began work in 1919, at a time when shortage of rolling stock (bus and tram) was acute, and one of its first recommendations was that all tramcars in London should be pooled. This was found impracticable on the grounds that no London operators had any spare cars except Leyton UDC, who had five, but curiously there was no mention of the forty or so London United Type X cars which were lying in store. Some were sold during 1919 to Blackpool Corporation.

In February 1920 the MET and LUT discussed the question of using surplus LUT cars on the MET system, and put the proposal to the MCC, who on 26 February agreed provided the terms were equitable and had county approval. On 26 March the MET board agreed to a rent of 10% per annum of the capital cost of any cars used on the other company's system, and the MCC agreed. The subject was then dropped, for reasons unknown, and instead of being drafted to the MET, fifty-eight LUT cars were scrapped during 1923 and others put into store until broken up some years later.

At the end of the 1914-18 war, traffic problems in London were acute and at some places the queue system was instituted, one being Golders Green station. No. 75 with a conductress in charge copes with heavy traffic for North Finchley on Whit Monday, 1919.

(Courtesy London Transport

During the war, James Devonshire had been a member of a Board of Trade committee which had taken a census of rolling stock with a view to the transfer of cars from one town to another where needed, but the Metropolitan Police had objected to the use of provincial tramcars in London. The LTAC tried to persuade the police to relax their objections so that provincial tramcars could be brought to London to alleviate the post-war shortage, but the police would not agree.

The LTAC also urged all London operators to adopt the queue system, which was being tried at a few places, including Golders Green on the MET. At most tram stops there were still chaotic scenes at peak travel times, with large crowds besieging the cars. The value of the fixed stopping places long adopted by the trams was recognised, and the LTAC urged its extension to the buses, by abolishing the right under the Hackney Carriage Act to compel an omnibus to stop anywhere.

LCC EXTENSION PLANS

At the end of the war, the London County Council again sought powers to extend their tramway system, and introduced in the Spring of 1919 a Bill which would have extended the Euston line along the whole length of Tottenham Court Road to Oxford Street. This failed, but the LCC tried again in 1920 with an ambitious scheme for tramways right across central London. These were not authorised, and the only new LCC construction to affect the MET was a line from Seven Sisters Road along Amhurst Park to Stamford Hill, opened in 1924.

The LCC's 1919 and 1920 Bills also contained an attempt to obtain powers to run buses anywhere in the county of London, or beyond the county to any area being developed under the council's housing Acts. Some of these estates were in the MET territory, and the MET board resolved on 17 October 1919 to oppose the Bill. The LCC said that they had no intention to run other bus operators off the streets, their aim evidently being to provide cheap transport for those whom they had rehoused, but the powers were not granted.

CONCLUSION

The Metropolitan Electric Tramways ended the war in a physically run-down condition, and recovery was slow to start. The track over much of the system had deteriorated to an extent that despite speed restrictions derailments were commonplace, and there were many complaints about bad services, poor riding, and noise.

The new manager, C. J. Spencer, did not shirk the issues and made the track his first priority, followed by re-equipment of the workshops to allow them to make good the backlog of car maintenance. Despite the company's poor financial position and the uncertainties surrounding future relations between the MCC and the company, it was realised by all concerned that the MET system had to be kept in operation, and the work of reconstructing the track and rehabilitating the rolling stock carried out as soon as practicable, albeit on the most economical basis. The MET board approved the programme towards the end of 1920, and its progress will be told in Volume 2.

METROPOLITAN ELECTRIC TRAMWAYS TRAFFIC STATISTICS

Year (to 31 Dec)	Traffic receipts	Working costs	Passengers carried	Car Miles (MET cars)	Number of cars	Miles open
1903	£66,793	£60,158	13,924,105	1,559,193	62	8.41
1904	£81,843	£64,123	17,631,257	1,713,770	95	19.89
1905	£140,040	£93,351	28,842,989	3,286,712	150	24.56
1906	£179,600	117,449	36,318,774	3,975,463	190	29.97
1907	£244,200	£147,652	48,242,404	5,037,204	187	42.02
1908	£300,013	£186,948	57,369,307	6,361,253	212	43.25
1909	£326,441	£200,680	62,357,947	7,033,186	237	52.45
1910	£393,869	£241,497	76,460,980	8,761,837	262	56.47
1911	£460,544	£279,039	89,908,677	10,433,113	292	57.80
1912	£460,750	£303,602	91,508,693	11,482,870	312	57.21
1913	£469,988	£327,103	94,426,011	12,255,429	312	57.21
1914	£462,415	£328,795	93,325,170	11,479,592	312	—
1915	£460,823	£306,740	89,656,054	9,686,525	312	—
1916	£504,338	£358,564	105,109,403	10,681,781	312	—
1917	£542,531	£407,157	106,593,495	10,446,566	312	—
1918	£627,334	£491,044	116,483,280	9,978,733	312	57.09
1919	£795,556	£649,415	125,805,992	10,219,168	312	57.09
1920	£940,751	£794,716	126,867,379	10,846,861	312	56.59
1921	£1,031,534	£820,044	116,092,650	10,310,353	313	57.00
1922	£980,787	£718,943	115,456,302	10,561,957	312	57.00
1923	£829,712	£693,230	114,413,178	11,216,294	312	57.00
1924	£744,811	£694,945	110,548,043	11,482,424	312	53.88
1925	£668,756	£659,586	102,815,807	11,594,081	312	53.88
1926	£628,569	£632,413	99,049,454	11,268,506	312	53.66
1927	£637,851	£652,555	104,357,045	11,933,524	312	53.46
1928	£679,369	£661,395	110,589,733	12,021,598	313	53.46
1929	£709,923	£693,679	114,362,387	12,337,892	314	53.49
1930	£768,434	£707,386	122,857,312	12,800,234	314	53.49
1931	£803,636	£722,000	122,709,031	12,654,391	316	53.51
1932	£781,180	£694,161	118,771,379	12,603,503	316	53.51

Figures for 1903 relate to horse traction.

Track-laying in Enfield, 1908-09. On the left, the new rails are in position for final levelling and concreting, the centre picture shows the wood blocks with which most MET and MCC tracks were paved, and the right hand view in Enfield Market Place shows the final tarring over of the wood-block paving.

(London Borough of Enfield Libraries

164

CHAPTER FOURTEEN
TRACK AND OVERHEAD

PERMANENT WAY AND PAVING

The MET/MCC system consisted in 1929-30 of 53.49 miles of line of which 42.61 miles were owned by Middlesex County Council, 9.38 miles by the MET and 1.50 miles by Hertfordshire. A further 2.76 miles in Harrow Road and Seven Sisters Road, formerly MET-owned, had been sold to the LCC, bringing the total length to 56.25 miles. The lines owned by Middlesex and Hertfordshire were light railways, built under the provisions of the Light Railways Act 1896, but were physically identical with the MET-owned tramways save for the 0.487-mile section of reserved sleeper track light railway in the grounds of the Alexandra Palace, the only example in the London area.

With this one exception, the entire system was laid along the centre of public roads, many of which had been widened at the tramways' expense when the lines were laid. Main roads had generally been widened to 60ft. between fences, with a 40ft. carriageway flanked by 10ft. footways, and other roads were widened to 50ft., with a 32ft. carriageway and 9ft. footways. Almost one-third of the total expenditure on the MET/MCC system was accounted for by highway improvements, of which road widening and the associated purchase of property had cost £972,457 by 1925. This programme was of immense and lasting benefit to north and northwest London.

Both the company and the county council used the form of track construction which became almost standard in Britain, with grooved girder rail laid on a continuous concrete foundation. The rails used on the MET tramways of 1904-5 weighed 101 lb./yd. in 45ft. lengths, and came from the Phoenix Steel Co. of Ruhrort, Germany, but the Middlesex County Council insisted on using British rails, and at the August 1904 opening gala there was applause at the statement that all the rails used were British 'with not a piece from Belgium'. These rails were of British Standard Section No. 3, 6½in. deep and weighing 100 lb./yd., with BSS No. 3C of 106 lb./yd. on curves with a thicker guard to withstand the wear, the first consignments coming from the North Eastern Steel Co. and Walter Scott Ltd. The special 85 lb./yd. dwarf rails used on the Alexandra Park sleeper track were supplied by the North Eastern Steel Co. Ltd.

The rails were held to standard 4ft. 8½in. gauge by steel tie bars, made initially by Bayliss, Jones and Bayliss Ltd. On straight sections the two tracks were normally laid with the centres eight feet apart (wider where centre poles were used) and on curves the spacing was increased as necessary to allow a minimum space of 15in. between passing cars. In two cases, curves had to be relaid to provide the 15in. clearance; one was at Pound Lane, Willesden, in December 1907, the other at Aldermans Hill, Palmers Green, when a curve had to be respaced before top-covered cars could run there.

The MET-MCC system was one of the best-engineered in Britain, but at a correspondingly high cost; by 1925 expenditure by all parties had reached £3,400,820. Virtually the entire system was laid with double track, the exceptions being so few that they can be listed in one paragraph. Two short pieces of interlaced track were never doubled, one in Station Road just north of Willesden

Junction and the other in Walm Lane near Willesden Green station. Until 1911 there was another section of interlaced track in High Road, Willesden. The railway bridges over the North London line at Kensal Green and the GNR main line in Friern Barnet Road carried only a single line until they were widened and a second track laid, respectively in November 1908 and the autumn of 1913. There were also nine cases in which single line working was necessary pending completion of road widening; these sections, which are detailed in the respective route chapters, were one in Seven Sisters Road, two in High Road Tottenham, four in Edmonton, one (additional to the railway bridge) in Harrow Road, and one at Whetstone.

All the special work (points and crossings) was supplied by Hadfields Steel Foundry Co. Ltd., whose 'Era' manganese steel was used from the start in 1904. Road points were double-tongue, of 100ft. radius, usually 12ft. 3in. long with 9ft. blades, but single-tongue points of sharper radius were laid in depots. Crossover roads were about 70ft. long, angled at 1 in 5½, and point blades were 8ft. long, all points and crossings being bolted together on to channel sleepers. The largest single installation was at Wood Green junction, where double track connections were provided for every movement between all four roads (in tramway parlance, a 'Grand Union') but this was later simplified; another complicated layout was that at Cricklewood Broadway, which had to be altered at least twice to permit different through services.

The standard rail joint used 2ft.-long six-hole fishplates, with a 2ft. soleplate 8in. wide and ⅝in. deep, secured by bolts and Eureka locknuts; later soleplates were 10in. wide. The rails were joined electrically by Neptune bonds, and the rails were cross-bonded at every 100 yards. County engineer H. T. Wakelam carried out a number of experiments (described in the *Light Railway and Tramway Journal* for March 1910) to determine the best form of rail joint; they included soleplates riveted to the rails, transverse steel sleepers, transverse or longitudinal pitch pine sleepers, and Dicker joints. Meanwhile, the MET in reconstructing the Harrow Road line in 1906 had begun to use Thermit welded joints, and from 1910 these became standard in new construction, other sections being done subsequently.

There was the usual obligation on the part of the tramway owner (even under the Middlesex Light Railway Orders) to maintain the road between the

Laying the crossover north of Totteridge Lane on the Great North Road in 1905, showing the concrete bed on which the wood-blocks are to be laid. (London Borough of Barnet Libraries

166

The rails used on the MET system were normally made in 45 ft. lengths, and were taken to the site by the company's two Foden steam wagons, one of which (NK 1671) was fitted with a swivelling hydraulic crane. They continued in use under London Transport.　　　(D. W. K. Jones

tracks and for 18 inches on either side. The MET would have preferred to use hard-wearing granite setts, but even on the 1904 lines was often obliged to use hardwood blocks on a 6in. concrete foundation.

There was a general agreement that wood block paving would be used outside schools and places of worship and other public buildings. A dispute arose over this when the Wembley—Sudbury line was being laid in 1910; the Commissioner of Police asked for wood paving outside Wembley police station, and the council replied that they had not previously considered a police station to be a public building. However, the county solicitor found that it was, and wood paving had to be laid.

In fact the use of setts was comparatively rare on the MCC lines; the district councils, particularly in the outer residential districts, nearly all put up a strong case against granite and usually got their way. In some cases they obtained wood paving across the whole width of the road, in others such as Friern Barnet there was wood block paving on the track and margin, separated by a line of setts from macadam haunches. James Devonshire of the MET contended that the light railways committee were under no obligation to pave with wood at all; he considered wood paving to be a highways improvement and therefore the responsibility of the Highways Committee. The Highways Committee disagreed and in 1907 asked that wood block paving should always be used in future. The minutes of the local councils at this period contain innumerable references to the paving question, and in three cases the parties had to resort to arbitration.

For the period up to 31 March 1908, track construction had cost the council an average £13,281 per mile. However, the 1910 extension from Warwick Crescent to Paddington cost nearly £20,000 per mile. Cabling, overhead construction and road widening costs were additional, and a 1926 MCC report quoted the total capital expenditure as over £60,000 per mile. The rent payable on this by the company was £3,000 per mile.

The Harrow Road was the scene of a dispute over clearances between passing cars. In December 1906 someone at the Board of Trade noticed that the Type C cars (151-165) were 6ft. 10in. wide, whereas the line had been built to allow 15in. between passing cars 6ft. 9in. wide. The company admitted this and said

Left: MET tracks were normally laid with the centres eight feet apart, slightly closer than those of the LCC tramways. The close spacing shows clearly in this 1930s view of Feltham 2092 (MET 348) in Ballards Lane, Finchley, on route 40.
(The late Dr. Hugh Nicol

Below: MET monogram on a section feeder box at the Manor House.
(D. A. Thompson

Right: An MET arc-welding set in use at Tottenham in 1927, taking its supply from the trolley wire. (London Transport

they had not allowed for the thickness of the upper deck wooden screen boards to which the advertisements were fixed. Photographs show that the boards were soon afterwards replaced by enamelled iron plates, but it was also necessary to move in the upper deck seats, stanchions and decency boards and to alter the cant rails and water beading. This caused the Harrow Road cars to stay in most cases on their own route instead of moving around the system.

When the Harrow Road line was reconstructed for electric traction, the LCC had wanted the tracks to be laid at 9ft. centres, but the Board of Trade had allowed the 8ft. spacing because it was standard on the rest of the MET system. There must have been some relaxation of the rules from 1912, for the LCC cars which began to participate in through running with the MET via Finsbury Park were 7ft. 1in. wide.

In 1909 the company installed its first set of electrically-operated points, at the Jubilee Clock, Harlesden. These were Turner's automatic point shifters, bought from Tramway Supplies Ltd., which were always set for the principal route and could be changed for the diverging route by taking power as the car passed under a skate. Further sets were bought in 1909 and 1910 and installed at Bruce Grove, Seven Sisters Corner, Turnpike Lane (2), Wood Green (2), North Finchley (2) and Craven Park. When the junctions at Cricklewood and Harlesden (Jubilee Clock) were remodelled in the 1920s they were equipped with Collins point turners, both types proving highly satisfactory.

When the first electrically-operated points were installed at Harlesden in 1909, the Commissioner of Police felt that the police should have been consulted, but MET secretary A. L. Barber held that they were solely a matter for the Board of Trade. The Board agreed, and decided that police responsibility ended at licensing the cars, motormen and conductors, and regulating traffic.

By 1911 Middlesex had benefited to the extent that some 50 miles of its principal roads had been widened and improved, often well in advance of building development, much of the work being done at the insistence of the local councils in return for their consent to the lines being taken through their areas. Prior to this even such important thoroughfares as the Edgware Road and parts of the Great North Road were largely unpaved and without kerbs or lighting. In addition to the widenings, drainage and paving, the light railways account had also paid for granite kerbing, and for footpaths paved with Victoria stone slabs.

During the war the government stopped the manufacture of tram rail, and one of the first measures taken by the MET after the war was to order 500 tons of rail in March 1919 from the United States Steel Products Co. at £18.6s. per ton; this compared with £7.10s. per ton before the war. It was needed to renew the one mile of track between Harringay Park station and Turnpike Lane, which was in very poor condition. The job cost £37,772 and was the first major track renewal on the system, though £17,235 was spent in 1919 on replacing points and crossings.

By this time, the MET was in a poor state financially, and nothing had been added to the Reconstruction and Renewals Fund since 1911. This fund was hopelessly inadequate to finance even a fraction of the outstanding arrears of track renewal. Discussions took place on the possibility of granting the company a non-repairing lease at a fixed rent, with the county council taking over responsibility for the repair, renewal and maintenance of the track, but the new lease did not materialise and the company's tenure remained unresolved for several years. Money was however found for a major programme of track renewal from 1921 onwards, and this will be described in Volume 2.

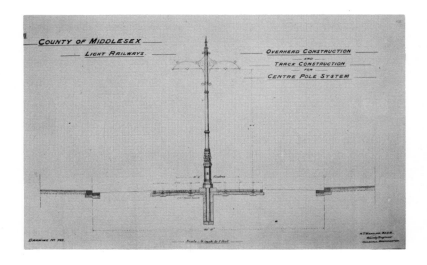

MET overhead construction, as designed by the Middlesex County Surveyor, H. T. Wakelam. Centre poles (above) were used only in Finchley and Tottenham, all other sections using side poles and span wires (below). The octagonal pole bases were probably unique to the MET.

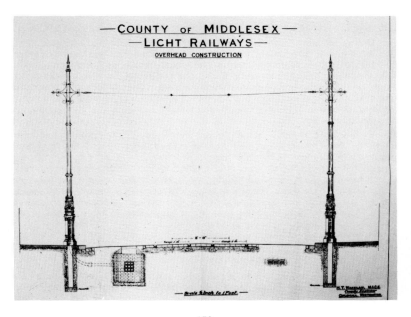

OVERHEAD CONSTRUCTION

The MET was unusual among tramways in possessing from the start its own overhead and building department which could erect the overhead equipment of the new lines and carry out such works as depot extensions. The MET acted as its own contractor for overhead equipment, though outside contractors were used at times of pressure. The MET engineer concerned, Sidney G. Smith, later joined Norman Clough (who had equipped the Potteries tramways) and set up the well-known electrical contracting firm of Clough, Smith & Co.

By the time the MET/MCC system was constructed, Board of Trade regulations for tramways had become fairly standardised. Power was supplied to the cars at 550V dc through a hard-drawn copper trolley wire suspended 20ft. above the track (lower under bridges) and strung from traction poles usually planted 120ft. apart on straight track and closer on curves. The overhead line was divided electrically into half-mile sections, each fed separately from the nearest substation by an underground low-tension feeder cable of the vulcanised bitumen type laid in wood or stoneware troughing, usually beneath the pavement.

The entire overhead layout was suspended from traction poles, no use being made of wall rosettes except for two solitary examples in the 1920s. The poles were supplied by John Spencer Ltd. of Wednesbury, one of whose directors was Sir Ernest Spencer, deputy chairman of the MET, this point being stated in the company's 1903 prospectus. The poles were 30ft. long, of which the bottom 5ft. was buried in the ground and set in concrete. Most poles were of the slender 840 lb. No. 1 type, but a slightly heavier 1050 lb. No. 2 type was used on curves and at feeder pillars, and a more robust 1200 lb. No. 3 type at junctions. In 1904 they cost about £5, £6 and £9 respectively.

The many local authorities involved with both the county scheme and the recon-struction of the MET tramways all had their own ideas on overhead construction and street furniture. Separate consultation with each would have led to a multiplicity of different designs, and late in 1902 the company erected sample poles, over-head fittings, feeder pillars and other items in the yard of Manor House depot, and invited the councils to inspect them. As a result a uniform design was adopted for the whole MET/MCC system, except for minor differences where the poles were also to be used for street lighting.

The pole design may have been unique to the MET, for it was designed jointly by the company and H. T. Wakelam, the county engineer. The poles were particularly elegant, with well-proportioned spiked cast-iron finials, ornamental collars at the shoulders, and octagonal bases surmounted in the case of the earlier routes by a Grecian urn decorated with finely cast acanthus leaves. The original drawings showed the urn surmounted by an ornamental studded collar, but this was omitted. The pole bases bore the MET monogram on the tramways, and the appropriate county arms on the light railways. Poles in Finchley and Tottenham which were to carry street lighting had elongated octagonal bases to contain the switches, again surmounted by the Grecian urn. Standard MET poles were used on the section of LCC-owned line in Archway Road, Highgate, but a different type of pole was used in Paddington, to the Borough Council's design.

Within a year of opening, the company asked the county to forego the Grecian urn which formed the upper part of each base. This and a second similar request were refused, but in February 1907 the council relented and allowed a smaller pole base in future construction, without the urn. The new bases were used on lines constructed after 1907, starting with Winchmore Hill to Enfield. Despite this saving, the cost of poles had risen by 1909 to £9, £11 and £14 for the three types. Some tramways dispensed with separate pole bases in later years, but on the MET most of them remained to the end.

The 1902 legislation allowed Wood Green and Tottenham councils to use the traction poles for street lighting without charge. Wood Green used these powers to mount pairs of gas lamps about half way up certain poles, mainly at inter-

This early view in High Street, North Finchley shows the centre-pole construction insisted on by Finchley UDC, but replaced by side poles and span wire construction from 1913.

(Commercial view, courtesy D. W. K. Jones

sections; in Tottenham's case the lighting was electric. Finchley obtained and used similar powers, but had to pay extra for the enlarged pole bases. The Alexandra Park Trustees at first wanted every tram pole in the park to be lit at the expense of the county council; they were told they could have free use of the poles for their own lighting and that the MET would supply the power at cost price, but did not take up the offer.

When the plans were being drawn up, Finchley, Tottenham, Wood Green and Southgate all demanded centre poles for their districts. Wood Green and Southgate soon dropped the demand, so did Tottenham in respect of Lordship Lane and Bruce Grove, but wanted centre poles in the High Road. The county opposed the idea as it would cost an extra £950 per mile, but the two councils insisted and asked the Board of Trade to arbitrate. Major Pringle inspected the routes, found them wide enough for either system and told the parties to reach agreement among themselves; if they could not, then the council request for centre poles should be granted. Centre poles were therefore used in Tottenham High Road and in Finchley's part of the Great North Road, and Finchley in 1906 insisted on their use just north of Tally Ho Corner where part of the line had been built with span wires.

In 1904 Finchley also demanded centre poles on its portions of the Golders Green and New Southgate routes. This time the MET brought in consulting engineer Stephen Sellon, who said he regarded centre poles as anathema and would never recommend them. Finchley persisted and said that centre poles would facilitate future road-widening, but the Board of Trade thought otherwise and allowed side poles and span wires.

On most of the system, the 0.4-in. diameter hard-drawn copper trolley wire was suspended in Estler Bros. ears from stranded galvanised steel span wires supplied by Rylands Bros. Ltd., of Warrington. Flexible bowstring suspension was used with the centre poles, and simple spans elsewhere. The span wires were suspended between short cross-arms, which had accompanying wrought-iron scroll-work, bought separately from sub-contractors. Guard wires were mounted above the trolley wires where GPO or railway signal wires crossed, and were earthed at one or more poles by being bonded to the rail. At about half-mile intervals, feeder wires ran up a pole and out to the two trolley wires from a cast-iron roadside section feeder box containing switches, fuses and lightning-arresters.

172

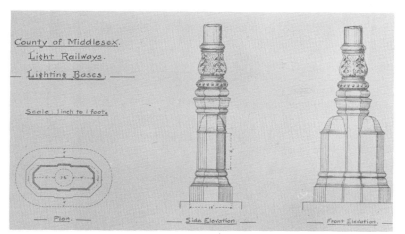

Where traction poles carried street lighting a special extended base was used to house the necessary terminals and switching. They were used with both centre and side poles.

Since construction of the system had generally been accompanied by widening of the roads to at least 50ft., there was little occasion to use side poles with extended bracket arms. A few were used at a narrow point in Bruce Grove, and there were five in Ballards Lane, North Finchley, between Tally Ho Corner and Old Nether Street on the approach to Finchley depot, which were replaced by span wire construction when the line to Golders Green opened. There was also a short length of side bracket construction at the Enfield Town end of the Southbury Road route, which had to be converted to span wire construction in the 1920s before top-covered cars could run there, and some in High Road, Willesden, on a section of interlaced track.

Automatic trolley reversers were used at several points, including Canons Park, Southbury Road (Enfield), Waltham Cross, North Finchley and Wood Green (Lordship Lane). They were installed at various dates between about 1911 and

Trolley reversers were used at several points on the MET until about 1927. This one was at Waltham Cross. (Commercial view, courtesy A. G. Forsyth

An MET pair-horse tower wagon ready for the road. The foot-gong was used when the crew were called out to an emergency such as a broken wire. (Courtesy London Transport

1920 and were used only by the open top cars which had the trolley rope wound round the pole. The reversers were removed by about 1927.

The London County Council, owners of the Colney Hatch Lunatic Asylum in Friern Barnet Road, wanted no traction poles on their side of the road, but the usual span wire system was used, each pole on the asylum side being fitted with formidable iron spikes to deter any would-be climbers. The MCC also had to build a new wall high enough to prevent upper deck passengers from seeing into the grounds.

From 1908 there were complaints about the centre poles in Finchley and Tottenham from other road users, including the secretary of the Automobile Association. Finchley council had taken the view that the centre poles would impose a discipline on 'automobilists' and reduce accidents, but events proved otherwise, and by 1909 they had already caused two fatal accidents in Tottenham. In 1912 it was decided to replace them with side poles and span wire, and the work was begun in January 1913 and completed in 1914. In the Great War luminous paint was applied to the poles.

In 1924 it was discovered that despite regular painting (always in dark green) many of the poles had become corroded, especially beneath the attachments. Later that year C. J. Spencer gave instructions that the scrolls, finials and collars were to be removed throughout the system, and the ornamental cast-iron finials were replaced by plain wooden ones produced by the wood-turner. The poles were reinforced by placing steel rods inside them and filling them with concrete, which involved hauling the mixture up in buckets by rope and pulley and pouring it into the pole through an outsized metal funnel. 51 poles in the Edgware Road were resited in 1924 to facilitate road improvements.

Renewals of the overhead line after the war were carried out in grooved wire with non-fouling ears, and by 1921 their use was sufficiently widespread to permit an experiment with trolley skids in place of wheels on the Stonebridge Park routes. Dewirements were nearly halved, but wear on the wire was doubled, so the MET decided to lubricate the trolley wire. This reduced the wear, but the skids were abandoned in 1924 or early 1925, perhaps because LCC cars were to run through to Wembley for the exhibition, or perhaps because of lubricant falling on to passengers riding on the open top cars. A later experiment with bow collectors will be described in Volume 2.

In 1908, the Board of Trade gave permission for the usual 120ft. interval between poles to be exceeded at two places. These were the railway bridges at Church End, Finchley and in Friern Barnet Road, where the overhead was taken over each bridge in one section by placing heavier poles at each end of the bridge and using additional bearer wires slung between the tops of the poles and brought together to form a rectangle in the bridge centre. This removed the need to place any poles on the bridges.

A further experiment was carried out in 1930 between the Orpheum cinema at Temple Fortune and Hoop Lane, Golders Green by removing each alternate pole and supporting the wires from span wires slung between the tops of the poles, the supporting wires being pulled into a nearby horizontal plane. The term used to describe this method of suspension was Horizontal Catenary. It was inspected by delegates to a Tramways and Light Railways Association conference, but shortly afterwards a motor bus working on the Golders Green—St. Albans service struck one of the poles and brought down about 100 yards of overhead. The tarred wooden paving caught fire, and within a matter of days the absent poles were re-positioned and the standard overhead suspension reinstated.

During the 1920s, the MET purchased a number of one-man arc-welding sets. Two of these are seen in this 1927 view during track welding in Regents Park Road, Church End, Finchley. Note the wood block paving.   (London Transport

Extract from MET Rule Book, January 1928 edition.

POINT CONTROLLERS

These are at the following junctions:—

Turner Point Controllers:—

1. Bruce Grove, set for Edmonton, operated for Wood Green.
2. Seven Sisters Corner, set for Finsbury Park, operated for Stamford Hill.
3. Turnpike Lane, set for Wood Green, operated for Muswell Hill.
4. Turnpike Lane, set for Finsbury Park, operated for Muswell Hill.
5. Wood Green, set for Enfield and Finchley, operated for Bruce Grove.
6. Jolly Butchers Hill (Wood Green), set for Enfield, operated for New Southgate and North Finchley.
7. Woodhouse Road, set for Highgate, operated for New Southgate.
8. Tally Ho, set for Highgate, operated for Golders Green.
9. Craven Park, set for Sudbury, operated for Willesden.

Collins Point Controllers:—

10. High Street, Harlesden, to Acton or Paddington.
11. Chichele Road, Cricklewood, to Hendon or Finchley.

OPERATION OF POINT CONTROLLERS

Turner Type. These points are always set in one direction, as stated. Motormen operate the points by putting handbrake on and controllers on the second or third notch of power when trolley is passing under the skate. The points are automatically reset again. Cars not requiring to operate the points coast under the skates with controller in 'off' position. The overhead frog is automatically operated at the same time as the points.

In the event of a defect rendering points inoperative or a car overrunning the skate, they can be worked by turning operating handle on the front of the pillar.

Collins Type. Unlike the Turner, these points are left in the direction taken by the previous car and are operated by cars for both directions in the following manner:—

Cars for Acton and Hendon pass underneath the skate on the first notch of power with the handbrake slightly on.

Cars for Paddington and Finchley pass underneath skate with the controller in 'off' position. The overhead frog is a drop lever pattern operated by the trolley boom.

In the event of a defect rendering points inoperative, or a car overrunning the skate, they can be moved with a point iron in either direction as required.

176

CHAPTER FIFTEEN
DEPOTS AND WORKS

The cars of the Metropolitan Electric Tramways were based at five large depots, at Edmonton, Finchley, Hendon, Stonebridge Park and Wood Green. Their combined capacities were quoted as 230 as built and 287 by mid-1908, and by 1912 they could accommodate 350 cars (312 MET cars, the works fleet, and vehicles hired at various times from the LCC and LUT). Unlike the LCC depots with their narrow entrances and traversers, the MET depots were open-fronted and entered through track fans allowing direct access to each road.

At the inception of the scheme it was anticipated that each part of the system would need its own local generating station, and several sites were chosen for their proximity to rivers and streams (for cooling water) and to railway sidings (for coal delivery), the best example being Stonebridge Park. By 1902 high-tension ac distribution had become practicable and the depots needed only a rotary substation, whilst Stonebridge Park did not even need this equipment as its routes could be fed direct from the nearby generating station.

WOOD GREEN DEPOT

This depot was located on the west side of High Road, Wood Green on the portion of road usually known as Jolly Butchers Hill. It does not appear on the 1894 Ordnance survey, though the site had been taken on lease and cleared in that year by the Metropolitan Tramways and Omnibus Co. Ltd., which had been set up to facilitate the continued operation of the horse tramways in Middlesex after those in London had been purchased by the LCC. The MTOC built a horse car depot and stables on the site in 1895, and leased them to the North Metropolitan Tramways Company, who worked the route with horse cars.

Wood Green depot was transferred to the MET in 1902 with a book value of £8,405. A contract to reconstruct it for electric traction was awarded that year to Clift Ford at £14,486, and a further £4,000 was voted to buy a site alongside the depot on which Brush would erect and equip a substation. The building was already well-constructed and the work consisted mainly of raising the roof, heightening the walls, and relaying the tracks, with pits on six of the seven tracks. It is likely that during this work most of the horse cars were based at the Manor House depot, with few if any at Wood Green.

Wood Green depot was rebuilt to accommodate sixty-two cars, of which forty-six had arrived by August or September 1904, at which time the depot also housed eight tower wagons. The first electric cars had arrived in April 1904 and were assembled there, and it was from here that the three cars carrying the MET directors and their guests set out to tour the system on the opening date, 22 July 1904. Until 1910 the depot also served as repair works and paint shop for the northern lines, using machine tools powered by traction motors, and continued to overhaul at least the bodies of the cars until the MET system was linked together in February 1910 and cars from all depots could reach Hendon Car Works.

As early as November 1904 the company had seen that it would be necessary to enlarge the depot, and offered Watney, Combe, Reid & Co. Ltd. £1,000 for a piece of land at the rear of the "Three Jolly Butchers". The owners held out for a higher price, and a figure of £1,150 was agreed on 18 May 1906. By June, 1908 the depot had been enlarged to accommodate 87 cars, its dimensions being given as

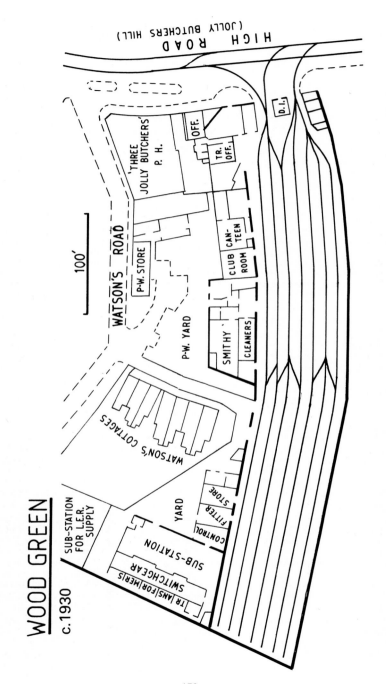

WOOD GREEN
c.1930

100'

HIGH ROAD
(JOLLY BUTCHERS HILL)

WATSON'S ROAD

'THREE JOLLY BUTCHERS' P. H.

OFF.

TR. OFF.

D. I.

P-W. STORE

CLUB CANTEEN

ROOM

CLEANERS

SMITHY

P-W. YARD

WATSON'S COTTAGES

CONTROL

FITTER STORE

YARD

SUB-STATION

SUB-STATION FOR L.E.R. SUPPLY

TRANSFORMERS

SWITCHGEAR

178

An early view of the entrance to Wood Green Depot from Jolly Butchers Hill. The structure over the entrance dates back to horse tramway days and was removed in the 1920s.
(London Borough of Haringey Libraries

about 84ft by 473ft. A further enlargement costing £711 was made in 1912, and pits were provided on the portions of track not already equipped. On 22 December 1909 the MET-owned portions of the site were transferred to the MCC for £6,295, but the older part of the depot was on land leased by the MET for 99 years from the Learoyd Trustees, and did not pass to the MCC.

Wood Green Depot was rebuilt for electric cars. This 1904 view shows some of the 35 Type B cars which opened the first line ready for service.
(Tramway Museum Society

179

EDMONTON

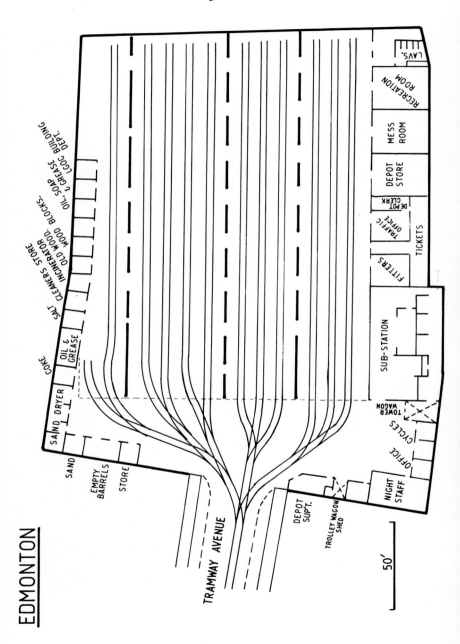

N

50'

TRAMWAY AVENUE

SAND
EMPTY BARRELS
STORE
DEPOT SUPT.
TROLLEY WAGON SHED
NIGHT STAFF
OFFICE
CYCLES
TOWER WAGON
SUB-STATION

SAND DRYER
COKE
OIL & GREASE
SALT
CLEANERS STORE
INCINERATOR
OLD WOOD BLOCKS
WOOD
OIL, SOAP & GREASE BUILDING
LOCO DEPT.

FITTERS
TRAFFIC OFFICE
DEPOT CLERK
DEPOT STORE
MESS ROOM
RECREATION ROOM
LAVS.
TICKETS

180

Two sand driers were purchased towards the end of 1920 at £219 the pair and were installed at Wood Green depot. From this time bagged sand was supplied from there to all the depots on the system, delivered by four-wheel sand van 05. Extra accommodation was provided in 1922 for motor tower wagons, at a cost of £131.

In February 1927 the MET board decided to buy and instal two mechanical car washing machines, consisting of pumps, pipework and high pressure hoses. The cost came to £390 and photographs were taken of them in use at Wood Green depot in summer 1927. The high pressure mains fed hoses fitted with brush heads that enabled one man to clean the exterior of a car in a fraction of the time taken by two or more men using the old method of hand-washing with sponges and buckets of water. Their use was extended in 1928 to the other depots. Vacuum cleaning plant for car interiors was installed at Wood Green in 1929.

Mechanical car washing equipment had just been installed at Wood Green Depot when this photograph was taken in 1927. Double-deck cars could be cleaned from the ground by use of high-pressure spray guns attached to hoses suspended from the roof trusses. The London United Tramways' car seen on the right was on a special working in connection with an inter-company social function.   (London Transport

EDMONTON DEPOT

These premises were built in 1880-1 to house the cars and horses of the North London Suburban Tramways which ran between Ponders End and Stamford Hill. The depot was about 250 yards east of the main Hertford Road and was reached by a new thoroughfare which was given the name Tramway Avenue, which it retains. From 1885 to 1891 the depot housed the steam tram engines and trailers of the North London Tramways Company. In 1891 the depot passed to the North Metropolitan Tramways Company and was again used by horse cars.

Edmonton Depot in the 1930s, showing a former B Type motor bus converted to an MET lorry.
(London Transport

The depot passed to Metropolitan Electric Tramways Ltd. on 26 November 1902 for £9,756. Unlike Wood Green, it had not previously been transferred to the MTOC. A £7,888 contract to reconstruct it for electric traction was awarded in July 1903 to Holliday & Greenwood, with electrical equipment and a substation to be installed by the Brush Electrical Engineering Co. Ltd. The sheds were in course of reconstruction when the MET inaugural party visited them on 22 July 1904, en route from Brimsdown to Wood Green, the roof being raised and walls extended.

Cars 36-70 were delivered to this depot late in 1904, but did not come into use until July 1905 when the reconstructed tramway through Edmonton reached Tramway Avenue. Until then, the MET retained eight horse cars and 97 horses to work the section in Edmonton. The depot was extended in 1907 at a cost of £5,515 to take a further 24 cars, and by July 1908 could accommodate 60 cars on ten tracks in a building 137ft by 217ft, all tracks having pits. A further extension was carried out for £888 in 1912 by roofing over part of the yard and laying extra track. Little further change was made to the premises during the period covered by this volume.

On 16 December 1930 the company purchased a strip of land on the north side of the depot from the British Land Company for £586, apparently to allow the stores to be relocated and so permit a full-length twelfth depot road in place of the stub track usually occupied by a works car. This would have been necessary if the depot had received an allocation of longer cars of the Feltham type, but the work was not carried out. At the same period, the siding at Edmonton Town Hall was extended for the specific purpose of accommodating longer cars.

Edmonton Depot was built on a site originally leased in 1880 to the North London Suburban Tramway Co. Ltd. by Thomas O'Hagan for 99 years, and did not form part of the "going concern" which could be purchased by the MCC at the end of the lease.

The area around Edmonton Depot consisted partly of market gardens, and on one occasion in the 1920s a donkey strayed into the depot and fell into the pits.

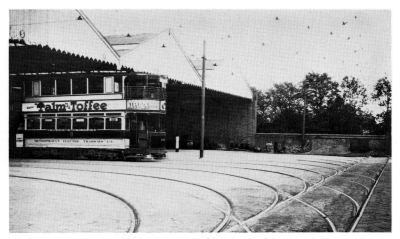

Finchley depot yard and track fan in August, 1929, showing the surrounding brick wall. The tram is No. 164.　　　　　　　　　　(G. N. Southerden, courtesy London Borough of Newham Libraries

FINCHLEY DEPOT

The Metropolitan Tramways & Omnibus Company's November 1898 application for light railway powers included a short branch in Church End, Finchley from Ballards Lane along Redbourne Avenue to the site of a proposed generating station and depot near the up line sidings of Finchley Church End GNR station. Negotiations fell through, and application was then made for a short line from the Great North Road in East Finchley to a site intended for a depot and generating station in East End Road, adjacent to the same railway. This was authorised in the 1901 MCC order, but Finchley UDC (who were planning their own generating station at Squires Lane) would not agree to a tramway power station in their district. By early 1903 the decision to centralise power generation at Brimsdown meant that Finchley would need only a car shed and substation.

During 1903 the MET found a more suitable site, only 400 yards from where the local routes would converge at Tally Ho Corner, and allowing each route to be served without dead mileage. The site was a curious one for a tram depot, being in the centre of a middle-class residential estate then being developed by a Finchley builder, C. F. Day, partly on the site of "Rosemont", the former residence of sometime Finchley UDC chairman Benjamin Todd.

Day agreed to sell 1¼ acres for £2,500, but the sale was not completed until 28 July 1904, and delayed the opening of the Great North Road route. A contract to build the depot and substation was awarded on 23 September 1904 to Willesden public works contractor Clift Ford for £14,365, plus £1,500 for trackwork. The depot and tramway opened on 7 June 1905, cars 111-130 having been delivered there and soon joined by other cars transferred from Hendon.

The site could only be reached by way of Woodberry Grove and other private roads which were owned by the Birkbeck Bank and the Birkbeck Building Society, who imposed various conditions. The MET had to build a high brick wall, with ornamental panels and terra-cotta coping stones, along the whole of the depot frontage, and in return for the entry wayleave they were required to buy for £1,000 the adjacent house on the south corner of Woodberry Grove and Ballards Lane (with the right to use it for offices) and pay an annual rent of two guineas for the right to lay cables. The MET also paid a small rental in respect of the traction poles in Woodberry Grove.

P. W. Yard

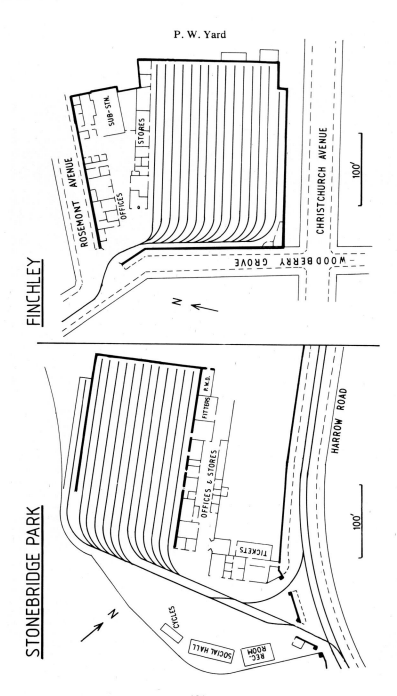

FINCHLEY

ROSEMONT AVENUE

SUB-STN.

OFFICES

STORES

WOODBERRY GROVE

CHRISTCHURCH AVENUE

100'

N

STONEBRIDGE PARK

FITTERS P.W.D.

OFFICES & STORES

TICKETS

CYCLES

SOCIAL HALL

REC. ROOM

HARROW ROAD

100'

N

It was intended to connect the depot both with the future Golders Green line in Ballards Lane and with the line in the Great North Road, and C. F. Day gave the MET permission to lay a line along the planned Rosemont Avenue. Woodberry Grove was very narrow, and in August 1908 Day, who owned the land on the north side, agreed to sell a 10ft strip to allow the MET to double the depot approach line. Against this, he would now allow only a 273ft siding in Rosemont Avenue, as far as the substation, which would still be 110 yards short of the Great North Road. The road was widened, but neither the double track nor the siding were ever constructed.

The lack of an access line from the Great North Road had a profound effect on MET operations in the Tally Ho Corner area, as all car movements between this line and the depot involved a reversal at the Percy Road crossover in the congested High Street. The arrangement remained unchanged throughout the existence of the MET.

During October 1906, a Middlesex County Council representative visiting Finchley depot noticed five cars there lettered "County Council of Hertfordshire". The committee asked the MET what charge was being made to that council for housing them, and arrangements were made to charge Hertfordshire an annual rent of 6% of the cost of the depot, plus a car maintenance charge of five-sixtieths of the depot total. The depot was built to accommodate 60 cars on 15 tracks, with a covered area about 175ft by 149ft. The Hertfordshire cars were stored ready to work on the Whetstone—Barnet line, which was behind schedule.

By 1907 the Middlesex County Council had adopted a policy of owning the sites on which the MET depots stood, these being considered as part of the "going concern" which the county could buy at the end of the company's lease. The Finchley site was conveyed to the county council on 4 December 1907 for £2,960.

Finchley Depot paying-in room in 1930, showing the desks at which the conductors checked their cash and tickets. The white discs are headway clocks which recorded the passage of trams on both tracks at Golders Green. (London Transport

Newly-installed moquette seating called for improved methods of interior cleaning. The first vacuum cleaning equipment was installed at Finchley Depot in 1928, using powerful suction hoses. The tram being cleaned (in both views) is No. 317. Following the success of these trials at Finchley, vacuum cleaning machines and high-pressure washers (first tried at Wood Green) were adopted at all MET depots.
(London Transport

186

By the end of 1908 Finchley UDC had adopted Woodberry Grove, so the trams no longer entered and left the depot by courtesy of the Birkbeck Permanent Benefit Building Society. In 1928 the company had to pay £599 in road charges when the council made up Rosemont Avenue and Christchurch Avenue.

To provide space for later extension, the depot area was nearly doubled on 21 August 1907 when the MET purchased Harwood Villa and its one acre of grounds from A. J. Sherrott and others for £1,850. Harwood Villa was retained, and leased to tenants; it still stood at the time this was written. The extension was not built until some time after the Finchley—Golders Green route opened in December 1909; it was extended at the rear on to this land during 1912, at a cost of £1,692, and now had a frontage, but no access, to the Great North Road, the difference in level being too great. Part of the land was used as a permament way store.

In 1922 a garage was provided for a motor car at £177, and in 1928 Finchley depot was chosen for an experiment with vacuum cleaning plant, supplied for £900 by the Sturtevant Fan Company. Two roads were fitted with this equipment, adjacent to the 1928 car-washing plant, and used 15hp turbo-exhausters with four vacuum hoses to each road. These successfully replaced the old method of sweeping car floors and hand-brushing the seats, and similar equipment was installed a year later at the other four depots.

Substantial alterations were needed at Finchley depot in 1930 to house the new Feltham cars, and will be described in Volume Two.

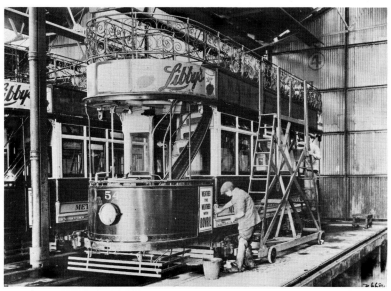

Washing cars by hand at Stonebridge Park Depot before the installation of high-pressure hoses in 1928. The rear walls of this and some other depots were in corrugated iron, to allow for possible extension.   (London Transport

187

Stonebridge Park Depot in 1906, with cars of Types A, C and D. In contrast to all other MET depots, the roads at Stonebridge Park were numbered from right to left.
(Tramway and Railway World

STONEBRIDGE PARK DEPOT

The first depot site acquired for the Middlesex Light Railways, though not the first to be built upon, was an eight acre site at Stonebridge Park in the Urban District of Wembley, situated on the Harrow Road between the Iron Bridge and the Stone Bridge and bounded at the rear by the River Brent. In this case the site was always county-owned, and the depot was built by the MET under the terms of the November 1900 agreement. The site was chosen for its suitability for a generating station, close to railway and river, but a change of MET policy meant that no generating station became necessary. A power station was however built on a nearby site in 1915 by the LNWR to supply its electric trains.

By early in 1906 it was clear that construction of the line between Harlesden and Stonebridge Park would be delayed. Completion of the depot had dropped behind schedule on account of winter flooding from the River Brent, though part of the building had been completed. It was opened on 10 October 1906 with the line from Harlesden to Stonebridge Park (Iron Bridge) and initially housed the 20 cars for this service. The building could accommodate 48 cars on twelve tracks in a covered area 140ft by 146ft, all tracks having pits. From the autumn of 1906 until about 1911 one of the Harrow Road horse cars was kept at Stonebridge Park depot to operate statutory journeys over the Chippenham Road branch described in Chapter Nine. Because of the different ownership of the lines served, the depot's costs were allocated five-eighths to the Harrow Road tramway and three-eighths to the MCC.

A large additional piece of land was bought in 1912 from the LNWR, almost doubling the area of the original site, the buildings and their environs occupying only a quarter of the land held, even after the depot was extended in 1912 at a cost of £1,692. Part of the extra land may have been intended for a bus garage but if so, this was not built. In the same year, the Local Government Board began planning what was to become the North Circular Road, and in the early 1920s the county council began work on this road at Stonebridge Park, appropriating part of the land bought in 1912 and leaving a piece isolated from the rest. As a result, some land was exchanged and the canal straightened.

Another early view of Stonebridge Park Depot. This one includes on the left the horse tram which was kept to use as a statutory car to retain the company's rights over the disused Chippenham Road branch.   (Courtesy D. W. K. Jones

A separate building was added in 1922 at a cost of £866 for a motor tower wagon, and two pieces of land to the rear of the depot were later leased away. The depot saw its busiest period in 1924 and 1925 when many extra cars were run to and from the Empire Exhibition at Wembley. Early in 1928 the River Brent overflowed after a rapid thaw and the depot was flooded, the pits being filled with water and the offices submerged. Trams were used as temporary offices until the water subsided.

Car washing equipment was installed in 1928, and vacuum cleaning gear in 1929.

HENDON DEPOT AND WORKS

On 15 May 1903 the MET board agreed to acquire from W. B. Fordham and others a 6½ acre site on the east side of the Edgware Road to the north of Annesley Avenue, in the part of West Hendon now known as Colindale. It was a roughly rectangular plot bounded on two sides by the Silk Stream. Two more acres were added in 1903, and the whole property was bought on 11 August 1903 for £4,462.

This site was intended for a car depot, repair works and motormen's school, and a £9,436 building contract was placed on 22 January 1904 with Holliday & Greenwood Ltd., with £3,930 authorised for equipment. First to be built was the car shed, holding 32 cars on eight tracks in a building 95ft by 144ft, the smallest of the five MET depots. The motormen's school was also built at this stage, and included a skeleton car and models. The depot was ready by November 1904, by which time cars 84-107 had been delivered and assembled there, entering service when the Cricklewood—Edgware route opened on 3 December. Cars 108-110 also started life at Hendon, but twelve cars (in two batches) soon migrated to Finchley.

The site had earlier been considered for a generating station, even though it was without railway access. Railway access would also be useful for the car works, and on 12 November 1903 the MCC committee recommended that a line should be built at an estimated cost of £1,987 from Edgware Road along Church Lane to the GNR sidings at Edgware station, for use by trams taking materials to the

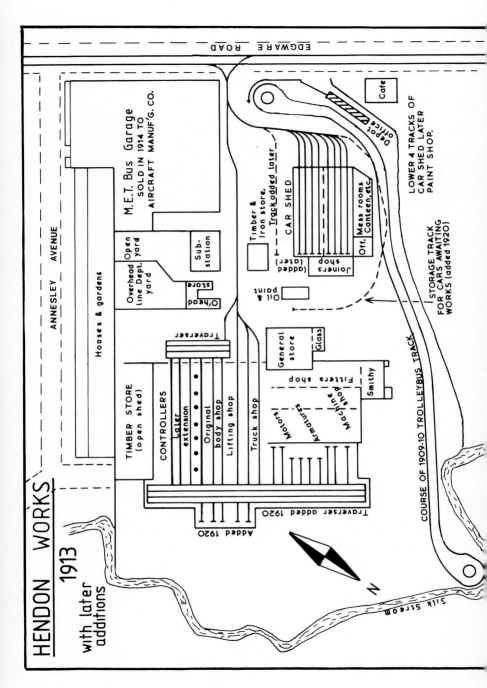

HENDON WORKS
1913
with later additions

EDGWARE ROAD

ANNESLEY AVENUE

Houses & gardens

M.E.T. Bus Garage
SOLD IN 1914 TO
AIRCRAFT MANUF'G. CO.

Open yard
Overhead Line Dept. yard

Sub-station

O/head store

TIMBER STORE
(open shed)

CONTROLLERS
Later extension
Original
body shop
Lifting shop
Truck shop

Traverser

Added 1920
Traverser Added 1920

General store
Glass

Fitters shop

Motors
Armatures
Machine shop
Smithy

Oil & paint

Timber & Iron store.
Track added later

CAR SHED

Joiners shop (added later)

Off. Mess rooms Canteen, etc.

Depot office

Cafe

LOWER 4 TRACKS OF CAR SHED LATER PAINT SHOP.

STORAGE TRACK FOR CARS AWAITING WORKS (added 1920)

COURSE OF 1909-10 TROLLEYBUS TRACK

Silk Stream

N

190

Hendon Depot in original state. Part of the car shed later became the paint shop of the tramcar overhaul works. (Courtesy London Transport

car works. The MET envisaged using either four wheel open trailers hauled by passenger cars, or special works trams. The Board of Trade agreed to the proposal in January 1905, with some limitation on the hours of use, but nothing more was done at this time, even though the car works would soon be ready for use.

The plan was revived in the MET's 1911 Bill, this time with alternatives. One application was for the line along Church Lane, Edgware (now Station Road) to the GNR goods yard, the other was for a similar branch from Edgware Road, Cricklewood south of Ashford Road into the goods yard and coal depot of the Midland Railway's Cricklewood station, with curves and crossovers allowing entry from either direction. The MET also asked the council to relax its weight limit on stores cars, which was considerably less than the weight of loaded passenger cars. The Cricklewood proposal was later withdrawn from the Bill, leaving only that at Edgware, which was sanctioned. However, due perhaps to the purchase of further road vehicles the line was not built.

For the same reason as at Finchley, the site of Hendon depot and works was sold to the Middlesex County Council on 4 December 1907, the price being £4,282.

During 1909, a U-shaped trolleybus "route" with turning circles at each end was built for demonstration purposes around Hendon depot, as described in Appendix Three. It was dismantled in 1911, and a part of its course was used in 1912 to extend the layout at a cost of £928. With the opening of the Golders Green—Cricklewood line in February 1910, cars from all parts of the MET system could reach Hendon works and all overhauls, repairs and repainting were carried out there, the repair shop and paint shop at Wood Green being closed down.

Since no generating station had been built at Hendon, and a proposal to relocate the MET head office there was not pursued, part of the site was still vacant and on 26 April 1912 this land was leased to the Tramways (M.E.T.) Omnibus Co. Ltd. for a bus garage, as described in Chapter Twelve. The subsequent arrangement with the LGOC meant that the garage would not be required and the last buses left on 13 March 1914. In April the garage was sold to the Aircraft Manufacturing Co Ltd.

As described in Chapter 13 on the wartime period, Hendon works from July 1915 to June 1919 maintained not only the MET tram fleet but also that of the London United Tramways, to enable the LUT repair works at Chiswick to be given over to munitions work. The cars were worked on at Hendon by LUT staff, for whom at least one daily special car was run. A daily staff car was also run for many years for the MET works staff, probably from Willesden Green or Cricklewood.

During the war, a huge backlog of car maintenance work had built up and the new MET manager, C. J. Spencer, asked the board in June 1919 for new equipment needed to speed up car overhauls. Purchases included electric hoists for raising car bodies, a 7 cwt. electric hammer, new metalworking and woodworking machines, and an additional wheel lathe, some equipment being bought second-hand.

The pooling of works resources between the MET and LUT during the war had proved effective and was resumed in 1926 as a permanent arrangement, extended also to the cars of the SMET, with some machines being transferred to Hendon from the LUT works at Chiswick. These and later developments will be described in Volume Two.

The entrance gates to Hendon Depot and Works bore heavy brass nameplates, which were common to all MET depots. The car shed is on the left and the extensive works buildings are to the rear. The buildings on the right became an aircraft factory in 1914. This view was taken in the mid-twenties. The gates were later re-used by Modern Electric Tramways Ltd. at Eastbourne.

(London Transport

MANOR HOUSE OFFICES

After the North Metropolitan Tramways Company took over the steam-operated lines of the North London Tramways Co., the formerly separate tracks were connected at the Manor House. In anticipation of retaining its Middlesex operations after the sale of its London lines to the LCC, the North Metropolitan company evidently decided to build a new depot, office and stables at this point and on 22 November 1898 took a lease from J. Swinyard of a site in Seven Sisters Road, with a separate rear entrance north of the Manor House hostelry on the corner. The premises could hold about 25 cars and 200 to 300 horses.

The property was included in the November 1902 sale to the MET and changed hands at £16,049, the price when compared with the £9,756 paid for Edmonton depot indicating that the Manor House premises were quite extensive. The building could not be used for electric cars because the tracks were in a semi-basement with low headroom, and at first it continued as traffic office and depot for the horse cars. After electric services began on 22 July 1904 Manor House depot became a permanent way, overhead and cable store, and it was here that the MET arranged a display of poles, overhead wires, feeder pillars and other items in the yard for the local authorities to inspect. The overhead department moved to Manor House from Wood Green, probably when space was required for further cars at Wood Green in 1906 or 1907.

When electric services commenced, the MET traffic office was located in two houses at 52 and 54 Lordship Lane, Wood Green which had been bought by the MCC for road-widening, and were let to the MET at £112 per year. By 1907 it had been decided to move back to the Manor House premises, and the building was altered in readiness. The front elevation was entirely altered, 32 windows being made in place of seven, terra-cotta stringers were put along the front elevation, and a front door and terra-cotta portico added. By 1910 the building was in full use by the traffic and engineering staff, including the engineering side of the NorthmeT power company. It also housed the MET's "in-house" building department, which was quite extensive and carried out most of the enlargements to depots, without the need to employ outside contractors. However, the rebuilding of the Manor House premises had been carried out by Holliday & Greenwood Ltd. under a contract of 30 November 1906, including reconstructing the depot siding for electric traction.

The siding was provided partly for the use of the engineer's department, but was later used also by two of the Alexandra Palace single deck cars when serving as ticket and punch vans, and to collect cash and ticket boxes from the depots, redistributing them to the depots afterwards. Motor vehicles were also used for this work but did not take over entirely until the later 1920s. New recruits to the MET service reported to the Manor House offices for their medical examination and to be measured for their uniform, to be issued from the clothing stores.

When the Hendon site was being laid out it was stated that the MET's administration would be based there, but this did not take place. A part of the premises was included briefly in the proposed sale of the boundary tramway to the LCC in 1912, but was soon withdrawn, perhaps because of the MET board's decision to become a bus operator with routes into central London. A fire occurred in the Manor House stores on 25 April 1919, but the offices were not affected thanks to the efforts of the local fire brigade assisted by members of the staff.

After the three company tramways had become subsidiaries of London & Suburban Traction in 1913 the new owners decided to bring together at the Manor House the headquarters of the three companies, MET, LUT and SMET. The correspondence with Acton UDC over the proposed tramway link at Horn Lane was conducted partly on London United notepaper bearing the Manor House address. This was in 1915, but shortly afterwards the management was transferred to Electric Railway House, Westminster. The day-to-day running of the three tramways remained at the Manor House until after the formation of London Transport.

WINCHMORE HILL DEPOT SITE

When the Middlesex Light Railways were planned, it was thought that there would be insufficient space at Wood Green depot to house the cars required for the Enfield route. The 1901 application included powers for an additional depot and generating station at Winchmore Hill, on a 4½ acre site bounded by Green Lanes, Green Dragon Lane and Salmon's Brook. The idea was revived in 1912 and the MCC allocated 5,333 square yards of county-owned land on the west corner of Bush Hill Park and Village Road, but the site was not built on, as the MET found it possible to accommodate the extra cars at Wood Green. The county sold the land to Edmonton UDC for £850 in 1925 for use as an open space.

TRENMAR GARDENS, COLLEGE PARK

In 1887 the Harrow Road and Paddington Tramways Company built a depot in Trenmar Gardens, College Park near the College Park Hotel, with a stables at the rear. The premises held a maximum of 21 cars and 157 horses (in 1901) and were purchased by the MET with the Harrow Road tramway in 1906. The depot was unsuitable for electric cars and was disposed of after the horse car service ceased, part becoming a cinema. The depot survives in industrial use and the manager's house was purchased by the LCC, sub-divided and leased to tenants.

ST. ANNS ROAD, SEVEN SISTERS ROAD

Prior to the opening of Wood Green Depot in 1895, the steam (later horse) trams used on the Wood Green route appear to have been kept at a small two-road depot in Kingsford Terrace, near St. Anns Road. The site was held on a lease granted by Thomas O'Hagan. The premises were vacated some time between 1895 and 1900.

PERMANENT WAY YARDS

Open yards for the storage of rail and paving materials were provided at Finchley, Stonebridge Park and Wood Green depots, and in the early years also at Manor House. In 1912 a piece of land in Southbury Road, Ponders End was rented to serve as a permanent way yard for the northern system, at a rental of £165 per annum. The site also had a frontage onto High Street, Ponders End, opposite Garfield Road, and had been acquired by the MCC about 1906 to facilitate road-widening. It was purchased by the MET from the MCC for £800 on 2 October 1916, re-conveyed to the MCC for the same sum on 2 November and thereafter rented to the Company for £32 per year. These yards did not have tramway sidings, as the work was carried out using Foden steam wagons.

REGISTERED OFFICE

The first registered office of the Metropolitan Electric Tramways Ltd. was at the BET headquarters at Donington House, Norfolk Street, London WC. It was transferred in 1902 to Evelyn House, 101 Finsbury Pavement, London EC, where directors and shareholders meetings were normally held. On 1 December 1908 the office was moved to the newly opened headquarters of the British Electrical Federation at 1 Kingsway, London WC.

On 18 May 1915 the registered office joined those of the "Combine" at Electric Railway House, Broadway, Westminster, London SW1. When some adjacent property was acquired it moved on 10 April 1924 to 55 Broadway, probably the best-known address of a transport headquarters in the world, but was moved again on 11 October 1926 to Broadway Buildings, Broadway, SW1 when site redevelopment began. All these were in reality offices in the same block of buildings, which were being rebuilt and extended.

The North Metropolitan Electric Power Supply Company shared the same offices as the MET until 1928, when the power company established its own head office at NorthmeT House, Cannon Hill, Southgate, London N.14.

CHAPTER SIXTEEN
NORTHMET POWER

When the Middlesex Light Railways were planned, it was proposed to build a separate generating station for each group of routes. The Hendon and Stonebridge Park depot sites were chosen for their suitability for generating stations, and other sites considered were at Finchley, Wood Green, Edmonton, Alexandra Park, Winchmore Hill and Friern Barnet. Most were in residential districts, and the district councils usually objected.

The British Electric Traction group, conversant with the rapid strides being made in ac transmission, saw an opportunity to serve the whole area from a central power station. On 19 January 1899 they registered the North Metropolitan Electrical Power Distribution Co. Ltd., and on 6 August 1900 obtained an Act incorporating the North Metropolitan Electric Power Supply Company. These companies between them obtained or purchased electric lighting orders for Hertford, Enfield, Barnet, St. Albans, Edmonton, Tottenham and Southgate, and later powers added Kingsbury, Friern Barnet, Chingford, Waltham Cross, Ware, Cheshunt, Harpenden, Hoddesden, Broxbourne, Hatfield, Harrow Weald and Stanmore. Their powers covered 325 square miles by 1906 and a further 250 miles were added by 1925.

The supply company acquired two sites for generating stations. The smaller one, which was developed first, was on the bank of the River Lee in Hertford near the GNR, and was opened on 20 November 1901. For the first few months it was operated by the Distribution company, who also had a small and short-lived (1900 to 1905) generating plant in Barnet. The larger 12.25-acre site, the freehold of which was owned by Trinity College, Cambridge, was alongside the River Lee Navigation at Brimsdown in the parish of Enfield. This was destined to become the large central station which supplied the power requirements of the MET and a large area of West Essex, South Hertfordshire and North Middlesex.

The first directors of the power supply company were Emile Garcke, W. L. Madgen, J. S. Raworth and R. P. Sellon, all well-known BET personalities. It was realised that substantial economies could be realised if the generating and distribution systems for traction, industrial and lighting power could be combined, and in the summer of 1902 the MET obtained the agreement of the MCC to this plan. Under the MET-MCC agreement of 16 November 1900, the MET was responsible for providing power for the light railways, and the method chosen was for the MET to buy the power supply company. The MET board approved the purchase on 2 October 1902, with prior BET approval, and the agreed price was £43,652 including £15,000 for Parliamentary powers and £13,552 for the power station in Hertford.

On 7 November 1902 BET chief engineer Stephen Sellon was appointed Consulting Engineer to the power supply company for Brimsdown. The directors decided to award the entire Brimsdown contract to the Brush Electrical Engineering Co. Ltd., another member of the BET group, on the understanding that Brush would, wherever possible, sub-let the electrical equipment to BTH with whom a prior agreement existed. Brush would also equip the substations at Edmonton, Wood Green and Finchley depots. On 24 October 1902 the directors accepted a report recommending the adoption of Parsons steam turbines.

Meanwhile, on 14 October 1902, Garcke, Barber and Pott had discussed the question of whether Brimsdown should burn coal or fuel oil. Babcock & Wilcox had quoted (via Brush) for six oil-fired boilers at £9,785, or coal-fired at £10,173. The Shell Trading and Transport Co. Ltd. had offered to supply 2,500 tons of oil (about six months' estimated supply) for testing purposes, and would offer two or three years' supply on the same terms. The MET offered Shell 28s. per ton, but in January 1903 Shell declined to accept a fixed price for more than nine months, and the MET board then decided that all boilers at Brimsdown should be coal fired, with automatic stokers. The proposal to use oil firing was very unusual at this early date, and until the late 1940s it was almost unknown for any British station to raise steam with oil except under duress, such as coal strikes.

Estimates for Brimsdown's other equipment were submitted to the board in December 1902. The structural steelwork and coal bunkers were awarded to Dorman, Long and Co. Ltd. and the building work to Clift Ford of Willesden, with a 125ft steel chimney by Piggott & Co. Ltd. and a landing dock by T. W. Pedrette. £20,300 was voted for Brush to supply and instal three Parsons steam turbines each coupled to 1,000 kW alternators made by Brown-Boveri of Baden, Switzerland, and one 2,000 kW vertical Curtis-BTH turbine and generator, though this did not come into use until 1906. Other equipment included four exciter sets (two of 50 kW and two of 100 kW) comprising Bellis & Morcom reciprocating steam engines coupled to BTH dynamos, three J. P. Hall compound feed-pumps delivering 4,000 gallons of water per hour, six Babcock & Wilcox automatic stokers, three Mirrlees-Watson condensers, steam piping by John Spencer Ltd., a storage tank by Piggott & Co., a BTH Pollak-type battery, and BTH high and low tension switchboards. The last of these contracts were awarded on 15 May 1903, and the station was expected to be ready in May 1904.

Brimsdown was to generate three-phase alternating current at 10,000V, 50 cycles, and distribute it to traction substations at Wood Green, Finchley and Edmonton depots, equipped with BTH rotary converters of 250 kW or 500 kW, plus transformers, meters and switchboards. BTH negative boosters were provided for the more remote sections, and Finchley and Wood Green each had an 800 ampere-hour battery. By 1922 there were some higher-output rotaries, two of 1,000 kW at Wood Green and one of 1,500 kW at Finchley. High tension cables on the first contracts were supplied and laid by British Insulated & Helsby Cable Co. Ltd., later ones mainly by Callenders.

When the northern MET lines opened, the traction substations at Wood Green and Edmonton depots were supplied from Brimsdown, but the mains did not yet reach to Finchley. Finchley UDC, who had earlier promoted their own tramway scheme with the aim of obtaining a traction load for their generating station, objected to the MET or NorthmeT laying cables in their area. They maintained their ban on public supply cables, but the NorthmeT applied to Parliament for authority to supply traction power for use outside its area, obtaining an Act in 1905. By this time work on the Highgate—Whetstone tramway was well in hand, and the MET decided to postpone the Brimsdown link until later and take a temporary supply from Finchley's generating station in Squires Lane, even though this meant spending £1,500 on a temporary low-tension main to Finchley depot. It was probably used for about three years.

A second generating station was planned to supply the western lines, and on 31 July 1902 the power supply company obtained an Act authorising a power station to the south of the Edgware Road, alongside the Midland Railway's Cricklewood curve. In addition to tramway and public supply, this would have provided power for a proposed tube railway from Cricklewood via Kilburn to Marble Arch, where it would connect with the Central London Railway. This North West London tube was authorised by an Act of 9 August 1899 and its powers although renewed in 1905 eventually lapsed. Its connection with the BET group is indicated by the fact that the tube company's chairman, Lord Vaux, was also chairman of Brush.

Three councils in the MET area, Finchley, Hornsey and Willesden, had obtained their own Electric Lighting Orders and were already building their own generating stations. When the North West London tube railway was deferred in 1903, the North Metropolitan Electric Power Supply Co. made an offer to buy

Brimsdown Power Station when new, showing the coal barges.

Willesden UDC's generating station at Taylor's Lane, Harlesden, which commenced supply on 24 June 1903. Terms were agreed, and after an Act had been obtained the NorthmeT took over the station for £72,649 on 8 February 1904, power being sold in bulk to Willesden UDC for distribution. A Brush 1,000 kW turbo-alternator was added to the plant to provide extra capacity for the traction load.

The Willesden station had been built to generate at 25 cycles per second, whereas Brimsdown was built to the (now) more commonly accepted 50 cycles. The MCC wished to have interchangeability of working from the Willesden and Brimsdown stations, which would have meant installing frequency converters and other plant at Willesden. In May 1903 the MET obtained advice from two prominent electrical engineers, Charles Merz and J. J. Steinitz, and decided that since the power was in any case rectified in substations to the standard tramway voltage, interchangeability on the ac side was not important.

In fact some years were to elapse before Brimsdown and Willesden were connected even through the traction supply, due in part to the opposition of Finchley UDC. The Hendon depot substation with its BTH rotaries was supplied initially from Taylors Lane, and a planned substation at Stonebridge Park was never built, for Taylors Lane was so well placed, just half a mile from the mid-point of the western MET lines at Craven Park, that it was decided to put the substation equipment in the power station and run 550V dc feeders direct from Taylors Lane to points along the Harrow Road and Willesden routes.

The traction substations were always owned by the North Metropolitan Electric Power Supply Company, but the low-tension mains (also laid by Callenders) from the substations to the section feeder boxes were owned by the MET. These were installed at about half-mile intervals along the MET and MCC routes, and were supplied by BTH and by R. W. Blackwell. Each box contained switch fuses, choke coils and lighting arresters for each section, plus test wire and telephone terminals. The MET shared a private telephone system with the NorthmeT; it was completed by contractor S. G. Smith in 1912. The two companies also shared directors, chief officers, and office premises.

The original feeder cables sufficed everywhere until 1911, when on 11 August the board authorised expenditure on additional low-tension mains in Tottenham, Wood Green and on the Great North Road. The latter was postponed until 1916, when the mains between North and East Finchley were replaced by new ones of double the capacity. Similar work became necessary on other heavily-trafficked sections, but early in 1920 the distribution system in the Finsbury Park area was so overloaded that at busy times the whole service was slowed down, with occasional breakdowns.

On 29 November 1913 a serious breakdown occurred at Taylors Lane generating station, and until 9 December the Harrow Road service was maintained by motor buses hired from the LGOC at 7½d per vehicle mile. The MET took the fares, but lost £130 on the operation. A much-reduced tram service was maintained on the other lines, probably by connecting the two feeder networks where they met at Cricklewood and thus using Brimsdown power on the Edgware Road and in Willesden, these sections being normally fed from Taylors Lane. The press reports do not indicate whether any trams ran to Acton.

This mishap probably drew attention to the fact that Brimsdown and Willesden were still not interconnected, and the connection was made in 1918, by which time some of Willesden's original equipment had been replaced by new sets generating at the standard 50 cycles. This new plant was the subject of widespread interest in the industry.

In 1912, the Brush company took up a manufacturing licence for the Swedish-designed Ljungström steam turbine which was more compact and economical than the other types then in use. The first example, a Swedish-made 1,000 kW unit, was used by Brush from 1912 as a pre-production model and was then installed at Taylors Lane early in 1914, where it attracted much attention. Generating at 3000 rev/min, it consumed on full load 25% less steam per kW than the older sets. It remained in service there until 1921 and was then transferred to Hertford. After

The North Metropolitan Electric Supply Company made extensive use of Brush-Ljungström turbo-generators, for which the Brush company held the British licence. These two 5,000 kW sets were phtographed at Brimsdown in 1923.   (The Electricity Council

Hertford ceased to generate in 1926, it was sold to Beckenham council who used it until their power station closed in 1960, after which it was returned to its Swedish makers for preservation. An early UK production model of the same general type (Brush-Ljungström turbine 691 of 1914) which was used at Loughborough power station from 1914 to 1960 is displayed outside the Leicester Museum of Technology. By 1924 Taylors Lane had two Brush-Ljungström sets of higher capacity, and four Brush-Ljungström sets were installed at Brimsdown, one of 3,000 kW in 1912, and one each of 5,000 kW in 1918, 1922 and 1925.

The Paddington extension of 1910 took the tramways for the first time outside the area of NorthmeT supply, and although the line was at first supplied through the 500v dc feeders from Taylors Lane, it became necessary in 1920 to arrange a supply from the Amberley Road substation of the Metropolitan Electric Supply Company near Lock Bridge. This company supplied the area south and west of the NorthmeT, including the borough of Paddington. Probably for administrative convenience, it was arranged that the NorthmeT should buy the power from the Metropolitan company (METESCO) and resell it at standard rate to the MET.

With this exception, the direct 550V dc supply from Taylors Lane to the Harrow Road line continued unchanged, and when planning for heavy traffic to the 1924 Wembley exhibition, the MET Board sanctioned new 550V feeder cables from Taylors Lane to Craven Park and Wembley. Meanwhile, a new substation was built at West Green Lane (South Grove) in Tottenham in readiness for the 1920 through running with the LCC via Stamford Hill. It contained two 500 kW BTH rotaries which may have been transferred from Wood Green to make room for 1,000 kW sets. The NorthmeT paid for the substation, and the MET laid the feeders, the MET share of the £25,000 cost being £9,207.

By 1924 the cost of coal transhipment from ship to barge and of lighterage on the River Lee Navigation had evidently become greater than the savings on sea freight from the northeast, and Brimsdown began to receive coal by rail at the sidings alongside the London—Cambridge main line, with a coal handling plant for transporting coal by the newly-developed method of air suction. Since there was an ample supply of steam from the power station, fireless locomotives were used as shunters. The first (No. 1) was an 0-6-0 (Andrew Barclay 1554 of 1917) bought from the Ministry of Munitions in 1924 and given the name SIR JAMES, for MET director Sir James Devonshire. A second similar locomotive, No. 2 (Andrew Barclay 1989 of 1930) was bought new and named LORD ASHFIELD, and both were still in daily use in 1968. Garcke's Manual for 1925 lists an electric locomotive, but there is no maker's record of any, either battery or overhead-wire, though there was a rail-mounted electric crane. Taylors Lane always received its coal by rail, the last two shunting locomotives being a steam one bought new in 1942 from Robert Stephenson & Hawthorns, and a 1930 battery locomotive transferred in 1963 from Luton.

To meet the demand resulting from the use of higher-powered motors in the trams, an additional rotary substation was commissioned at Llanvanor Road, Childs Hill in 1926. When mercury arc rectifiers became generally available, it became practicable to house these units in existing NorthmeT lighting substations, and this was done in 1930 at Kensal Rise and Enfield Wash (Elmshurst Road) to reinforce the tramway supply at those points. A similar step was probably taken at Barnet, for although an early MET map shows an intended traction substation at Barnet, that built by the NorthmeT was originally a lighting station only.

Brimsdown was one of the relatively efficient base-load generating stations selected by the Electricity Commissioners in the 1920s to supply the proposed national grid. Its original turbo-alternators had been entirely replaced by 1924, mostly paid for out of revenue, and the NorthmeT's area had been extended to include the rest of Hertfordshire. The separate North Metropolitan Electric Power Distribution Company was wound up under an Act of 1922 and its undertaking vested in the Supply company.

Fireless 0-4-0T *Sir James* (Andrew Barclay 1554 of 1927) was used by the NorthmeT at Brimsdown power station from 1924, and was named after MET director Sir James Devonshire. A second similar locomotive was bought in 1930 and named *Lord Ashfield*.   (J. H. Meredith

When the MET system opened in 1904, *The Tramway and Railway World* wrote that the NorthmeT could provide local councils with a bulk supply at low rates by means of the cables laid down for the tramways, and that electric light and power would thus be available as a cheap by-product of the traction scheme. Electric power had to be cheap if it was to compete with gas engines and steam coal, but the method used by the NorthmeT (and by many municipal undertakings) was to make the tram passengers subsidise the price of electricity. This was to be the cause of conflict with the MCC in later years.

The original agreement between the MCC, MET and NorthmeT was signed on 13 October 1903 and authorised the MET to buy all its power from the NorthmeT at a rate of 1.4 pence per unit for the first five million units per half-year, reducing by 0.04 pence per unit for each additional million units with a minimum price of 1d per unit for the total current used. A similar agreement was signed with Hertford-shire on 6 November 1903, but in their case the starting price was 1.5 pence per unit. In October 1904 the MCC had asked that power used on the Middlesex Light Railways be metered separately from that used on the MET tramways, but were told that this was impracticable and that power costs would be apportioned between MCC, MET and Hertfordshire on the basis of car miles worked.

The company clearly had some room for manoeuvre on power costs, for in 1911 the MET offered to reduce the unit charge to 0.8 pence if Middlesex would extend the company's lease from 1930 to 1946. However, no agreement resulted.

By 1915 things had changed and on 30 December 1915 the NorthmeT wrote to the MET asking for a revision of the power tariff because of increased coal prices, but no change was made at that time. By July 1919 wages had doubled since 1914 and coal had increased by 70% since 1915, and the NorthmeT proposed a new tariff with a fixed charge per quarter subject to a wage clause linked to the pay of substation attendants, and a price of 0.7 pence per unit subject to a coal clause with a mid-point of 30s. per ton. The MCC committee sought an independent opinion from J. H. Rider of Preece, Cardew, Snell and Rider, who found the company's request justified, and a new agreement including coal and wages clauses and a maximum demand charge came into force in July 1921.

The introduction of a maximum demand clause in the tariff made it desirable to check power consumption on the cars, and eight Arthur power recorders were bought for £59 in 1921, to indicate to motormen the power consumed by the car. Following trials the entire MET passenger fleet was equipped, costing £1,885, but their use was discontinued in 1925 because armature and magnetic brake defects had increased as a result of motormen's attempts to reduce current consumption. When the recorders were removed, armature and brake defects reverted to their 1921 level.

So long as the MET owned the power company, profits from high power charges came back to the MET in the form of dividend. The MET held 40,000 of the 40,002 NorthmeT shares, and this investment of £400,020 had yielded £281,750 in dividends between 1910 and 1917, the dividend for 1917 being 6%. No dividend was paid in 1918, possibly because of new plant being charged to revenue, but the position soon recovered, to 4½% in 1919, 7½% in 1920 and 10% in 1921-4. The NorthmeT dividend was of vital importance to the MET, since the financial position of the tramways was steadily deteriorating. Some shares were sold to London & Suburban Traction in 1926, but the MET's holding was still £387,707.

MET power costs in 1926 averaged 1.46 pence per unit, the tramway load (23¼ million units in 1925) being about one-fifth of NorthmeT's total output, though originally the proportion had been much higher. The MCC noticed, however, that power costs on the MET in 1925 were 2.659 pence per car mile, against 1.579 pence on the LCC and only 1.401 pence in Glasgow. Of the ten largest tramways, only Liverpool at 2.761 pence paid more than the MET for its power, and this was eventually reduced. Challenged by Middlesex, Emile Garcke said that no two power companies were alike and the comparison was therefore unreasonable.

In 1927 the MET was in arrears with its rent to the county, and the MCC asked that the shares in the power company should be lodged with the county council as security for the rent due. Emile Garcke explained that since the MET itself had no physical assets, its holding in the power company was almost all pledged as security for the debenture holders. The issue became embroiled in negotiations for a new lease, but a result was that the average price per unit, already reduced to 1.20 pence per unit in 1927, was further reduced to 0.8197 pence per unit from 1 January 1928, facilitated by the commissioning of more efficient generating plant.

The size of the 1927-28 tariff reductions shows that there was some truth in the county council's view of the power charges, and their committee chairman said in 1926 that it now appeared to him that building up the profitable power company based on the monopoly concession granted by the county council may have been the real objective of the BET group when the Middlesex lease was obtained. Two years later, the BET sold its interest in the MET and in London and Suburban Traction to the Underground group, and on 6 November 1930 the MET board voted to sell all its shares in the power company (then valued at £351,820) to the UERL, who were planning to use Brimsdown power for the tube railway extension to Cockfosters. Part of the proceeds were invested in government securities on behalf of the debenture holders, and the rest was used to help buy the Feltham cars.

The NorthmeT company developed further in the late 1920s and the 1930s, building up domestic and industrial sales and opening up new areas. Around Brimsdown itself, further industries were attracted by the offers of cheap electricity and steam from the power station, and this may well have been a factor in the siting of the Edison Swan lamp factory at Ponders End in 1906 and the Enfield Cable Works in 1914. A second generating station (Brimsdown B) was built in 1926-28, with a first-stage capacity of 50,000 kW against the 28,750 kW of Brimsdown A and the 39,500 kW of Willesden. A further 50,000 kW became available from Brimsdown B in 1932, after which Brimsdown A was closed in 1935-37 for modernisation. Brimsdown B was a thoroughly modern station, burning pulverised coal and generating at 33,000v.

During 1928, the company's headquarters were moved from the UERL offices in Westminster to a former mansion near Arnos Grove which became known as NorthmeT House. There was great rivalry between NorthmeT's chief engineer, Captain J. M. Donaldson, and his opposite number in the London Power Company to instal the most up-to-date equipment, and the NorthmeT were pioneers in the use of the frequency master clock system (for electric clocks), 5-core distribution cables (for centralised public lighting switching), outdoor ironclad switchgear, and in the use (from 1922) of the 24-hour clock. The 1930s saw a forthright commercial policy, with an increase from 12 to 40 showrooms (plus mobile units) and a vast increase in the hire purchase business (mainly cookers) forming 50% of equipment sales. The traction load, which had been 50% in 1914, was still 9.5% in 1945 (one-third trolleybus, two thirds tube railways). Brimsdown A and Willesden remained in operation until closed down by the CEGB in December 1971 and March 1972 respectively, and Brimsdown B closed in March 1976.

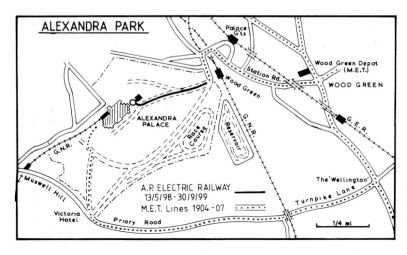

Appendix 1

The Alexandra Park Electric Railway

On 27 May 1898, Hugh Godfray, solicitor to the Metropolitan Tramways and Omnibus Company attended a meeting of Wood Green council to ask their support for his company's light railway scheme. He extolled the virtues of the overhead trolley system, and quoted examples from the USA and from Coventry, Douglas Head, Douglas and Laxey, Dover, Dublin, Bristol, Walsall, Leeds and Hartlepool. He failed to tell them that they could sample the system just half a mile away in Alexandra Park, presumably because he did not know about it.

This interesting little line, just under half a mile in length, was constructed and operated by the Elektrizitäts-gesellschaft Wandruszka of Berlin, who were general agents in Europe of the Steel Motor Company and the Johnson Steel Rail Company, both of Lorain, Ohio, USA. Victor Wandruszka was a Hungarian engineer who joined the Compagnie Francaise Thomson-Houston in 1893; his appointment as agent of the two American concerns followed a visit to America in 1897, and the Alexandra Park tramway is described in an American account as primarily a demonstration line for their products. They may have borne part of the construction costs, but no evidence of this is known.

The consulting engineers were Messrs Taylor & Field, and construction of the 660 yards of line commenced in February, 1898. There were considerable gradients, the average being 1 in 13, with a short section as steep as 1 in 9.75, and the continuous rise from the Park gates to the east entrance to the Palace amounted to 130 feet. The line was standard gauge, the 60 ft. grooved rails of 85 lb/yd being spiked to wooden sleepers. The original intention was for a single track, but before construction commenced it was decided to build a double track, the final cost being £11,000. The tracks were only 3 ft. apart, too close together for operating open-sided cars; a trailing crossover was laid in at the lower terminus and there was a 90 ft. radius turning loop at the Palace end. The loop was the only section of level track, the overhead line here being of span-wire construction, whilst the overhead on the remainder of the line was carried by centre poles, of German manufacture. A shed holding four cars was built at the upper terminus facing the Palace, with a generating station to the rear; this was a corrugated iron structure.

The generating equipment which, like the tracks, had been doubled in capacity before construction commenced, was of British manufacture. There were two 140 lb multi-tubular boilers by Ransomes, Sims & Jefferies, which supplied two 30 hp compound engines by the same maker, each coupled to a Johnson & Phillips four-pole compound-wound dynamo capable of producing 140 amp. at 550 volts and 600 rev/min. One engine and dynamo sufficed for normal operation, but the two sets could be used together in parallel when required. A fully loaded car with fifty seated and fourteen standing passengers required a current of 37 amp. at 510 volts to climb the hill.

The new tramway, known as the Alexandra Park Electric Railway, was included as one of the attractions in the announcement of the reopening of the Palace on 8 April 1898, but the work was not completed on time, and the line did not open until the ominous day of Friday 13 May 1898.

The four single-deck semi-open electric cars, built by Waggonfabrik Falkenried of Hamburg seated fifty passengers, thirty on six full-width cross benches and the remainder in a central unglazed saloon. The car sides were at first open above the waistline, but later wire mesh was fitted along the sides owing to the limited

The four cars of the 1898-99 Alexandra Park Electric Railway were built at the Falkenried tramway workshops in Hamburg, Germany, where this 1898 photograph was taken.

(Hamburger Hochbahn AG, courtesy J. H. Price.

clearance between the cars and the traction poles. Warning notices respecting the danger from the poles were displayed in the cars. A footboard was fitted on each side of the cars and there were full-width glazed bulkheads at each end. Roofboards reading 'Alexandra Park Electric Railway' were fitted. The livery is uncertain, but was probably dark green.

The wheelbase of the cars was 6 ft., and there was no separately-constructed truck, the running gear being integral with the main structure of the car. Each car was fitted with two 25 h.p. motors of the Steel Motor Company's type 22; the controller was also of American make, the Johnson 20-22 design. Current collection was by a single trolley-pole and braking was by hand, and owing to the steep gradients the cast-iron brake shoes required renewal every four weeks. Cars on the descent were found to be liable to skid on wet rails and following a collision on 30 May 1898 involving a fully laden car operation was generally suspended in wet weather. Three persons were injured in this accident and were awarded damages against the proprietors, but as the status of the line was that of miniature railways operated in fairgrounds it was outside the jurisdiction of the Board of Trade and therefore does not figure in the Board's records. Accounts of this accident reveal that the manager of the tramway was Mr. Robert Wray.

The dangerous spacing of the centre poles in the 3 ft. space between the tracks took its toll on 17 June 1898 when Mark Steinhaus, a fitter engaged in Berlin by Wandruszka, struck his head on one of the poles when attempting to alight from the off-side of a moving car, receiving injuries from which he died in hospital three days later.

There were no further incidents in the tramway's first season; from the opening in May until the closing firework display on 5 November some 172,000 passengers were carried, an average of 1,142 per day. For the first part of the season takings averaged £12 5s. per day, fares being twopence for the uphill journey and a penny down. There were some unfavourable comments in the local press on these fares; a comparison was made with the pennyworth from the Archway Tavern to the top of Highgate Hill and the twopenny ride of "one mile and a quarter and seven yards" along Southend Pier. It was suggested that a uniform 1d each way would attract more riders on the majority of days when no big events were taking place at the Palace.

These criticisms notwithstanding, the fares remained unchanged during the first season of operation; each car carried a conductor, who collected fares and issued Bell-Punch tickets, usually as passengers boarded. Monthly season tickets at 2s. 6d.

were issued to Palace staff. The opening hours of the Palace and Park, which applied also to the tramway, were 10 a.m. to 10.30 p.m. on Monday to Friday and 10 a.m. to 11 p.m. on Saturday, the Palace and park being closed on Sundays. Two cars normally sufficed in service, but at busy times such as on Bank Holidays all four would be in use, providing a maximum possible service of a car every three minutes, the round trip including loading and unloading taking twelve minutes for each car, there being no intermediate stops.

Details of the financial relations between Thomas Hawkins, lessee of the Palace and park, and Wandruszka are not known, but it is clear that the latter was mainly a manufacturer's agent and considered the line as a demonstration line for his principals' equipment; he did not wish to continue indefinitely in the role of operator. This was the source of some difference of opinion between the two parties in October 1898 but a new agreement appears to have been negotiated under which Hawkins paid Wandruszka a further £3,000 and the latter continued to work the line for a further season.

The Palace reopened for a week at Christmas and then closed again until the start of the 1899 season on 31 March. The tramway fare was now reduced to 1d in either direction and the line worked throughout the spring and summer of 1899, this time without any reported accident. Admissions to the Palace were markedly fewer than in 1898, with bad weather and lack of attractions being given as the cause. The Palace, and the tramway, closed for the winter on 30 September 1899 (five weeks earlier than in 1898), and although Hawkins intended to reopen in 1900 the tramway never ran again.

The 1899 season had been a financial disaster with receipts insufficient to cover outgoings, including rent and rates, and following pressure from creditors Hawkins filed a petition in bankruptcy. His public examination commenced at Edmonton Bankruptcy Court on 18 December 1899, and reports of this provide the main source of information on his affairs.

The tramway and its equipment were sold during the autumn of 1899. Wood Green UDC, a creditor for rates had obtained possession of it, and disposed of the cars to the Great Grimsby Street Tramways Co. Ltd., a Provincial Tramways subsidiary. The Grimsby company converted the cars to double-deckers, three with open tops and the fourth top-covered, and later they were mounted on Brill 21E trucks, continuing in service at Grimsby until about 1925.

The Alexandra Park Electric Railway, although little-known, has an important place in the history of electric tramways in London. With the exception of some battery-operated cars on horse tramways and a short-lived experiment at Northfleet, the first electric tramway to operate on public roads was that of the London United Tramways from Shepherds Bush to Acton and Kew Bridge and from Hammersmith to Kew Bridge, opened on 4 April 1901. The Alexandra Park line pre-dated this by three years, and although situated on private land must be regarded as the first true electric tramway in the London area. The course it followed was the same as that of the 1906 MET/MCC line to Alexandra Palace East.

This account is based, with permission, on the notes of a lecture by J. H. Price to the London area of the Light Railway Transport League on 10 March 1955, which later appeared in shortened form in the *Journal of Transport History* for November 1958.

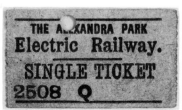

Appendix 2

Highgate Hill

The Highgate Hill Tramways Company, successors to the Steep Grade Tramways and Works Co. Ltd., of 1881, operated a 3 ft. 6 in. gauge cable-worked tramway between the Archway Tavern and Highgate Hill, a distance of three-quarters of a mile with a maximum gradient of 1 in 11. The line opened on 29 May 1884, but a serious accident on 5 December 1892 led to its closure until 19 April 1897 when it reopened under new management, being worked by four bogie cable cars and two sets consisting of a four-wheel dummy and four-wheel trailer.

On 14 November 1884, the Steep Grade Tramways and Works Co. Ltd. announced their intention to apply to Parliament for powers to extend the line by no less than 6.5 miles, from Highgate Village down North Hill to reach the Great North Road at The Wellington and continue through East Finchley, North Finchley, Whetstone and New Barnet to High Street, Chipping Barnet. Powers would be sought for cable, animal and mechanical traction, but the scheme was soon abandoned.

By 1906 the Highgate Hill company was in financial difficulties and its property was mortgaged for £2,100 to a trustee, James McDonald Garland. Since cable traction was unprofitable, the owners applied in May 1906 to the Light Railway Commissioners for powers to rebuild it as a standard gauge electric tramway and extend it from Highgate Village along High Street, North Road and North Hill to join the MCC/MET line in the Great North Road at The Wellington. This would bring the total length to 1.5 miles, of which the extension and a short piece of the existing line were in Middlesex. The MCC decided to oppose the scheme, and the cable company withdrew their application and decided to proceed by way of a Parliamentary Bill, seeking a new 25-year tenure.

In 1907 the LCC offered to buy the line for £13,000, to convert to electric traction, but opposition from Middlesex and Hornsey caused this to be deferred. 1,209 ft. of single track at the Highgate Village terminus were in Middlesex, and the MCC in April 1908 took up its right of purchase, granted under the Middlesex County Council Act 1902 and subject to Hornsey's consent. The LCC also wished to buy the entire cable tramway, but Middlesex were not prepared to agree to the LCC buying the section in Hornsey. A compromise was reached in May 1909 under which Middlesex would buy the part in its area after reconstruction by the LCC, and would lease it back to the LCC for thirty years. This was done, and the last cable car ran on 23 August 1909 and the first LCC electric car ran on 25 March 1910.

The LCC paid £13,099 to buy the cable tramway and £23,687 to reconstruct it for electric (conduit) operation. On a mileage basis the MCC's share would have been £6,084, but the LCC also asked Middlesex to pay the cost of some alterations to road levels in its area, and the final purchase price agreed in January 1912 was £6,377, the rent to the LCC being £357 per year. This small piece of line appears to have generated quite strong feelings, but the County of Middlesex had lost large areas to the LCC in 1889, and wished to maintain the principle that the two counties should keep to their respective territories.

Appendix 3

Trolleybuses

On 25 September 1909, at its Hendon depot, the MET demonstrated the first trolleybus to be built in Britain. So far as is known, it never ran on the public highway in the London area, but it carried a route board reading "Golders Green Station—The Burroughs—Hendon". This route had previously been proposed more than once as a light railway, so we must first explain why this was not built.

On 23 October 1897, the Finchley District Electric Traction Co. Ltd. (mentioned in Chapter 2) applied for a light railway from Golders Green Cross

Roads via Golders Green Road, Brent Street, Church Road, The Burroughs and Station Road to Hendon station, with an alternative line along Brampton Grove. An inquiry was held in March 1898, and the application failed. A similar application by the MTOC in November 1898 was equally unsuccessful; this had also included a direct line from Hendon to Finchley along Finchley Lane and Hendon Lane.

In May 1902 the MCC applied for a similar line from Golders Green crossroads along North End Road (now Golders Green Road), Brent Street and Brampton Grove to a point near Hendon Town Hall, then along The Burroughs and Station Road to join the proposed Edgware Road line. The inquiry was held on 20 October, and the main opposition came from residents in Golders Green Road and All Souls College which owned the Brampton Grove estate. Those opposing held that the proposed Edgware and Hampstead Railway, whose Bill had passed its third reading in Parliament on 16 October, would be capable of handling all the traffic in the district. Its engineer told the Light Railway Commissioners that the railway would be built "at the earliest possible moment" and for this reason the Commissioners rejected the light railway application as unnecessary.

In the event the tube trains did not reach Golders Green until 22 June 1907 and the terminus remained there until 1923. To develop traffic to Hendon, the railway company put on a bus service on 28 July 1907 between Golders Green and The Bell at Hendon, using two motor buses and drivers supplied by Birch Brothers, but with railway employees as conductors, and through road-rail tickets. The motor buses proved unreliable and were soon replaced by horse buses.

Railless electric vehicles offered the chance of a more reliable service, but it would first be necessary to conduct a trial, since at that time this form of transport had not been adopted anywhere in Britain. It would be unwise to promote a light railway again, since the eventual opening of the planned tube railway extension would capture its traffic. This objection would not apply to railless electric traction (trolleybuses) whose equipment could if necessary be dismantled and re-used elsewhere. The MET board also felt that there was a better chance of obtaining powers for a railless service from Canons Park terminus to the Hertfordshire boundary than obtaining light railway powers.

James Devonshire had visited some European trolley vehicle undertakings and early in 1909 the MET board had agreed to the Railless Electric Traction Co. Ltd. demonstrating its system within the limits of Hendon depot and works. A roadway with twin overhead was prepared, and the Railless company supplied a demonstration vehicle. This had been built by G. C. Milnes, Voss & Co. of Birkenhead and tested with a trailing skate on the Birkenhead tramways. It had chain drive to the rear wheels, two BTH 25 h.p. motors, and an ordinary BTH B18 tram controller mounted horizontally below the driver's seat and operated by his left hand. The single-deck body had seats for 22, and was painted in the standard MET red and white livery, with fleet number 1. The twin trolley poles (mounted one above the other) supported a single large trolley head resembling a small bogie truck with four wheels, two for each wire (patent 1077 of 1909) but this idea was not repeated.

The trolleybus was demonstrated on 25 and 29 September 1909 to members of the Municipal Tramways Association during their annual conference, and on 19 October to the Middlesex County Council Light Railways and Tramways Committee. The MET company then commenced negotiations with Hendon UDC for a proposed Railless service between Golders Green Station and West Hendon Broadway, the equipment to be installed by the North Metropolitan Electric Power Supply Company. These negotiations became protracted, as the Council wanted the power supply company to contribute towards upkeep of roads, and shopkeepers in Church Road had petitioned for the route to go along Church Road instead of Brampton Grove.

James Devonshire, A. H. Pott and A. L. Barber of the MET met Hendon UDC Works Committee in January 1911 and undertook to provide a ten-minute service and to remove the installation at the end of the three years if the council felt it to be unsatisfactory. The Council met on 13 February 1911 and agreed to a

The Railless Electric Traction demonstrator trolleybus at Hendon Depot in 1909. The 24-seat vehicle was built for the Railless company by G. C. Milnes, Voss & Co., with BTH equipment.
(Courtesy London Transport)

three-year trial, subject to a satisfactory agreement with the MET. The Clerk submitted a draft agreement with the Power Supply Company to the full Council on 6 March, and after some revision was instructed to send it to the power company. The MET records make no further mention of it, and it was not discussed again by the Council, but it appears likely that the Council had inserted conditions that were not acceptable to the companies.

As to what these conditions were, we can hazard a guess. There was as yet no specific legislation for trolleybuses, and it is possible that the BET, who were watching developments closely, had told the MET not to agree to make any contribution to road maintenance lest this be taken as a precedent. Many other railless schemes were being proposed, and this point was often in dispute until a House of Commons Select Committee when considering the Keighley Bill ruled in 1912 that trackless trolley vehicles should not be penalised in this way. By then it was too late, for on 30 March 1911 the London General Omnibus Company had begun to operate a service between Golders Green and Hendon with its new B type motor buses.

Proof that the Hendon trials were sponsored by the MET rather than by the Railless company is afforded by the expenditure incurred. The overhead, roadway, stores and wages were all paid for by the MET, the overhead alone costing £562, this being erected by Sidney G. Smith who had left MET service in 1908 and gone into business as a contractor. The Railless bus was borrowed without charge, but the MET incurred total costs (to 1911) of £1,173, some of which was recouped in that year when the overhead was dismantled. Part of the roadway was incorporated into a new access road to the various shops of the works.

The MET were still interested in the Railless system, for early in 1913 they promoted the M.E.T. Railless Traction Bill that would give them powers for a route from Wood Green tramway depot along Green Lanes, West Green Road, across High Road Tottenham and then along Broad Lane and Ferry Lane to terminate at the Essex/Middlesex county boundary. This covered the Tottenham—Walthamstow link for which Light Railway powers had been obtained in 1906 (see Chapter Five). The portion from Wood Green to Turnpike Lane would be used for depot access only.

The attraction of this idea to the MET was that it would use the planned new bridge across the River Lee, of which the MET were committed to pay half the cost under the terms of their 1911 Act, while at the same time rendering less necessary the expensive road widenings in Tottenham Hale which would be essential in order to build a light railway. The Bill became law on 15 August 1913 as the Metropolitan Electric Tramways (Railless Traction) Act.

This Act provided for widenings in Broad Lane and Ferry Lane, and for wood block paving and Plascom surfacing on the roads. No service was to be worked to within 100 yards of the bridge across the Lee Navigation until this was widened to 42 ft. Middlesex County Council had the right to purchase the line as a going concern every seven years from 1931 if they paid the widening and bridge costs, and could then grant a lease.

Owing to the war, the railless service did not materialise, though the bridge was opened on 30 March 1915 and the MET bought a portion of the roadway leading to the old bridge to serve as a trolleybus terminus. The MET kept the powers alive in their Act of July 1916, extending the powers in the 1913 Act to three years after the end of the war. A further five-year extension was sought in 1920, but was not granted because the MCC were now planning to build the line as a light railway, as recounted in Chapter Five.

Previous researchers into British trolleybus history have expressed doubts about the Golders Green-Hendon railless project because of the lack of reference to it in MET board minutes. The explanation is to be found in the close control exercised by the MCC over MET capital expenditure, all items in excess of £100 having to be referred to the MCC committee for approval. To avoid the delays that this would cause, the BET arranged for the planning and negotiations to be carried out by the North Metropolitan Electric Power Supply Company, with whom the MET was associated.

Appendix 4

Watford & District Tramways

Although the town of Watford in Hertfordshire lies well clear of the London conurbation, it was the subject of tramway proposals which would have been linked with the Metropolitan Electric system if certain other lines had been built, and must therefore be included.

At the turn of the century there was something of a "tramway mania" in Britain as rival groups of promoters sought to obtain tramway concessions for those urban areas not already provided with tramways. One such group was Pritchard, Green & Co. of 37 Waterloo Street, Birmingham, a partnership of consulting engineers Edward Pritchard and Robert Green, who were involved in many tramway and electric supply schemes. Their financial backers included contractor John Fell, Samuel Hunter and Walter James Kershaw, who in 1901 became the first directors of the Watford & District Tramways Company.

In November 1900, this group deposited a Bill in Parliament for 8.8 miles of tramway in and around Watford. From St. Albans Road in the town centre, lines were projected northwards to Bushey Mill Lane, Garston: southeastwards beyond Bushey Arches through High Street, Bushey to the Hertfordshire-Middlesex county boundary at Bushey Heath; and south-westwards to Church Street, Rickmansworth, all single line and passing loops. A depot and generating station would be built on the south side of Chalk Hill near Bushey Arches, adjoining Villiers Road

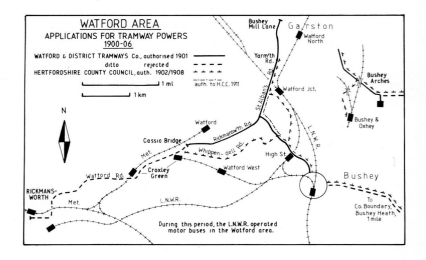

Watford UDC gave their consent to the lines in their district, but Watford Rural District Council and Bushey Rural District Council would not. The lines in their districts were struck out, and so the company withdrew the line in Rickmansworth, which would have been isolated. This left the line from Garston through the town to Bushey Arches and a branch from the town centre to Cassio Bridge, and these were authorised in the Watford and District Tramways Act of 17 August 1901.

The company realised that the truncated system they were left with was hardly likely to be a financial success, and decided to re-apply for the powers denied to them by Parliament, this time using the Light Railways Act. In September they made a fresh attempt to gain the consent of the neighbouring councils, with some success, though Watford Rural District Council still opposed. Two short sections were approved and authorised by the Board of Trade on 31 December 1903, but the rest was rejected.

The time taken to obtain the Light Railway powers meant that the Company's powers under their 1901 Act had to be renewed if construction had not commenced by August 1904. Insufficient capital had been raised to allow work to start, and accordingly the company applied to Parliament at the end of 1903 for an Act to extend the time. Detailed plans had been deposited with Watford UDC, and the company was ready to place contracts. Extensions of time were usually granted in such cases, but for some reason the House of Lords threw out their Bill and the company were left with only their Light Railway extensions, which were of course useless.

The promoters came to the conclusion that there was nothing further to be done, and by October 1904 the company had been voluntarily wound up. It is thought that the British Electric Traction Group had been prepared to back the scheme financially, but this is unconfirmed.

A full account of the Watford & District scheme by Jonathan P. Neale appeared in Journal No. 8, of the Watford and District Industrial History Society, published in 1978.

Appendix 5

The Hertfordshire Light Railways

During 1899 the Highways Committee of Hertfordshire County Council appointed a Light Railways Sub-Committee under the chairmanship of Arthur L. Stride to report on whether the county should follow Middlesex in promoting light railways. Its report of 29 September 1899 advocated this course and recommended that the lines should be leased to the MTOC on similar terms to those planned in Middlesex.

On 5 October 1899 MTOC consulting engineer V. B. D. Cooper told the HCC that his company was willing to operate county-owned light railways in Hertfordshire on a 42-year lease. He sent a map showing possible lines from Great Stanmore through Bushey to Watford, Garston and St. Albans with a branch to Rickmansworth, from Whetstone to High Barnet, and from Freezywater through Waltham Cross, Cheshunt, Broxbourne, Hoddesdon and Ware to Hertford, with an alternative route from Hoddesdon through Haileybury to Hertford. The map also showed the North Metropolitan and MCC lines of which these would form extensions. The Hertford proposals were probably influenced by the fact that the BET-owned NorthmeT power company was planning to build a generating station there.

Hertfordshire County Council on 23 October 1899 decided to go ahead with those sections for which they saw an existing need, and in November 1899 applied jointly with the MTOC for light railway powers from Great Stanmore to Watford and Rickmansworth, Whetstone to Barnet, Freezywater to Cheshunt and Hemel Hempstead to Kings Langley. The intended branch to St. Albans was not applied for, and it was felt that there was nothing to gain by continuing north of Cheshunt. Parts of the Stanmore and Whetstone lines would be in Middlesex.

Since none of the Middlesex applications had yet been granted, these applications were somewhat premature, and the only one to be approved (after an inquiry on 29 March 1900 at Cheshunt) was the section from Freezywater to the Cheshunt UDC boundary at Wormley (3½ miles), the continuation to Hoddesdon having been withdrawn. The Watford lines were rejected at an inquiry on 16 March 1900, and the rest withdrawn.

By mid-1901 the situation in Middlesex had become clearer and Hertfordshire decided to apply again, this time alone, for the lines in Barnet and Watford. The line from the county boundary to Barnet Church was approved at an inquiry on 29 and 31 January 1902, the portion in Middlesex having been transferred to the MCC, but the inquiry into the Watford lines was adjourned to March 1902. Meanwhile, the MTOC had agreed to sell its interest in the Cheshunt line to the county.

The position in Watford was complicated by the formation in 1901 of the Watford and District Tramways Company, whose 1901 Act empowered it to build a tramway from Bushey Arches to Garston with a branch to Cassio Bridge. The company's Act had given the HCC running powers over the company lines in Watford, and so the HCC application was now for a line from the county boundary at Bushey Heath to the company's terminus at Bushey Arches, with a branch to Bushey station.

The Watford company had submitted a rival application in November 1901 for light railway powers to Bushey Heath and Rickmansworth, the latter using a different route from that rejected previously, and the Light Railway Commissioners had to choose between the two proposals. Watford and Bushey RDC's both preferred the county scheme, because the county proposed to spend more on road improvements, and while the company obtained a short extension in North Watford, and part of a line to Rickmansworth, its Bushey application was rejected in favour of the county line, which was approved in March 1902.

As explained in Appendix 4, the Watford company's powers for the main part of its proposed tramway system expired in 1904 and were not renewed, perhaps because Hertfordshire were still interested in building the line themselves. The HCC

Only two cars bearing the Hertfordshire lettering remained by the early 1920s, Nos. 207 and 208. No. 208 stands at Barnet Church in 1921, ready to return to Tottenham Court Road.

(Courtesy A. G. Forsyth

applied for the Watford lines in 1906, and were authorised on 21 August 1908 to build from Bushey Arches along High Street, Queens Road, Woodford Road, Station Road and St. Albans Road to a terminus near Yarmouth Road, plus a branch to Bushey station.

Discussions on the county council's proposals in Bushey and Watford continued, but with the decisive rejection of its connecting line through Stanmore the MET was now less interested in Watford. In 1910 the HCC and MET proposed a Railless service from Edgware to Watford, but Watford UDC and the Watford Tradesmen's Association still wanted a tramway. The county obtained a quotation from Dick, Kerr & Co. Ltd. early in 1911 to build a line from St. Albans Road at Yarmouth Road through the town to the depot site in London Road, at a cost of £31,478, with a deviation authorised by the Board of Trade on 25 May 1911, and an extension of the earlier powers to 21 August 1913. However, on 13 January 1913 the county decided to take no further action, and an Abandonment Order was obtained on 11 February 1914. The MET had objected to the high cost of street-widenings and would only agree to a more modest scheme, but Watford UDC had refused to modify its demands.

Reverting now to 1904, the county's Barnet line was authorised by the Board of Trade on 26 February and terms were agreed with the MET for operating it. Under this agreement (signed on 9 June 1905) the county would grant the MET a 42-year lease at a rent of 4½% per year of the county's capital outlay and a share of revenue in excess of that which enabled the MET to declare a dividend of 6½%, with allowances for the company's own expenditure similar to those agreed between the MET and Middlesex. Power would be supplied by the North Metropolitan Electric Power Supply Company on the same terms as in Middlesex.

The Barnet line was built by Dick, Kerr & Co. Ltd. for £21,652 and opened on 28 March 1907, by which time county council was in dispute with Cheshunt UDC over the Wormley line. Cheshunt demanded a 50ft widening at Eleanor Cross, involving some very expensive property, and on 25 March 1907 Hertfordshire decided to cut the line back to end eighty yards south of this point. The contract was placed with Dick, Kerr & Co. Ltd. at £4,176 and the line to Waltham Cross terminus opened on 17 April 1908. No further construction was carried out in Hertfordshire.

Hertfordshire received a modest profit from its 1.50 miles of light railways, in addition to the fixed annual rent of £1,987, and in 1913 received £19,762 as the MET's share of the county's costs in obtaining powers for Bushey and Watford. The county's Light Railways Committee met for the last time on 23 March 1914 and the county council tacitly agreed to interfere as little as possible in the running of their lines. The only subsequent references in their minutes concern the Common Pool and the formation of the LPTB.

In 1907 five Type C cars (almost certainly Nos. 159-163) were allocated to (and lettered) Hertfordshire County Council. In December 1909 this was reduced to four cars at the county's request, and later there were only two, Type C/1 cars 207 and 208. This would have been the minimum number to enable Hertfordshire to retain a presence on each line, but the minutes do not reveal whether this was a requirement.

Appendix 6

No Trams to Harrow

The public inquiry into proposals by a government department or statutory undertaking is part of the democratic process in Britain. Today the inquiries which generate most controversy are those into the siting of airports or the building of motorways and nuclear, power-stations. At the turn of the century, similar controversy was sometimes aroused by proposals to build tramways.

In the period when the Middlesex Light Railways were being planned, the inquiries were held, usually at the town hall in the affected area, by the Light Railway Commissioners, who reported their decision to the Board of Trade. The Commissioners in this case were the Earl of Jersey, Colonel George Boughey and Mr Henry Allan Steward, and on three occasions they conducted inquiries into proposals to bring trams to Harrow.

Almost from the start of the joint MTOC/MCC scheme, it had been the intention to extend the Harrow Road and Paddington tramway through Harlesden, Wembley and Sudbury to Harrow. The first inquiry took place at the Middlesex Guildhall on 21 and 25 March 1900, and the proposals for Harrow were fiercely contested by almost all the local interests except, surprisingly, Harrow UDC. The Harrow School authorities were aghast at the proposal, even though the proposal was for a Sudbury-Stanmore line along Watford Road through Greenhill and Harrow Weald, passing the school at a distance of about half a mile. Concern was expressed at an influx of Sunday excursionists, whose undesirable character was already known from the weekend services run by the horse bus proprietors. The Commissioners refused to sanction the line, taking the view that although the local council supported the application, there was clearly a great weight of local opinion against it.

During 1901 the MCC applied again for various lines which had been rejected or withdrawn, including a line from Stonebridge Park through Wembley, Sudbury, Harrow and Harrow Weald to Stanmore, entering Harrow via Sudbury Hill and leaving via Station Road and High Road, Wealdstone. The inquiry was held at the Middlesex Guildhall on 6 November 1901, after Harrow School and other interested parties had persuaded the county council to withdraw the line through Harrow and revert to the 1899 Watford Road route. Dr. Wood, the headmaster, the Earl Spencer who was chairman of the school Governors, and senior housemaster Mr. Charles Colbeck all spoke against the proposal, Mr. Colbeck saying that the School would be killed because many fathers would no longer send their sons there. Fears were expressed that an influx of trippers would invade the town at weekends, and that a slum would be created around the school. The Commissioners approved the section from Stonebridge Park to Wembley & Sudbury LNWR station, but rejected the remainder.

This rebuff did not deter the county council, and in May 1902 they applied again for a line from Wembley station along Harrow Road to Greenford Road, then through Harrow and Wealdstone to the Red Lion at Harrow Weald. The inquiry took place on 21 and 31 October 1902 at the Harrow Assembly Rooms, and was long and acrimonious.

This time, Harrow UDC, Wealdstone UDC, the *Harrow Observer* and the local Tradesmen's Association favoured the scheme, but the county council trod very carefully, realising that they were now the centre of a "town versus gown" controversy. They now planned to keep the line well clear of the school, by-passing the town centre to the west and following Bessborough Road, College Road and Station Road to reach Harrow Weald. Counsel for the MCC did however point out that opposition from the school when the LNWR company were laying their line had meant that the railway station was so far from Harrow as to be largely useless.

Speaking for Harrow School was Lord George Hamilton, a cabinet minister who was a Harrow School governor, an Old Harrovian and the local MP. He claimed that if the light railway scheme went through, Harrow would become a suburb. If the country aspect were lost, the same class of boy would not come to Harrow and the School would degenerate. The trams would run between two areas of playing fields, part of which would be taken for widening, and the passage of trams would be a danger to the boys. The School had not up to this time had to impose "bounds" on the boys, but if trams came then bounds would have to be set. At this, the county representative offered to forbid the carrying of boys in Harrow School uniform on the cars, but Lord George was sure the boys would evade this.

The Earl Spencer, chairman of the Governors, said the new scheme was less objectionable than the previous one, but the governors did not want the Metropolis creeping closer to Harrow. Evidence was given that the line would never pay its way, and the Commissioners diplomatically rejected the application, not on emotive grounds, but because in their view, promoters should not put forward schemes involving heavy expenditure with the prospect of only small returns. The battle for Harrow was lost, and no further applications were made for that part of the county.

Appendix 7

The Kilburn proposals

Among the applications under The County of Middlesex Light Railways (Extensions) Order No. 3, lodged with the Light Railway Commissioners in May 1901, was one from The Crown, Cricklewood, south-eastwards along Edgware Road through Brondesbury and Maida Vale to Elgin Avenue, then along Elgin Avenue to join the Harrow Road & Paddington Tramways Company's line in Harrow Road. Most of this line would have been in the County of London, and when the Light Railway Commissioners considered it on 1 and 6 November 1901 the London County Council opposed it, as did Hampstead Metropolitan Borough Council and Willesden Urban District Council. The part south of Bridge Terrace, Kilburn was withdrawn before the inquiry, but the LCC, the LNWR and the local councils kept up their objections and the Commissioners refused to sanction any part of the line.

During 1902, the Middlesex County Council applied again for the 1.5 miles from Cricklewood via Shoot-Up Hill and Kilburn High Road as far as Bridge Terrace, Kilburn. The Middlesex-London boundary ran down the centre of the road for almost the whole of this route, so one track of the double line would be in Hampstead, in the County of London, and the other in Willesden Urban District, in Middlesex. The inquiry commenced at Willesden Council offices on 20 October, but it was learned that the LCC proposed to apply to Parliament for a similar line and in view of the joint interest of the county councils the Commissioners suggested that Middlesex should do likewise.

Nothing more was done for three years, but late in 1905 the MCC prepared a Bill in Parliament seeking powers for a tramway from Cricklewood to Kilburn to join an intended LCC tramway continuing along the Edgware Road from Kilburn to the

Marble Arch. At a meeting in November 1905 with the LCC it was tentatively agreed that to obviate boundary difficulties a "repairing boundary" between the two county tramways would be established mid-way along the joint section at Netherwood Street, Brondesbury. A further meeting on 15 December between MCC, LCC, MET, Willesden and Hampstead was less productive, Willesden and Hampstead demanding conduit track throughout, 60 ft. minimum width roads and wood block paving. The cost of widening the roads to 60 ft. was found to be prohibitive, and both Bills were lost.

The idea was revived at a meeting between the two county councils on 13 May 1909, when the LCC announced its wish to revive the scheme. The line would now be built on the overhead system from Cricklewood to a change pit at Brondesbury (Netherwood Street) and then dual system conduit and overhead to Bridge Terrace, beyond which the line would be conduit and wholly in London. Estimates were prepared for the MCC portion, and the line was included in the 1910 LCC and MCC Parliamentary Bills, though the MCC were told that Paddington council were objecting to the London end of the route, and Willesden still insisted on the road being widened to 60 ft., the cost of which would have been astronomical. The MCC thereupon withdrew and left matters to the LCC.

The LCC tried again in the 1911 session of Parliament for Cricklewood—Marble Arch and also for lines from the county boundary along Finchley Road and Adelaide Road to Chalk Farm, from Maida Vale to Adelaide Road and from Swiss Cottage via Finchley Road to Baker Street station then along Marylebone Road to the Edgware Road. Willesden and Hampstead still demanded costly road widenings, and the LCC wished to own the line as far as Netherwood Street; Middlesex told the London representatives that in this event they must carry out all the widenings. Willesden had declined to contribute towards them as a road improvement, but by June 1911 all these lines had been struck out of the Bill.

The London County Council revived the scheme in its 1920 Bill, but with a difference. The difficulty was the narrow and congested High Road, Kilburn, the centre of a busy shopping and commercial quarter that would require extensive widenings at enormous expense. To avoid this the LCC now proposed that the 0.333 miles between Dyne Road (Brondesbury Station) and Priory Park Road should be one-way north to south with single track, the northbound line using Priory Park Road, St. Julian's Road and a proposed new road into Dunster Gardens, to reach High Road again via Dyne Road. All these side roads were in Willesden (Middlesex) and would be widened, but would cost far less than widening Kilburn High Road.

The LCC's 1920 scheme was more ambitious than any of its predecessors, as it proposed to continue the line from Marble Arch to Victoria Station with a branch along Victoria Street to Westminster. The Bill also included a line from the end of the Harrow Road tramway across Edgware Road and along Marylebone Road to meet the lines radiating from Kings Cross Station, and various shorter lines to link up the dead ends of the LCC system in central London.

Because the LCC now proposed to build part of its Edgware Road line wholly within Middlesex, the Middlesex County Council decided to apply for similar powers to build this portion (including the one-way part in Kilburn) and promoted their own Middlesex County Council (Tramways and Improvements) Bill 1920. The two councils met at the Middlesex Guildhall on 18 November 1919 and after much bargaining agreed that the LCC would pay for, equip, operate and maintain the whole line south from Cricklewood (including the whole cost of widenings) and would maintain the roads in Middlesex along which the tramways would run.

The LCC's 1920 Bill was however defeated by the opposition of the Metropolitan borough councils, and the Middlesex Bill was then withdrawn. This was the last attempt to build a Cricklewood—Marble Arch tramway and bypass the busy Kilburn High Road shopping centre, still a traffic bottleneck today. The MET's stub end track at the Crown Hotel in Cricklewood, which would have formed the start of the Kilburn line, was subsequently tarred over and eventually removed.

Appendix 8

M.E.T. Inspection and Opening Dates

	Date of Inspection	Date of Certificate	Formal Opening	Public Opening
Finsbury Park to Wood Green	19 July 1904	20 July 1904	22 July 1904	22 July 1904
Manor House to Seven Sisters Corner	19 July 1904	20 July 1904	22 July 1904	22 July 1904
Wood Green to Bruce Grove (W. of GER Bdg.)	6 Aug. 1904	9 Aug. 1904	20 Aug. 1904	20 Aug. 1904
Seven Sisters Corner to Brantwood Rd.	19 Aug. 1904	19 Aug. 1904	20 Aug. 1904	24 Aug. 1904
Seven Sisters Corner to Stamford Hill	19 Aug. 1904	19 Aug. 1904	—	12 Apr. 1905
Brantwood Rd. to Tottenham/Edmonton bdy.	(note a)	3 Nov. 1904	—	?29 Oct. 1904
Cricklewood to Hendon Depot	15 Nov. 1904	18 Nov. 1904	—	3 Dec. 1904
Hendon Depot to Edgware	30 Nov. 1904	3 Dec. 1904	—	3 Dec. 1904
Tottenham/Edmonton bdy. to Angel Bridge	22 Mar. 1905	10 Apr. 1905	—	12 Apr. 1905
Highgate Archway to Whetstone	30 May 1905	5 June 1905	7 June 1905	7 June 1905
Angel Bridge to Tramway Avenue	5 July 1905	7 July 1905	—	19 July 1905
The Wellington to Alexandra Palace West	22 Nov. 1905	24 Nov. 1905	6 Dec. 1905	6 Dec. 1905
Highgate Archway to Archway Tavern	21 Dec. 1905	21 Dec. 1905	—	22 Dec. 1905
Cricklewood to Willesden Green Station	20 Mar. 1906	23 Mar. 1906	30 Mar. 1906	31 Mar. 1906
Wood Green to Alexandra Palace East	6 Apr. 1906	7 Apr. 1906	9 Apr. 1906	11 Apr. 1906
Bruce Grove to High Road Tottenham	6 Apr. 1906	7 Apr. 1906	9 Apr. 1906	11 Apr. 1906
Whetstone to Hertfordshire boundary	26 July 1906	1 Aug. 1906	—	4 Aug. 1906
Harlesden (Royal Oak) to Stonebridge Park	10 Aug. 1906	15 Aug. 1906	10 Oct. 1906	10 Oct. 1906
Wood Green to The Ranelagh, Bounds Green	23 Nov. 1906	26 Nov. 1906	28 Nov. 1906	28 Nov. 1906
Harlesden (Royal Oak) to Lock Bridge	17 Dec. 1906	19 Dec. 1906	—	22 Dec. 1906
County boundary to Barnet	26 Mar. 1907	28 Mar. 1907	—	28 Mar. 1907
Bounds Green to New Southgate Station	7 May 1907	9 May 1907	10 May 1907	10 May 1907
Wood Green to Palmers Green	4 June 1907	5 June 1907	6 June 1907	7 June 1907
Willesden Green Stn. to Dudden Hill Lane	25 June 1907	5 July 1907	—	23 Dec. 1907

Edgware to Canons Park	5 Oct. 1907	7 Oct. 1907	—	31 Oct. 1907
Tramway Avenue to Freezywater (boundary)	26 Nov. 1907	28 Nov. 1907	11 Dec. 1907	11 Dec. 1907
Dudden Hill Lane to Craven Park Jct.	20 Dec. 1907	24 Dec. 1907	—	23 Dec. 1907
Stonebridge Park to Wembley	7 Apr. 1908	9 Apr. 1908	—	15 Apr. 1908
County boundary to Waltham Cross	15 Apr. 1908	16 Apr. 1908	17 Apr. 1908	17 Apr. 1908
Jubilee Clock to Willesden Jct. Stn.	7 Apr. 1908	9 Apr. 1908	—	30 June 1908
Palmers Green to Winchmore Hill	23 July 1908	26 July 1908	—	1 Aug. 1908
New Southgate Stn. to North Finchley	7 Apr. 1909	7 Apr. 1909	—	8 Apr. 1909
Winchmore Hill to Enfield	21 June 1909	24 June 1909	1 July 1909	3 July 1909
Willesden Junction Stn. to Acton	23 Sept. 1909	27 Sept. 1909	7 Oct. 1909	8 Oct. 1909
North Finchley to Golders Green	10 Dec. 1909	13 Dec. 1909	16 Dec. 1909	17 Dec. 1909
Golders Green to Hampstead boundary	14 Feb. 1910	18 Feb. 1910	21 Feb. 1910	21 Feb. 1910
Cricklewood to Childs Hill (The Castle)	14 Feb. 1910	18 Feb. 1910	21 Feb. 1910	21 Feb. 1910
Lock Bridge to Warwick Avenue	13 July 1910	18 July 1910	—	14 July 1910
Wembley to Sudbury	10 Sept. 1910	27 Sept. 1910	—	24 Sept. 1910
Warwick Avenue to Paddington	30 Nov. 1910	3 Dec. 1910	—	6 Dec. 1910
Ponders End to Enfield	6 Feb. 1911	10 Feb. 1911	20 Feb. 1911	20 Feb. 1911

(a) opened under temporary Board of Trade Licence pending inspection on 22 March 1905.

Appendix 9

Speed Limits

In sanctioning the opening for public traffic of a new tramway, the Board of Trade inspecting officers would lay down the maximum speeds at which cars were allowed to travel over each section of the line, and these would be printed in the rule-book issued to drivers. Compulsory stops, known generally as Board of Trade stops, would be imposed at points on the system such as the top of a gradient or the entry to a junction or a narrow section of road. In the case of steam tramways, the maximum permitted was generally eight miles per hour, but electric cars were capable of higher speeds than this.

The inspecting officer who normally dealt with the MET was Major J. W. Pringle, RE. When in July 1904 he inspected the first MET lines, the most he would allow was 10 miles/h, reduced to 4 miles/h over facing points and 6 miles/h descending the hill at Wood Green. The same limits were applied to the line through Tottenham to Tramway Avenue, Edmonton, which ran wholly through built-up areas.

However, when Major Pringle inspected the line from Hendon to Edgware on 30 November 1904, he allowed 14 miles/h, probably because the route was in open country. 12 miles/h was allowed in 1905 along most of the Great North Road route, with 14 miles/h from North Finchley to Whetstone, and in 1906 he allowed 16 miles/h on the semi-rural section from Whetstone to the county boundary near Barnet. These higher speeds may also reflect the fact that the Great North Road had been widened when the lines were laid.

This set a precedent and from 1907 onwards, 16 miles/h was generally allowed on straight track and in wide roads, though the Harrow Road in the metropolitan area was mostly limited to 12 miles/h, and congested thoroughfares such as part of High Road, Willesden were restricted to speeds as low as 8 miles/h. The most severely restricted lines on the MET system were the two Alexandra Palace hills, where cars were to descend the gradients at not more than 4 miles/h, with compulsory stops at top and bottom.

16 miles/h was more than the pre-1914 motor bus was allowed, and this coupled with its superior acceleration gave the tram an advantage. By 1925, bus competition and the prospect of more powerful motors prompted the MET to apply for an increase in the maximum speed limit from 16 to 20 miles/h. Major G. L. Hall, RE, inspected the routes in July 1925 and recommended that 20 miles/h should be allowed on all suitable sections of route, despite objections from Finchley UDC who claimed that trams had been clocked on the Great North Road at 33 miles/h. The Minister of Transport confirmed the new speed limits on 20 April 1926.

Appendix 10

Advertisements

On 24 February 1904, while the first MET cars were being built, the MET told the county council that they proposed to accept revenue advertising on the cars. They would charge £20 per year for an upper deck side, £10 for an end panel (canopy or stairhead) and 10s. for a window transparency. Two sides, four end panels and twelve transparencies would bring in £36 per year of which £29 would be profit. 150 cars would thus yield net revenue of £4,350 per year, of which the county would receive 45% under the terms of the lease.

The county sub-committee was opposed to advertisements, and in March told the MET that the idea must be abandoned, whereupon James Devonshire said the company would require compensation for loss of revenue. His board suggested £15 per car per year, but this must have been too much for the council, for on 14 July they rescinded their earlier decision. The result was an agreement to accept interior advertisements from the start and hold the matter of exterior displays over until 1905.

The subject was next raised in March 1905, when MET secretary A. L. Barber pointed out to the MCC that the London United cars (which operated in Middlesex) carried external advertising, as did those of the LCC. If they were not allowed on the MET, the company would claim from the council a sum equal to 55% of the comparable advertising revenue earned by the LUT, deducting it before paying the council's share of receipts.

The MCC decided to seek Counsel's opinion, and this was that the MET could not be prohibited from taking advertising on the cars except under specifically-framed byelaws. This settled the matter, and on 19 October the committee resolved that advertising be allowed and invited the MET to submit sample advertisements and "a model car". On 10 November the MET board sanctioned £100 for building a model car fitted with specimen advertisements.

On 5 April James Devonshire met the MCC committee and showed them the model tram demonstrating the advertising scheme proposed. The committee approved it, and exterior displays began to appear on the cars soon afterwards. By this time the upper deck side panels were vacant, because the detachable route boards formerly carried there had been moved higher up on to the wrought-iron grille work, probably so that the crew could reach and change them. The model tram appears to have been stored away at the Manor House offices, and appeared regularly until at least 1930 in the company's inventory of insured effects, at a value of £120.

Details of the displays will be seen in various illustrations. There was a main panel on each upper deck side, with four short displays on the canopy bends of canopied cars, and a panel advertisement at the top of the stairs of uncanopied cars 71-130. The earlier intention to use the main stairhead panel on these cars was not adopted, since most of them carried a headlamp there, these having been repositioned from the dash. Inside the car, there were transparencies near the tops of the windows and on the lower parts of the saloon door windows. Some of the enamelled iron exterior advertisements seem to have lasted as long as the cars that carried them.

The single deck cars had little space for external advertising, as the route boards were carried along the roof, but when these were dispensed with after the 1914-18 war they were replaced by advertisement boards. From about 1911, poster-board announcements of special events and places to visit were hung on the car dashes near the body side end, and these boards were later fixed permanently and used for any kind of advertising. On cars 71-130 the boards covered the grille between the dash and the offside front corner pillar, and further advertisements appeared later on the landing panel of the stairs.

The advertising was handled by an agent, R. Frost-Smith, on 15% commission. A provisional contract was concluded in 1905, then cancelled, and a new one signed on 15 June 1906. This was renewed regularly until 30 June 1916, after which the company's advertising was handled by the Underground group. At that time many exterior panels were untenanted, but they were soon filled again after the war and in 1921 the advertising revenue amounted to £6,295, about £22 per car.

There is no record of the council or the board placing restrictions on the subjects that could be advertised, but in 1909 a New Southgate resident objected to advertisements for ales and stout on the back of the tickets.

Appendix 11

Biographies

Membership of the board of directors of Metropolitan Electric Tramways Ltd. was as follows: Emile Garcke (chairman 1902-1929, deputy chairman 1929-1930); Sir James Devonshire (1902-1933, managing director to 1919); Sir Ernest Spencer (deputy chairman 1902-1916); C. G. Tegetmeier (1902-1933); W. L. Madgen (1902-1923); W. C. Burton (August 1919 only); Sir Albert Stanley, later Lord Ashfield (managing director 1919-1929, chairman 1929-1933); Sir William Acworth (1919-1925); E. R. Soames (1923-1933); H. A. Vernet (1925-1933); Frank Pick (1929-1933).

The chairmen of the Light Railways and Tramways Committee (or sub-committee) of the Middlesex County Council were Sir Francis Cory-Wright (1901-1909); Henry Burt (1909-1919); Col. Sir Charles Pinkham (1919-1923); Benjamin Todd (1923-1924 and 1927-1929); W. B. Pinching (1924-1927 and 1929-1933). Each term of office commenced in April.

ACWORTH, W. M.

William Mitchell Acworth, a barrister who was also a well-known railway economist and statistician, was a director of the Underground Electric Railways Company of London Ltd. and its subsidiary companies. He became chairman of the London United Tramways in January 1913 and a director of the MET in 1919. He was knighted in 1923 and died on 13 April 1925.

BARBER, A. L.

On 1 June 1902 Arthur Lea Barber, who had held various appointments in the BET group, was appointed full-time secretary to the MET at £275 per year. Unlike most tramways the MET at first had no general manager, management being shared between Barber (secretary), A. H. Pott-(chief engineer) and W. E. Hammond (traffic manager), all reporting directly to managing director James Devonshire. Barber's duties were therefore wider than those of most company secretaries and he helped to lead the MET company through many financial, legal and commercial difficulties. Until 1913 his name appeared in full at the bottom right corner of the rocker panel of each MET car, and in 1912-13 also on the nearside front lower panel of each MET omnibus. From 1913 he was also secretary of the LUT, SMET and L&ST. In January 1921 he relinquished these posts to become Commercial Manager of the Underground Group in succession to Frank Pick. He retired as Commercial Manager of the LPTB on 15 September 1939 and is still remembered for his old-world courtesy and charm.

BOYS, Major E., MC, FCIS.

Evelyn Boys joined the MET in 1903 as assistant to James Devonshire; from 1908 he was also secretary of the NorthmeT power company. After active service he rejoined the MET and became assistant secretary on 14 November 1919, then secretary in January 1921 in succession to A. L. Barber, with A. C. Ingram as assistant secretary. From this date he was also secretary of London & Suburban Traction. When the NorthmeT was separated from the Underground group in 1933 he remained with the power company, and in 1946 wrote (with E. T. Kingsbury) an unpublished history of the NorthmeT which is preserved in the Electricity Council Archives.

BURT, H.

Henry Burt was a member of Middlesex County Council and Hornsey Council who became secretary of the Alexandra Palace Acquisition Committee and led the campaign for its purchase in 1900-01, becoming first Chairman of the Alexandra Park Trustees. His personal album of the campaign is preserved in Hornsey Library, of which he was chief benefactor. He was vice-chairman of the county council from 1909 to 1930, and High Sheriff of Middlesex in 1917-18. Henry Burt was a leading member of the MCC Light Railways and Tramways Committee from its formation in 1901, becoming chairman in 1909 in succession to Sir Francis Cory-Wright and continuing in this post until 1919. He died in May 1940 at the age of 95.

COOPER, V. B. D.

Vivian Bolton Douglas Cooper was a consulting engineer in private practice who was concerned in many tramway promotions. He acted as consulting engineer to the MTOC, MCC and HCC for their light railway scheme, though his fees often gave rise to debate in the two councils. He had been engineer to the syndicate which provided electric lighting in the Houses of Parliament, joint engineer for the electrical equipment of the Dover Corporation Tramways and North Staffordshire Tramways, and had acted jointly with Sir Douglas Fox in renewing the roof of the central transept of the Crystal Palace.

CORY-WRIGHT, C. F., DL, JP.

Alderman Cory Francis Cory-Wright, who was knighted in June, 1903, was the first chairman of the Light Railways and Tramways Committee of the Middlesex County Council, a post he held from 1901 to 1909. He was born in 1838 and joined the family coal business in 1860, playing a leading part in the amalgamation of the coal distribution trade in 1896 and heading the firm of William Cory & Sons Ltd. He was chairman of Hornsey Council, and was High Sheriff of Middlesex in 1902-3. He was one of the small group of men who subscribed the money necessary to secure the option to buy the Alexandra Park and Palace in 1900, and he held numerous other public offices in Middlesex and elsewhere. He appears to have had a liking for driving trams, for on those occasions when he officiated at opening ceremonies he frequently drove throughout the trip, as for instance on the non-stop run from

Highgate to Finchley when the Highgate-Whetstone line opened. He was taken ill in the spring of 1909 and died on 30 May at the age of 70.

DEVONSHIRE, J. L., MIEE.

James Lyne Devonshire began his career in 1888 with the Laing, Wharton & Down Construction Syndicate, predecessor of the British Thomson-Houston Co. Ltd., of which he became manager and secretary in 1891. He later joined the BET group, and was one of the original directors of the MET, becoming managing director in July 1902. He became managing director of the NorthmeT power company in 1905, chairman of the SMET in 1906, managing director of the Tramways (MET) Omnibus Co. Ltd. in 1912 and of the LUT and SMET from 1913. During the war he served on the Board of Trade Committee on Tramways, for which he received a knighthood. In 1919, following the integration of the MET into the Underground group, Sir Albert Stanley (Lord Ashfield) become managing director of the three combine tramway companies, but in practice the duties of that office were still carried out by James Devonshire. He remained a director of the MET until 1933. As chairman and managing director of the NorthmeT power company he was a leading figure in the electrical industry.

GARCKE, E.

Emile Garcke was born in Saxony in 1856 and became a naturalised British subject in 1880. He joined the Anglo-American Brush Electric Light Corporation Ltd. as secretary in 1883, becoming manager in 1887 and managing director of its successor company, The Brush Electrical Engineering Co. Ltd., in 1891. He was a firm believer in the possibilities of electric traction and with his financial friends, including other Brush directors, set up the British Electric Traction Co. Ltd. in 1896, becoming its managing director. By 1904 the BET group consisted of 66 companies, mostly concerned with tramways and electric power, with Emile Garcke as the moving spirit of the whole vast enterprise, which in 1906 operated 15% of all British tramways and carried 11% of passengers. He was chairman of the MET from its formation to 1929 and then deputy chairman until his death on 14 November 1930.

HAMMOND, W. E.

William Ernest Hammond spent a lifetime in the service of London's tramways, joining the London Tramways Company in 1872 and moving to the North Metropolitan Tramways Company in 1882. He became traffic manager of the MET from the time of electrification, and continued in this post until his retirement in December 1918. A full account of his career, with some interesting sidelights on horse tram operation, appeared in *The Tramway and Railway World* for February 1919.

MACKINNON, J. B.

James Buchanan Mackinnon became traffic superintendent to the MET, LUT and SMET on the retirement of W. E. Hammond in December 1918. He was the younger brother of Lachlan Mackinnon, the well known Glasgow tramway manager, and began his career with 8½ years in the service of Glasgow Corporation. He moved to London in 1904, becoming Staff Assistant to the Metropolitan District Railway, and became Traffic Assistant to the London United Tramways in 1912. After some years with the MET, he became Schedules Superintendent to the LGOC and continued in a similar position with the LPTB. In May 1936 he was appointed Schedules Superintendent (Road Services), but he died suddenly on 13 September 1939.

MADGEN, W. L., MIEE.

William Leonard Madgen was born in 1862 and became a pupil at the School of Electrical Engineering in London. In 1882 he became a district manager with the National Telephone Company, and in 1892 founded the journal *Lightning,* later the *Electrical Times.* From 1893 he was engaged in developing the Ferranti meter business, and in 1896 helped to found the Municipal Electrical Association. He helped to set up the BET-owned North Metropolitan Electrical Power Distribution

Co. Ltd., becoming a BET director in 1899. After the Brush Electrical Engineering Co. Ltd. joined the BET group he became a director of Brush in 1902, managing director from 1903 to 1908, then vice-Chairman until 1924. He was one of the original directors of the MET, continuing in office until 22 June 1923. He died in January 1925.

MASON, A. V., MIEE.

Archibald Victor Mason was educated at Sherborne School and became a pupil at the Brush Electrical Engineering Company's works at Loughborough in 1898. He served briefly as resident engineer on the BET tramway at Kidderminster and was then sent out to Canada by the BET group as secretary of the Nelson (British Columbia) tramways. He returned to Britain in 1903 and after supervising the layout of the Belfast Corporation tramways became manager of the BET-owned Devonport tramways, then in July 1908 manager of the South Metropolitan Electric Tramways & Lighting Co. Ltd., continuing in this post until 1919. When the SMET management was merged with that of the MET and LUT under C. J. Spencer, Mason became Deputy Manager and Engineer to the group's three tramway companies, his title being changed on 28 January 1921 to Deputy General Manager and Engineer. He played a leading part in the development and commissioning of the Feltham type cars, and retained his engineering appointment with London Transport until his retirement in July 1939. He died in 1948 at the age of 74.

PICK, F.

Frank Pick was born at Spalding in 1878. He joined the North Eastern Railway, transferred to the UERL in London in 1906 and became traffic officer in charge of advertising in 1909 and Commercial Manager in 1912. He was seconded to the Board of Trade from 1916 to 1919, and became assistant managing director of the UERL in 1921 and managing director in 1929. He was a director of the MET from 1929 to 1933, and was vice-chairman of the LPTB from 1933 to 1940; he died in November 1941. His career is chronicled in the recent book *Frank Pick—The Man Who Built London Transport* by Christian Barman (David & Charles Ltd.) which confirms that he was largely responsible for the replacement of the North London trams by trolleybuses.

PINCHING, W. B.

Middlesex County Councillor William Benjamin Pinching, who from 1919 represented the Southgate North Division, was an electrical and mechanical engineer who was appointed chairman of the council's Light Railways and Tramways Sub-Committee in April 1924. He was one of a new generation of county councillors who inherited the problems of the MET lease in the changed postwar circumstances. Although some councillors were pressing for the abandonment of the system, Pinching was a firm believer in the tram as the main provider of transport, and led an MCC delegation to Birmingham to study the new Bristol Road reserved track line. He was critical of the relationship between the MET and the NorthmeT power company, but was not unsympathetic towards the MET, whose management he considered superior to that of the LCC trams. His 1926 report on the Light Railways undertaking will be described and discussed in Volume Two. After a two-year break he resumed the committee chairmanship in April 1929, and brought to a conclusion the negotiations for the new lease which enabled the MET to invest in new rolling stock.

POTT, A. H., MICE, MIEE.

Arthur Henry Pott was born in 1865 and joined Crompton and Co. in Chelmsford as a pupil in 1886, becoming head of the test room in 1889, assistant outside engineer in 1892 and assistant manager in 1896. After service in South Africa with the Electrical Engineers, RE, he joined consulting engineers Preece & Cardew until appointed Engineer to the MET on 31 May 1902 at £600 per year, the appointment being restyled Chief Engineer by 1905. From the formation of London & Suburban Traction in 1913, Pott became General Manager and Engineer to the MET and LUT, and his name appeared on the cars, replacing that of A. L. Barber.

A. H. Pott built up the MET system from the reconstruction and electrification of the North Metropolitan horse tramways through the electrical equipping of the county lines to the reconstruction and electrification of the Harrow Road and Paddington Tramways. With Stephen Sellon he also designed and supervised the construction of Brimsdown power station. As well as being a well-qualified technical man, he was a practical man of the highest calibre.

The MET board must have been surprised to learn on 16 October 1918 that Pott, then aged 53, had tendered his resignation from 31 October. The post was not advertised, and it seems likely that Pott had been persuaded by Sir Albert Stanley to take early retirement in order to obtain the services of C. J. Spencer. The London and Suburban Traction Company's directors voted Pott an honorarium of £1,500, equal to one year's salary, and appointed him consulting engineer to the three Combine tramway companies at £250 per year, a position he held until 31 October 1924. From October 1918, he also served on the Board of Trade committee on tramways. He died on 4 June 1945 at the age of 80.

SELLON, S. d'A., AMICE.

Stephen d'Alte Sellon was an associate of Emile Garcke in the Brush company and in the formation of the BET, becoming BET chief engineer. In addition to his many other tramway interests he was appointed consulting engineer to the MET in October 1902, and was closely involved in the planning and design of the system, including Brimsdown power station. He died in December 1918.

SMITH, S. G.

Sidney G. Smith after being engaged in the electrification of the BET-owned Potteries tramways was appointed engineer in charge of MET permanent way, overhead and power distribution in June 1902 at a salary of £300 per year. As the construction of the system neared completion, he left the MET in 1908 to set up his own electrical contracting business, and in this capacity he installed the MET demonstration trolleybus line at Hendon depot in 1909. In June 1910 he joined another BET engineer, Norman Clough, to set up the firm of Clough & Smith, later Clough Smith & Co. Ltd. (now Clough Smith Ltd.), which carried out many trolleybus installations during the next half century. In 1912 the firm extended and completed the MET's private telephone system.

SPENCER, C. J., OBE, MIEE.

Christopher John Spencer was born in 1876, the son of a tramways manager, and in 1889 was apprenticed to the Blackpool Electric Tramway Company. Whilst there he devised the carbon brush for use in traction motors, which had hitherto had brushes of brass, and the directors awarded him a sovereign for this invention. In 1892 he became electrician to the South Staffordshire Tramways, where his father was resident engineer, and in 1898, at the early age of 22, he became general manager of Bradford Corporation Tramways. During his 20 years at Bradford he designed, with the help of his father, the Spencer Slipper Brake for use on steep gradients, and the variable-gauge equipment which enabled cars to work from the 4 ft. Bradford system onto the standard gauge Leeds tramways. He was President of the Municipal Tramways Association in 1910.

During the 1914-18 war Spencer was seconded to the Admiralty as an assistant director of its labour division. Whilst there, he doubtless met Sir Albert Stanley (later Lord Ashfield), chairman of the Underground group of companies, who was then President of the Board of Trade. During 1918 Bradford Corporation pressed for Spencer's release from the Admiralty but it seems probable that Spencer was approached by Sir Albert Stanley and invited to accept the post of tramways manager to the London & Suburban Traction group. Spencer never returned to Bradford, being succeeded there by R. H. Wilkinson.

Spencer's appointment took effect from 1 November 1918, at a salary of £1,500, as manager of the MET and LUT; on 24 January 1919 he was also appointed manager of the SMET. His name thereafter appeared on the cars, and his title was changed to General Manager from 28 January 1921. The many developments on the

MET during his managership are evidence of his progressive outlook and his 1926 paper on tramcar design foreshadowed the research programme which culminated in the Feltham cars. On the formation of the LPTB in 1933 he was designated Tramways Manager (Northern and Western Areas) but resigned later that year, becoming a director of the NorthmeT power company (until 1940) and visiting South Africa in 1934 to head the Spencer Commission into Johannesburg Transport. He died in 1950 at the age of 75.

STANLEY, A. H.

Albert Henry Stanley was born in Derbyshire in 1874 as Albert Knattriess but the family emigrated to the USA and he was educated in Detroit. He entered the tramway industry at the age of 14 and rose quickly to become manager of the Public Service Corporation of New Jersey in 1904. In 1907 the American shareholders in the UERL persuaded him to return to Britain as UERL general manager (a director from 1908, managing director from 1910). With Sir Edgar Speyer he brought about the mergers of 1911-1913 between UERL, LGOC, MET, LUT and SMET, and was knighted in 1914. In 1916 he became director-general of mechanical transport at the Ministry of Munitions, and was chosen as President of the Board of Trade later that year. On returning to the UERL in 1919 as chairman and managing director, he was elevated to the peerage, becoming Lord Ashfield of Southwell. He was chairman and managing director of the London & Suburban Traction Co. (owners of the MET) for most of its life, and managing director of the MET from November 1919, though his many other committments meant that James Devonshire usually acted on his behalf. As Lord Ashfield he became chairman of the LPTB on its formation in 1933 and continued in this post until 1947. He died in November 1948.

TEGETMEIER, C. G.

Charles George Tegetmeier was a director of the British Electric Traction Co. Ltd. and many of its subsidiaries, including Auckland, NorthmeT Power and the MET and SMET and chairman of the BET companies at Swansea, Merthyr and Weston-super-Mare. He was the moving spirit in the 1929 electrification of the Swansea and Mumbles Railway, and was a council member of the Federation of British Industries. He was an MET director until 1933, and died in 1949.

WAKELAM, H. T.

Henry Titus Wakelam was born in 1858 and commenced his career in municipal engineering in 1874, becoming county surveyor of Herefordshire in 1892 and county engineer and surveyor of Middlesex in 1898. He was county engineer throughout the period when the Light Railways were being planned and constructed, his salary being increased in recognition of the extra work, after an alternative request for payment by commission had been rejected by the council. He was given an assistant engineer and a draughtsman from 1901 to cope with the work. He devised several experimental types of tramway rail joint, which were tried on the MET-MCC system prior to the general adoption of Thermit welding. He died on 20 January 1920, and W. E. Froome Crook became acting surveyor and engineer pending a permanent appointment. The new county engineer was Alfred Dryland.

WANDRUSZKA, V.

Victor Wandruszka, proprietor of the Alexandra Park Electric Railway described in Appendix 1, was born in Nyiregyhaza, Hungary on 24 July 1862 and trained as an electrical engineer. He served with AEG from 1890 to 1895 and with Felix Singer of Berlin in 1895-97 before setting up his own company (Electrizitätsgesellschaft Wandruszka) as European agents for some American traction equipment manufacturers, including those whose products were used at Alexandra Park. He remained in Britain, becoming engineer (foreign department) to Babcock & Wilcox in 1899 and moving to the BET in 1900, becoming manager at Hartlepool. He resigned in 1903 due to ill-health.

Further Appendices, Bibliography, Index and Source Notes will appear in Volume 2.

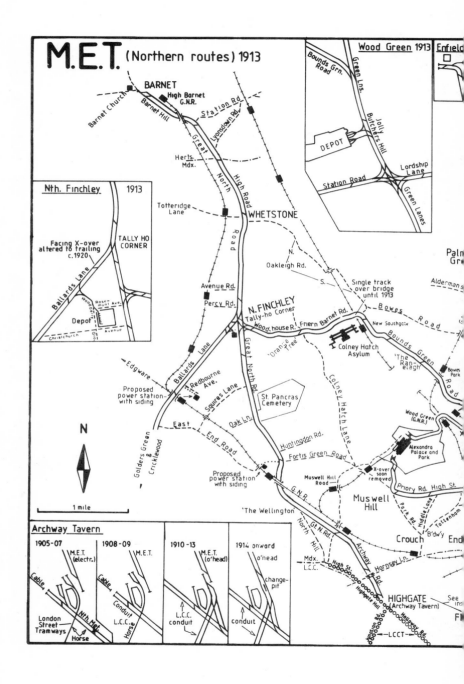

M.E.T. (Northern routes) 1913

BARNET

High Barnet G.N.R.

Barnet Church

Barnet Hill

Station Rd.

Lyonsdown Rd.

Great North Road

High Road

Herts.
Mdx.

Totteridge Lane

WHETSTONE

Avenue Rd.

Percy Rd.

N. FINCHLEY
Tally-ho Corner

Wood house R.

Oakleigh Rd.

N.

S.

Single track
over bridge
until 1913

Bowes Road

Alderman's...

Friern Barnet Rd.

New Southgate

Colney Hatch
Asylum

'The
Ran-
elagh'

Bowes
Park

'Orange Tree'

Great North Rd.

St. Pancras
Cemetery

Colney Hatch Lane

Bounds Green Road

Wood Green
(G.N.R.)

Wood Green 1913

Bounds Grn.
Road

Green Lns.

Jolly Butchers Hill

DEPOT

Station Road

Lordship
Lane

Green Lanes

Enfield

Palmers
Green

Nth. Finchley   1913

Facing X-over
altered to trailing
c.1920

TALLY HO
CORNER

Ballards Lane

Woodhouse Rd.

Rose-
munt Ave.

Depot

Christchurch

Avenue

Edgware

Ballards Lane

Redbourne
Ave.

Proposed
power station
with siding

Squires Lane

East   End Road

Oak Ln.

Golders Green &
Cricklewood

N

1 mile

Proposed
power station
with siding

Huntingdon Rd.

Fortis Green Road

'The Wellington'

G.N.R.

North Hill

Muswell Hill
Road

X-over
soon
removed

Priory Rd.

Muswell
Hill

High St.

Park Rd.

Hurdle Lane

Alexandra
Palace and
Park

Crouch End

Tottenham

B'dwy.

Archway Tavern

1905-07

M.E.T.
(electr.)

Cable

London
Street
Tramways

Horse

Nth. Met.

1908-09

M.E.T.

Cable

Conduit

L.C.C.

Horse

1910-13

M.E.T.
(o'head)

L.C.C. conduit

1914 onward

o'head

change-
pit

conduit

Mdx.
L.C.C.

Gt. N Rd.

High St.

Archway Rd.

Highgate Hill

Hornsey Ln.

HIGHGATE
(Archway Tavern)

Holloway Rd.

LCCT

See
ins...

F...